COMPLETE BOOK OF OUTDOOR

D.I.Y.

THE COMPLETE BOOK OF OUTDOOR

D.I.Y.

PENNY SWIFT & JANEK SZYMANOWSKI

First published in the UK in 1996 by
New Holland (Publishers) Ltd
London • Cape Town • Sydney • Singapore

24 Nutford Place
London W1H 6DQ

80 McKenzie Street
Cape Town 8001
South Africa

3/2 Aquatic Drive
Frenchs Forest, NSW 2086
Australia

Managing Editor Richard Pooler
Editors Sally D. Rutherford, Jenny Barrett, Cherie Hawes.
Design Manager Petal Palmer

Designer Julie Farquhar, Darren Maclean, Dean Pollard
Cover design Darren Maclean
Design assistant Lellyn Creamer
Illustrator Clarence Clarke
DTP conversion Jacques le Roux, Darren Maclean,
Dean Pollard
Reproduction by cmyk Pre-press, Cape Town and
Unifoto (Pty) Ltd, Cape Town
Printed and bound by Tien Wah Press (Pte) Ltd, Singapore

ISBN 1 85368 732 4

ACKNOWLEDGEMENTS

A book of this nature takes time to produce, and there are always a number of people to thank when production is eventually complete. Some provide us with locations to photograph, others assist with the projects, while professionals in various fields also offer advice and share their expertise. We cannot note them all in print, but our gratitude goes to every one.

Specific companies we wish to acknowledge are Corobrik, manufacturers of bricks and pavers; Terraforce, a leader in the field of earth retaining systems; Klapmuts Concrete, manufacturers of Terraforce and other concrete blocks; Smartstone, manufacturers of a range of reconstituted stone products; Cape Gate Fence and Wire Works, manufacturers of fencing materials; Centrecore, manufacturers of timber fencing; Logo Homes, which builds timber-frame houses and has a range available in kit form; timber merchants, Federated Timber Industries and Airton Timbers, as well as Mondi Timbers; Youngman Roofing; and Kaytech Geotechnical and Industrial Fabrics, which introduced us to the fin drain system.

More specifically, we thank Mike Ingram, a regional director of Corobrik; Holger Rust, inventor of Terraforce blocks (now available worldwide); Andy van Niekerk of Smartstone; Neville White of Cape Gate; Harvey Downes of Centrecore; Alan Cruickshank and Alan Paine of Logo Homes; Wayne Brown, a timber-frame builder with extensive experience in both South Africa and the United States of America; Brian Reid, group product manager of Federated Timbers; Graham Retief of Airton Timbers, who is also a chairman of the Institute for Timber Construction Limited; Dave Reeves, general manager of Mondi; both Brian Buddle and John Marshall of Youngman Roofing; and John Mortimer, executive director of the South African Lumber Millers' Association.

Holger Rust, Andy van Niekerk and Wayne Brown feature in some of the step-by-step photographs; namely building the concrete block wall, the reconstituted stone wall, and the stud-frame structure respectively. Other people who posed for pictures in the section on Paths, Steps and Patios include John Forbes, Paddy Kelly and the late "Morgie" Morgan. Janek Szymanowski is seen in the rest of the step-by-step pictures.

Numerous experts from the United Kingdom, United States of America, Australia and South Africa checked the manuscript for accuracy. Our thanks go to them all; in particular Steve Crosswell, a regional director of the Portland Cement Institute; Lewis Silberbauer, technical manager of Mondi Timbers; Richard Bailey, an engineer with the CSIR; and Mike Ingram.

Many of the structures featured were built by ardent DIYers, others were professionally constructed. We do not always know which companies or individuals are responsible, and so we may have inadvertantly omitted some names. In the section on Wooden Structures, four designed by landscape architects Gouws, Uys and White are featured, and a deck designed and built by Mike Lister. In the Plans section, the Garden Shed was designed and built by Janek Szymanowski; the Timber Umbrella was designed and built by Arne Schaffer of Cape Lumber; the Perfect Pergola was designed by architect Margie Walsh; A Place to Play was created by Cerf's Adventure Playground; the Stylish Entrance was designed and built by Allan Pearson; and the Tiptop Tree-house, constructed by Tony Mansfield. In the section on Walls and Fences, Graham Viney designed the Lattice Screen for Tom and Sheila Boardman, and André Pugin assisted Grant and Desireé Byram with the design and construction of the charming Pole Pattern Fence.

METRIC/IMPERIAL CONVERSION TABLE

To convert the measurements given in this book to imperial measurements, simply multiply the figure given in the text by the relevant number shown in the table alongside. Bear in mind that conversions will not necessarily work out exactly, and you will need to round the figure up or down slightly. (Do not use a combination of metric and imperial measurements – for accuracy, rather stick to one or the other system.)

TO CONVERT	MULTIPLY BY
millimetres to inches	0.0394
metres to feet	3.28
metres to yards	1.093
square millimetres to square inches	0.00155
square metres to square feet	10.76
square metres to square yards	1.195
cubic metres to cubic feet	35.31
cubic metres to cubic yards	1.308
grams to pounds	0.0022
kilograms to pounds	2.2046
litres to gallons	0.22

CONTENTS

INTRODUCTION

We have been designing, creating and developing outdoor spaces for centuries; building walls and fences; laying paths; designing courtyards and patios; and constructing a variety of both useful and decorative features from the materials available to us. Some of us do it ourselves, others employ professionals to do it for them.

Much of this activity involves building and woodworking skills, and this simple, easy-to-read book offers the reader hands-on advice and information which may be adapted to just about any environment, anywhere in the world. Whether you are starting from scratch or modifying an existing property, you will find these pages crammed with hints, ideas and useful instructions to help you do-it-yourself or simply increase your knowledge so that you can hire or contract the right person to assist you achieve your goal.

Of course some projects are challenging, even daunting, but most of those illustrated here can be tackled by any DIY homeowner who is both capable and enthusiastic. A proper tool kit is important, often making light work of seemingly complicated tasks, while a knowledge of building principles and techniques is essential.

Although various building skills will help you improve your property, we all know that planting is important too; after all without flowers, shrubs and trees, what would a garden be? Although this is not a gardening book, it does give some advice and guidance which will help you plan the development of your outdoor spaces. Hundreds of full colour photographs also offer inspiration and suggest a myriad of possibilities which you can adapt for your own property.

The examples shown here illustrate a wide range of types, varying not only in size and style, but in geographic location as well. The aim is to provide as great a cross-section of imaginative and inspirational options as possible.

Most people want a well-designed garden which incorporates walls, fences, paths, steps, patios. This may include other features and facilities where they can sit, play, entertain, or simply enjoy their little patch of nature in peace and quiet, away from neighbours and passers-by. At the same time, designing or remodelling a garden or a part of any outdoor area presents a tremendous challenge, particularly if you have never done it before. It takes time, but the results can be highly rewarding. Not only can you transform your property beyond all expectations, but you can also improve your lifestyle. Better still, the improvements you make could increase the value of your property.

With some basic knowledge of materials, tools and techniques, you will find that building your own garden features and structures in a logical and well planned manner can be one of the most rewarding and enjoyable aspects of home improvement.

Before you start, you will need to have a proposed layout of the garden, including a general planting plan, and a good idea of the preferred ground surfaces and shelter possibilities. You will also need to know, more or less, how the entire outdoor area will be used. If there are specific spaces for washing lines, water features, a rose garden, seating or anything else, these must all be indicated.

Only then should you decide where the more permanent features will go. Each will have its own particular

A small patio creates an ideal entertainment area.

The casual appearance of these steps and walkway conceals careful planning.

function; a factor which will help decide where the structure is to be sited. Proper planning, described in some detail in this book, is essential.

Walls, fences and other enclosures provide privacy. They also screen the garden from wind and noise, and, depending on the materials used, may filter sunlight. Whilst some are decorative, often visually defining a boundary or section of the garden, most are functional. Paths, steps and walkways are also practical elements with very distinct functions, for instance steps enable us to traverse a change in level safely. They are part of what is termed the 'hard landscaping' scheme. They provide a dry, solid surface to the house and through the garden. Often linked to patios, paths and steps are an important design feature within any garden, and should be planned with care.

Like paths and steps, patios have a hard surface, and are also part of the hard landscaping scheme. These are

all elements which ideally should be tackled in the early stages of establishing any outdoor area. More than anything else, it is the patio (as well as courtyards and formal terraces) which will enable you to use the garden as an extenion of your house in fine weather.

Although some people incorporate a patio when they build their house, this feature is more frequently added on later. Walls, fences and screens also form part of the overall design, as do pergolas, arbours and gazebos which are usually built for shelter. Although the various elements are constructed at different times, they all form part of the overall plan.

When it comes to planting, or 'soft landscaping', as it is known, the secret is to consider it in the context of your overall plan. Not only do flowers provide colour and scent, but they are an integral part of the design scheme. They may be used in conjunction with other more formal features; they may also be planted alongside paths or

steps, around the perimeter of a patio, or, in the case of creepers or climbers, used to create shelter over a pergola or arbour.

Trees provide shade and introduce essential form to an area. They may also be used to create a backdrop for other plants or features, and as a part of the basic framework of the garden. Positioning them correctly is important. If you are planning walls and fences around a property, large trees with sprawling root systems should not be planted near the boundary. On the other hand, shrubs and certain framework plants may be used for hedging and screening in place of walls and fences.

This book explores the possibilities of all these elements, from the planning stages to completion, offering a huge range of options for every type of garden, big or small. Divided into three distinct sections, it looks independently at walls and fences; paths, steps and patios; and finally, simple wooden structures designed to add interest to the garden, and greatly increase the usefulness of your outdoor area.

Each section includes basic details on planning, design, materials, tools, construction principles and the various techniques required to do the work yourself. However, the emphasis and scope of each of the three parts varies considerably. Similar headings simply make the text easier to follow. For instance, having grasped the basic skills required to erect a lattice screen or picket fence (in the section on walls and fences), you will not necessarily be fully equipped to build a garden shed or pretty gazebo. Foundation requirements differ and more complicated fixing and joining procedures have to be followed for structures like gazebos and pergolas. Your timber needs may also vary somewhat.

Similarly, having built a solid garden wall from brick, you will hopefully have mastered the essential techniques required for bricklaying, but there are additional elements to be considered when constructing a flight of steps.

This book may be approached several ways, depending on your needs. First, browse through it and try to assimilate as much as you can. This will help you identify how you can improve your own particular outdoor space and what your options are. Then you can decide which jobs you feel competent to tackle yourself, and which jobs you would rather leave to the professionals.

If you are interested in one particular section of the book, it makes sense to concentrate on that area. But do not disregard the others; by dipping into each of them, you will find you gain a much clearer insight into the possibilities for your property as a whole. You may even be inspired to tackle a completely different project to that originally envisaged.

Each of the three parts in the book begins with an introduction and a section which relates to planning. Essential aspects are discussed here, including the role a variety of professionals may play in your project, and the possible need for plans. Building codes are discussed in some detail in the section on wooden structures, which also contains a page relating to the essentials of plumbing and electrics. There is less detail on this subject matter elsewhere. Since budget is an important factor for most people about to tackle any type of home improvement, the issue of quantifying and costing materials is discussed in all the planning sections.

Design is also discussed in all three sections, but the approach in each is quite different and entirely specific to the subject. In Walls and Fences, the focus is on finish and the effect this has. Of course this relates to the style of structure you are planning, and also to finishing touches and design details – pillars, alcoves and niches, built-in planters and so on. Design in the section on Paths, Steps and Patios looks at floor surfaces, screening materials, lighting, seating and

Only basic skills are need for this picket fence and planter.

A simple covered patio well within the skills of the home enthusiast.

A simple timber deck with steps leading into the garden is ideal for outdoor entertaining and adds value to any property.

planting. The section relating to outdoor Wooden Structures, discusses flooring, roofing and cladding with reference to both open structures and more substantial timber structures.

Throughout all the Design sections, there are boxes of information which any home improver will find interesting. These cover decking, gates and doors, essential security, traditional wooden structures, play structures which will appeal to children of all ages, additions and reasonably simple extensions. All are highlighted on the contents pages.

The construction sections focus on a range of materials, tools, methods and techniques which will show you how to tackle the project of your choice.

Although timber is discussed briefly in Walls and Fences, the emphasis is on fencing types and methods of construction rather than the timber itself. For more information on the use of softwoods, hardwoods, poles and sawn timber, you can turn to page154 in the section on Wooden Structures.

A pre-cast fountain forms a focal point at the end of a charming flagstone path.

Imaginative design transforms a rendered boundary wall with a tiled portico.

Lattice screens and a simple roof create a delightful garden shelter.

Some hints on suitable timber preservatives are included.

Although concrete and mortar are discussed in several sections, suggested ratios differ, depending on the work undertaken. Similarly, basic principles are interpreted and executed differently, depending on the project tackled. Furthermore the techniques used when tackling a brick wall, and erecting a pole structure, are quite different, simply because of the variation in materials.

If you have a particular project in mind, it is best to read all you can about the specific materials you plan to use and then to study the building methods carefully. Nothing works as well as trial and error, and, unless you are familiar with construction basics, you are advised to practise the techniques shown photographically in the step-by-step sections.

The projects featured in these sequences have been photographed step-by-step while in the process of being built, and they have been chosen to show generic methods, as much as the projects themselves. They show you how to form joints and connect pieces of timber, and how to lay bricks and blocks; how to erect simple timber panels which may become the walls of a shed or simple garden building.

The reason for this approach is to illustrate techniques as clearly as possible. The idea, too, is for readers to adapt the step-by-step building methods, and use the skills shown to build a variety of structures, including those featured as plans at the back of each of the three main sections.

A wide range of materials and methods is shown for all the projects; these include timber, wire mesh, both pre-cast and concrete cast *in situ,* bricks, blocks, slabs and pavers.

Before starting your project, it is a good idea to experiment if you can. If you are working with bricks or blocks and mortar for the first time, mix a little of the cement with sand and water in ratios as described in the text, and try laying a few bricks on a solid concrete surface. Once you get the hang of using the trowel, and become familiar with handling bricks, you should be confident to tackle the real thing.

If you are new to woodwork, use timber offcuts to try out tools before you get started. Drill a few holes and screw two pieces of wood together. Then practise using a saw. Once you feel confident, there will be absolutely nothing to hold you back. Ideally work with someone who has some experience; if you watch closely you may be surprised how quickly you get the hang of the different techniques.

Of course many people like to design their own structures; but for those who do not have the experience, or prefer to follow plans, the book contains a total of 28 detailed projects. Each of these is accompanied by a full list of materials and a brief description of the steps that should be followed during construction. The plans themselves are varied, showing a number of different styles and structure types. While some are demanding, most are well within the reach of a competent handyman, including beginners with little previous building experience. All may be used as they are, or altered to suit the demands of your own property.

In some instances the exact materials specified may not be available. For instance a particular kind of retaining block or paver may not be manufactured in your area. Bricks, and especially blocks, may be available in a slightly different size. In most cases something similar can be substituted without any adverse effects at all. Wherever possible, alternatives are suggested.

Timber dimensions may also differ (particularly if you are using hardwoods), but this is seldom a problem when it comes to actual construction. Slight variations are easily adapted. The exact sizes of nails and screws are also not a problem. Once you understand the principles involved, it is a reasonably simple matter to find something which will work just as well.

Ultimately it is your own imagination and creativity which will make your DIY project special and rewarding for you.

A pre-cast foundation forms a strong focal point in an informal garden.

A simple brick path and attractive gazebo add charm to a garden.

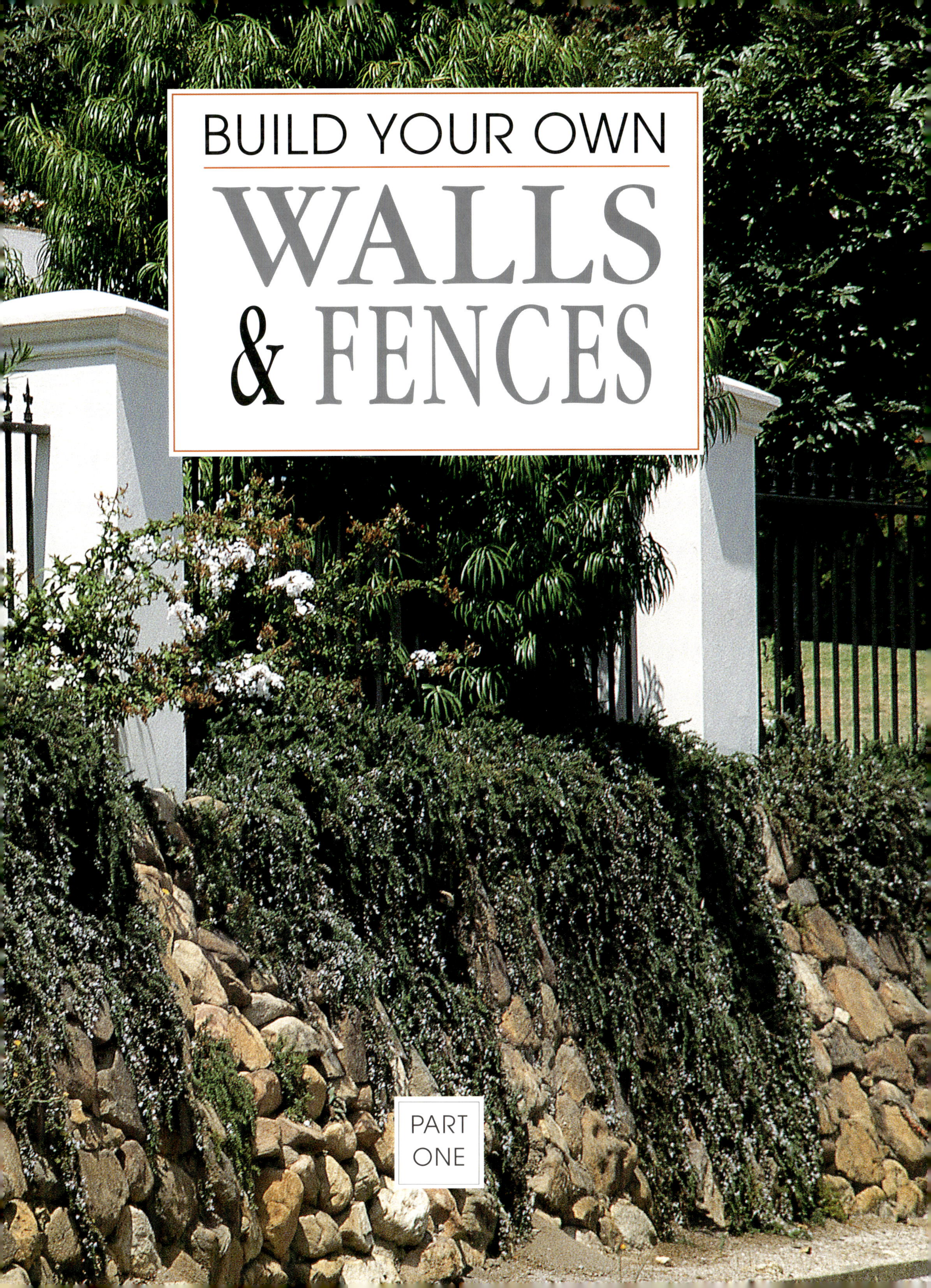

BUILD YOUR OWN WALLS & FENCES

PART ONE

INTRODUCTION

Garden walls and fences are invaluable elements within all garden schemes. They provide security, add privacy, and are frequently used to define the boundary of a property. They may also be erected specifically to block out unsightly views or service areas, to furnish some protection from the elements, or to provide a perfect backdrop or support for plants. Whatever the size or style of your garden, these varied structures also give you the opportunity to subdivide and re-organise the shape and function of your outdoor space.

The concept of enclosing areas around homes and dividing parts of the garden to create separate, often private, areas is nothing new. Ancient civilisations used walls and hedges to create secluded courtyards and kitchen gardens. The most famous wall is probably the Great Wall of China, built in about 200 BC, a monumental 2.414 km masonry structure which still stands today. In medieval times, enclosures were largely constructed as a means of defence, and walled paradise gardens (or parks) were popular. Early European gardens often included walls and neatly clipped hedges to introduce a feeling of formality, while the cottage gardens of 18th-century Britain featured rustic fences, stone walls and hedgerows planted with a mix of shrubs and trees. Many of the most famous late-Victorian gardeners used walls, fences, screens and hedges to create secret gardens and a series of 'rooms' outdoors. The materials chosen for these structures have varied over time depending on availability and cost, as well as the purpose of the barrier. Whilst the earliest walls were made of stone, bricks have been used for many centuries: as long ago as the Middle Ages walls were built from irregular, handmade bricks. Rustic timber fencing and hedges have been used for thousands of years.

Nowadays expense is a primary consideration, but the design, size and style of your garden, as well as the type of barrier you prefer, are all vital factors. Furthermore, the architecture of your house should also be considered, especially if you are planning a solid structure.

The method of construction is another very important consideration. If you plan to build or erect your own wall or fence, it is important to have (or to learn) the necessary skills. Some materials are more difficult to work with than others, but most structures can be tackled successfully by the competent handyman. Alternatively, if you feel you cannot lay your own bricks or erect the fencing of your choice, or do not have the time to do so, you can always employ someone to do the work for you. And whether you plan to do-it-yourself or to use the services of professionals, this book will be an invaluable guide, offering good ideas and advice from the design and planning stages right through to the construction phase.

The first part of the book will help you choose the best type of wall or fencing for your particular needs. It illustrates a range of effective finishes and recommends a wide variety of suitable materials for every building method. There are also many imaginative suggestions for combining materials and incorporating distinctive features to tranform an ordinary design into something special.

A timber panel fence forms a perfect backdrop for pretty plants.

A simple, precast picket fence.

Post-and-rail fences are popular.

Elaborate cast-ironwork may be set between plain, rendered brick pillars for a period look.

Critical cost implications are considered in general terms and the most common building codes, regulations and restrictions which affect DIY builders are discussed in the relevant sections.

With the information supplied, you will be in a position to site the structure most effectively within the constraints of boundaries and any servitudes, liens or other legal restrictions.

Since most walls and fences incorporate gates or doors, this aspect is considered in some detail, as is the importance of including these elements in the landscaping plan as a whole. Security, which can be a vital factor, is dealt with separately, with an emphasis on maintaining an attractive façade. Retaining walls as well as some less substantial screens are discussed, along with hedges and other planted barriers and borders.

A comprehensive range of accepted construction methods is explained,

from blockwork and bricklaying to basic carpentry and simple metalwork. The necessary tools are clearly itemised, and a table is given on page 46 to help you to estimate the quantities of materials needed.

To simplify construction for beginners, photographic step-by-step instructions are featured in some detail. These illustrate how to lay both a facebrick and a stone block wall with supporting pillars; a simple method of building a substantial boundary wall with hollow concrete blocks, and how to render it; how to erect an attractive timber picket fence and hang a homemade gate; as well as how to make an open lattice screen from timber laths. Also shown are proven techniques commonly used to install a wire-mesh fence, so that it is properly tensioned and braced, and the procedure for the construction of a 1.2 m-high retaining wall from interlocking concrete terrace blocks.

In the latter half of the book, a total of 10 project plans are provided, together with a detailed list of materials required for each, and a simple list of guidelines to help you tackle it systematically.

Since dimensions, boundary lines and other factors will be sure to vary, most of the plans relate to a section of the structure; for instance, one panel of a fence, or the length of wall between two pillars. The designs are suitable for most gardens, but formal building plans will be necessary in many areas. You are advised to check with your local authority before putting any of the plans into action.

The designs chosen incorporate a variety of materials and range from a simple yet attractive trellis screen suitable for use alongside a patio, to a solid boundary wall with generous planters. A picket gate is included in one of the plans, and pillars in several. All may be adapted to meet your particular needs.

Walls and fences are used to enclose properties and frequently to divide gardens into several distinct areas. Most are permanent in nature, although some less substantial screens and enclosures may be moved and resited with reasonably little effort. The motivations for building a wall or erecting a fence or screen vary but, whatever your needs, the value of thorough planning and careful preparation must never be underestimated. Every property and each individual garden plan is different, so it is vital to ensure that any structure, however simple, blends with the general scheme and that it complements your home. It is essential to consider the full range of available materials at an early stage, and to cost the project before work begins.

FUNCTION

Even though the two most obvious functions of any type of wall or fence are enclosure and division, every structure you build will have a more specific role to play.

Those constructed around your property may screen the garden from passing traffic, effectively reducing the noise of the traffic and at the same time creating a welcome feeling of privacy. They also may provide a practical shield from prevailing winds, and may filter the sun. On the other hand, walls and fences may simply define your boundaries, or act as a support for climbers and creepers, or security may be their primary function.

Walls or fences built within the garden itself have even more functions. Walls may be built to establish courtyards or secluded areas within the garden. A low wall may be purely decorative, visually dividing one section of the garden from another, or it may be functional, perhaps incorporating a planter, water feature or a simple seating design. Even small and apparently insignificant structures

may play an important role in the landscape plan, defining flower beds or perhaps demarcating a patio.

If you live in a rural area and have livestock (horses, cows or sheep, for instance), or even if you have dogs, suitable fencing will contain the animals and prevent them from roaming. If you have a swimming pool, pool fencing and self-closing gates are essential to protect toddlers and children from possible harm.

Retaining walls have a practical function, and are a frequent component of sloping gardens. They must be designed and built with care to ensure that they are strong enough to support the earth they will retain, and will not collapse unexpectedly (see page 33).

SITE

While the function of a fence or wall will to some extent determine its site, you will find there are usually many location options and a host of other factors which must be examined.

One of the most important considerations will be any legal restrictions which affect the location of walls and fences. The most obvious is the demarcated boundary line of any property. However, there may be other factors which prevent you from building a wall or fencing an area at a particular spot. There may also be a legal requirement compelling you to erect some form of barrier, for instance around a swimming pool.

The first step is to check your own boundaries. If necessary have them

This picket fence around the boundary is painted white to match an internal lattice screen.

professionally surveyed to avoid any future disputes with neighbours. If you intend building on the actual boundary line, you will share ownership of the structure, even if your neighbour does not contribute towards the cost of it. The ideal situation is to get the cooperation of your neighbour, to mutually agree on the design and to share the costs. If this is not possible and the situation is unacceptable, a possible solution would be to site the wall or fence at least 150 mm in from your side of the boundary.

The next step is to check any other restrictions. Most of these are imposed by local authorities and relate to all residential land in an area, even though it is sometimes possible to obtain a variance or waiver to disregard them. In some case there may be a servitude, lien or other legal restraint which relates to your property in particular. For instance, a registered servitude or lien could allow other people access to an established footpath on your property. This would, in effect, prevent you from fencing it off unless a gate was provided.

Having determined the limitations, you can explore all the remaining possibilities in relation to your needs. If, for instance, you are building a wall for privacy, the front boundary line may seem at first to be the most obvious place to site it. Many people, however, prefer to leave the front garden open to the road, and to enclose a more secluded area for relaxation and entertainment. This is usually the cheaper option and a viable one, unless the need for security is the main priority. Similarly, a pool fence may be sited two or three metres from the perimeter of a swimming pool, or you may include more of the garden in this area and use an existing garden wall as one side of the enclosure.

DRAWING PLANS
Unless you already have a site plan, drawing one will make the planning much easier. Draw it to scale using ordinary graph paper, indicating where all buildings and existing structures are located. You will need to know the

A semi-detached house relies on a timber structure to screen the front garden for privacy.

Although a low wall defines this boundary, it does not shield the roses from view.

A low facebrick wall combines beautifully with shrubs and trees along a boundary.

The curved design of an unusual brick-and-stone wall adds character to the entrance.

dimensions of the site itself and of buildings, and distances between the various structures and boundaries. Mark these and the direction of true north. Draw in any landscaping features (trees, pathways, large rocks and so on). Existing walls, fences and hedges should also be shown, along with established shrubs and flower beds, and good view sites which you do not want to obstruct. Then mark in and label any sections of the garden which have a specific function, such as a patio, vegetable or herb garden, utility area with washing line and so on. If possible, spend some time in the garden noting sun patterns and prevailing winds, and indicate these on the scale plan too.

If it is done accurately, this plan will give a very good picture of the site and will help you to decide exactly where the garden should be enclosed or divided. Do not draw the position of any proposed walls, fencing or screens directly onto your plan. Instead, mark them on tracing paper and make several overlays of the various options that appeal to you.

A sloping property is a little more difficult to deal with, particularly if walls or fencing are to traverse steep or undulating ground. If you have a contour map of the site, refer to this; otherwise you may be able to simply label areas which could pose problems. If you do have a slope, you must decide whether you wish to step your wall or fence, or whether you need to build a retaining wall.

Neither walls nor fences have to be straight, and this is something you should remember when siting the structure. Furthermore, you do not have to remove all obstacles: a tree or attractive rock could be incorporated very effectively into the plan, often creating a unique feature.

Once you have decided where you are going to build your walls or fences, you should do more accurate drawings indicating the dimensions of posts, pillars, rails and so on. This will not only help you to visualise the design, but will enable you to accurately cost the project (see page 12).

HEIGHT AND DIMENSIONS

There are certain practical points to consider when determining wall or fence height, ranging from personal needs to the requirements of any local authority, and the necessity to use sound building principles.

If, for instance, you want to build a wall that will give you privacy from neighbours and passing traffic, it will have to be reasonably high with adequate foundations, expansion joints and supporting pillars or piers. You may also need to build in brick reinforcement. If you want to build something that will shield an entertainment patio from the wind, it is often better to opt for a structure that will allow the wind to pass through it. A perforated screen wall or slatted fence is often the best solution here, although it is important to ensure that it will withstand buffeting from strong winds. Solid walls sometimes precipitate turbulence, which can be very unpleasant and may cause damage to plants and patio furniture.

The height of any wall or fence is usually covered in local codes and planning or building regulations, although requirements and restrictions vary. Check how high you can build without plans and whether there will be any special steps your local council will insist you take when building it.

Even if there are no official constraints, common sense will tell you to adhere to fundamental building principles, and to seek advice if you are not sure what height and dimensions are acceptable. Local conditions, including wind and snow, are a vital consideration.

A low wall – around a flower bed, for example – can be built as a single thickness of stretcher-bond brickwork, but high boundary walls must not only be thicker, they should also incorporate reinforcing piers at regular intervals.

If you do not have any guidelines, you can safely build a half-brick garden wall about 100 mm thick to a height of 450 mm without piers, and to about 700 mm if two-brick piers are provided at 3 m centres. A thicker

The strong lines of a metal fence add interest and provide security rather than privacy.

Flower boxes follow the stepped lines of a solid brick wall which has been rendered.

Precast concrete panels, moulded to look like facebrick, were chosen for their texture.

one-brick wall may be built to a height of at least 1.35 m (or 18 courses) without piers, and to 1.8 m with 440 mm square piers at 3 m centres.

Half-brick walls should never be built to retain soil. Retaining walls should be at least 200 mm thick and must always incorporate weep holes for drainage, to prevent excessive accumulation of water behind the structure. Limitations on height, wall thickness and pier size are generally stringent, as severe damage may result from the collapse of even the lowest retaining wall.

Certain fence types and styles are better suited to different heights. A picket or post-and-rail fence can form an attractive boundary line, but these designs are both low. A panel fence, on the other hand, may be built substantially higher, as long as you provide adequate support for the material used.

MATERIALS

Having decided what to build, you will have to choose suitable materials for construction. The factors already discussed will all influence your choice, but you should also be guided by a thorough knowledge of all the available options (see pages 20–29).

While some materials will blend with any style of house, continuity is an important factor which should not be overlooked. Aim for harmony, and select materials which complement one another. For instance, if yours is a facebrick house, the same brick will be an obvious choice for the garden wall. If you want fencing, consider a neat palisade fence, which will suit the more formal finish of facebrick, but add a touch of rusticity. For a cottage-style home with walls smothered in pretty creepers and climbers, a hedge, stone wall or picket fence will be more complementary and appropriate.

In certain instances, there may be a variety of suitable and appropriate materials. For instance, a wall that is to be rendered can be built with clay bricks or concrete blocks, and screen walls with any number of perforated block designs. Similarly, a panel fence can be constructed with wooden slats, exterior-grade plywood, tempered hardboard (masonite) or even water-resistant particle board (chipboard). If you opt for wire fencing, there will be a range of options for both the support posts and the wire mesh or netting. Consider both appearance and cost before making a decision.

COST

There is rarely a time when cost is not a major consideration in a building programme. It is sometimes possible to stagger the building, doing essential projects first (for example, security fencing or boundary walling), and then building additional features like screen walls and other dividing structures within the garden at a later stage, when additional funds are available. Or you can divide each project itself into several stages.

Budget constraints may mean that you are forced to opt for one of the cheaper wall or fencing types, particularly if you cannot complete the project in stages. If you do have to compromise, make sure that whatever you build still meets your needs and fulfils the function for which it was intended (see page 8). You will not be saving money if you have to replace what you have built in a few years' time, simply because it does not provide adequate privacy or is not an effective barrier to strong winds. A brick wall will certainly be more expensive than a picket fence, but if security is your principal motive for building a barrier, you cannot even consider this type of fencing. On the other hand, a relatively inexpensive 1.8 m-high wire-mesh fence may be an acceptable alternative, even though it will not create privacy without the addition of a plant screen.

A sensible approach is to cost the project thoroughly in the planning stage. To do this properly, you will have to establish exactly what quantity of materials is required (see page 36). Everything should be included, from cement, sand and aggregate or crushed stone for foundations and footings, to all the nails, screws and other hardware you are likely to need. If you are building a wall that is to be rendered, do not forget to include paint, and if you are working with timber, allow a sum for any necessary wood coatings or preservatives. If you are planning to use the services of professionals or to employ labour to assist you, be sure to include these amounts in your total costing.

There are numerous professionals who can assist by offering valuable advice, designing structures and drawing up plans, undertaking the actual construction or by organising and overseeing the entire project for you. You will need to decide how much of the work you want to do yourself, and then identify the areas where help is needed.

Design

If yours is to be a purely functional fence or wall, without any special features, you probably will not require any assistance to design it. However, input from a professional can make all the difference, not only to the appearance of the finished product, but also in the choice of location and type of structure you build. It will also be helpful if the structure is a substantial one which requires special skills.

If you are involving a landscape architect or designer in the garden scheme, it makes sense to ask the same person to design your walls and fences. Similarly, if you have used the services of an architect to design the house or any additional building work, you can ensure a continuity of style if you hire the same professional now.

Specialist companies sometimes have their own designers, although many concentrate on structural rather than aesthetic elements.

Plans

If plans are required, these will identify the position of walls or fences and specify their height on a site plan. You may need to indicate the contours of the land and, depending on the type of construction used, include various sections and elevations. Whilst there is unlikely to be anything to stop you from drawing these up yourself, official rules and regulations are usually quite specific in their requirements. Unless you are familiar with these, it is therefore often wise to ask for professional assistance.

Since an architect often includes these elements in a house plan, and a landscaper incorporates them in his or her garden layout, either of these professionals may be approached. Most will work on an hourly basis as a consultant, or get as involved as you want them to be, even ordering materials and overseeing construction if necessary.

If you know exactly what you want, a draughtsman will draw up the plans on your behalf. This is a particularly good option if you are going to do the building yourself, or even hire sub-contractors, as their fees are generally much lower than the other professionals.

Building contractors and specialist fencing companies will usually include the submission of plans in their service, but they do not always have design skills.

Building

Apart from major retaining structures which frequently require the services of an engineer, most brick, block or stone walls can be built by competent DIYers. Fences, too, may be erected by handymen without any special skills. But there are basic building methods and techniques which must be adhered to if you hope to achieve a professional finish (see pages 30–35). It is imperative that you do not hire untrained or inexperienced labourers (however enthusiastic) to do the building work for you. If you do not have the confidence to tackle the project yourself, a fencing or building contractor may be the answer. However, this will cost more and so you must be sure you are paying for quality work. Ask for references and look at other structures built by this person.

Another option is to employ independent artisans. Bricklayers, plasterers, pavers and carpenters will work at an hourly rate or set a fee for the job. You will need to order the materials and supervise your labour force, so it pays to familiarise yourself with basic building principles. These people are not usually difficult to locate, although you will need to obtain reliable references. Ideally, employ artisans who are known to you or to associates; or check the classified advertisements in your local newspaper.

An ambitious rendered wall designed by a professional.

Concrete facebrick and metalwork installed by a specialist.

The importance of the design and style of walls and fences should not be underestimated. These are permanent, often costly, structures which form the framework of any garden. Once in place, they are not easily removed, so it is important that whatever you decide to construct, erect or, in the case of hedging, plant, suits your house and your garden.

Unfortunately, the visual impact of enclosures and dividing barriers is often overlooked, with the result that many of them do nothing much to enhance the look of a garden. Yet, with a little extra thought, effort and imagination, even the simplest, most inexpensive type of barrier can be improved by imaginative design.

Whilst there is no doubt that most boundary walls and fences have a primarily practical function, the very fact that they surround the property means they provide visitors with their first impression of your home.

Boundary structures are highly visible, so attention should be given to both the exterior façade and the appearance of the inside surfaces. The positioning of gates and doors is also very important.

Materials do not have to match those used elsewhere, but they should always complement the finish of the house. Furthermore, the design and style should be consistent with existing architectural elements and with any theme which is apparent in the garden.

Enclosures and screens located within the garden have a variety of functions (see page 39), and some will be more conspicuous than others. The trick is to aim for a pleasing visual effect and continuity. Remember that whatever you construct must form a natural part of the landscaping plan as a whole.

DESIGN BASICS

There are no rigid rules when it comes to garden design, but the importance of a good basic plan cannot be overemphasized. As trees and shrubs take years to develop, it is important to create a sound framework so that they are integrated in the best possible way into any structures you build.

Colourful pencil crayons are an enticement to what lies beyond.

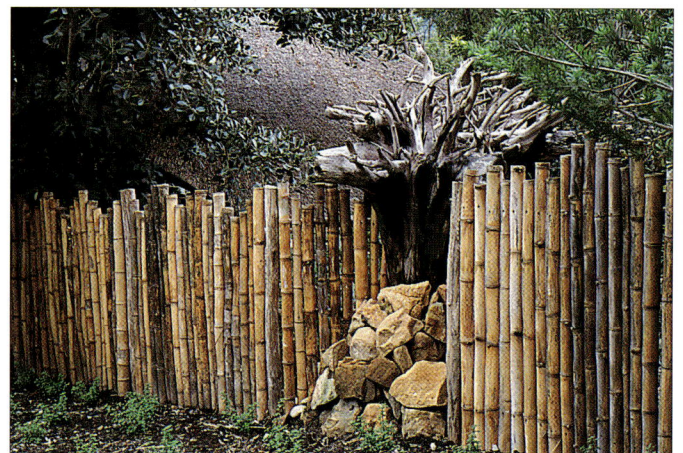
A bamboo palisade fence sets the style for an unusual garden.

Latticework set between brick pillars screens a parking area.

Whether you are starting from scratch or adding to or even simply enclosing an old garden, successful design demands a clear plan of action. On pages 19–20, the importance of an accurate site plan is discussed. In addition to this, you will need to establish whether the layout you are planning is to be essentially formal or informal, and then decide if you are going to follow a theme or establish a particular style.

Garden designers talk about two types of landscaping – hard and soft. The first, which includes the erection of fences and construction of walls, relates to all the hard, rigid materials which may be used to create a basic, static shell. Soft landscaping, on the other hand, refers to trees, foliage, flowers, hedges and so on; in other words, the natural elements which provide a vital softening effect.

Since structural work is, by its very nature, messy and often disruptive, you will need to complete as much hard landscaping as possible before starting to plant.

A modern metal fence is both functional and attractive.

Layout
The layout of any garden will be determined by numerous factors, ranging from the size and shape of the plot to personal preference. It will also be affected by the style, if any, you choose to follow.

It is important to decide whether this arrangement will, in general, be formal or informal. Not only will this help you select the shape and form of flower beds and the type of plants to be included, but also the manner in which the property should be enclosed and, if necessary, divided.

Formal gardens are characterised by symmetry and a carefully planned balance of all the elements involved. All except the most rustic types of material may be used.

There is usually little you can do to correct or alter the position of a boundary wall unless you choose to move it in from the actual perimeter of the property. Facebrick or neatly rendered walls may be used to good effect around the perimeter, while clipped hedges and neat latticework fences are perfect for internal screens. If planters and other features are to be incorporated in a wall, ensure that these fit the formal look.

Informal gardens are typified by irregular-shaped flower beds and gentle curves. However, even though straight lines should generally be avoided in garden design, this principle need not apply to the walls and fences which are built or erected within this area. A simple brick wall will provide a good backdrop to any scheme, while a straightforward post-and-panel fence will provide a good, solid surface for supporting climbing plants.

An informal garden is a good place to use really rustic materials, including random stone and waney board. Wire mesh is not particularly attractive on its own, but if covered with plants or shielded by a screen of foliage, it will complement the informal appearance of your garden.

Style
There are a several readily identifiable garden styles, ranging from the typical cottage garden to classical designs which imitate those laid out by various French and Italian landscapers during the Renaissance.

If your house is built in a specific architectural style, you may wish to continue the theme to the garden. If so, both hard and soft landscaping should be in keeping with the genre. For instance, it would be a pity to build a high wall around a quaint thatched cabin if you plan to plant a traditional cottage garden. Here, a picket fence or low hedge will be a more appropriate choice, as passers-by will be able to see the haphazard abundance of colour which typifies this style. Whitewashed walls which shelter private patios and enclose intimate courtyards are a feature of Mediterranean-style homes, while bamboo screens and latticework will fit a Japanese theme. Post-and-rail fencing will lend a rural feel, and decorative wrought iron can help introduce a touch of Victorian style.

If you are not certain which approach to take, the best advice is to keep walls and fences functional and simple. That way they are more likely to blend with your scheme and to keep your garden stylish.

Theme
In addition to style, which is in itself a theme of sorts, there are many other themes which can be either carried throughout the garden or confined to individual areas.

The best places to get ideas for garden themes are local public gardens and parks, and, of course, gardening books and magazines.

There is little doubt that one of the most popular themes is colour. One can use either a single hue or a combination of several. The question is whether to limit the theme to flowering shrubs and blooms, or to extend it to accessories and man-made structures. It is a personal choice, but garden walls and fences are rarely designed to match a colour scheme. It is usually better to allow these structures to act as a natural foil to the plants and other features which display the chosen shades.

Where several themes are introduced within a garden, a variety of partitions and borders may be considered. A screen wall may be the choice alongside an entertainment patio, while a pretty picket fence may be considered a more appropriate means of separating and shielding the kitchen garden. A latticework structure or wrought-iron fence might be the preferred option around a rose garden, particularly if it is to be smothered with rambling roses or climbers.

Where the theme is herbs and the layout is formal, it makes sense to introduce a clipped hedge of lavender, box or myrtle. If you do not have the patience to plant and tend to these, a low wall is an option. Or consider a plain fence, perhaps to be used as a frame for some climbing plants.

FINISH AND EFFECT

Walls and fences may be as plain or ornate as you wish. This will depend partly on the style, if any, you have chosen to emulate, as well as the materials you decide to use. For instance, planters may be incorporated into the design of just about any brick or concrete block wall design, but they will not be feasible if precast panels are to be used. Similarly, the finish chosen for the top of a picket fence may be quite elaborate, whilst the posts of most other types of fencing are usually kept simple.

If you want to introduce colour by painting the structure, it stands to reason that a suitable material must be used for its construction; avoid facebricks, rustic timber that has not been debarked, uneven waney board and stone.

Capping

Laid along the top of brick or stone walls to aid drainage, capping is often the most decorative feature of these otherwise plain structures, and attention should be paid to its detail. Materials used are often the same as those employed for the wall itself, although this is not always the case. For instance, facebricks may be laid to finish a wall that has been rendered (plastered) and painted, or quarry tiles

may be set atop a plain brick wall. Since capping which is slightly wider than the wall will effectively direct water away from the vertical surface, sloping roof tiles or shaped precast concrete capping set on a neatly rendered structure are particularly suitable materials and usually very attractive options.

Where matching capping bricks are available, these may be preferred, or you can fashion a shaped top with bricks and mortar. For solid facebrick walls, it is quite effective to use bricks laid on-edge. Similarly, pieces of split stone may be set on-edge atop a natural or dressed stone wall to finish it off. When building pierced or open screen walls, a continuous capping of stretcher bond will produce a nice, clean finish.

In previous centuries, walls were sometimes designed with a much wider, rooflike capping than we would use today. Although modern materials generally negate the need for a bulky protective capping, this finishing touch can add authenticity to certain styles. For instance, formal Oriental cappings were traditionally ornate, with flat or half-round tiles laid to create a narrow peaked cap along the entire length of the wall, and the Victorians sometimes created a pitch along the tops of walls and used tiles for capping.

A splash of colour adds interest to this gate.

Reconstituted stone blocks are used to create a visual theme.

This traditional hurdle archway combines well with a simple picket fence.

A modern and unusual gateway.

The entrance to a garden will always give the first impression of what lies beyond. The entrance may also set the style of the property, including the house itself. A door within the garden adds interest and tempts one to enter, even if its very purpose is to prevent one from doing so; and most gates will allow a glimpse, at the very least, of what is on the other side.

Most properties have at least one gate or external door which is located either on the boundary or, less frequently, within the garden itself. These are planned in numerous styles and constructed from a wide variety of materials. Although each has the obvious function of allowing people to pass through the wall or fence of which it is a part, its specific purpose should be carefully considered.

Do you want to encourage people to enter the door or gate, or would you prefer a design which obstructs access? Is this an entry point for vehicles? If so, will pedestrians also use it? Even if security is not a major factor, do you need a secure gate to keep children and animals inside?

While the fence or wall will be the initial guide to the type of gate or door you provide, you will need to decide how secure or substantial the arrangement you provide must be to meet your needs.

Many gardens have more than one entrance, and not all of these are through a gate or door. Even if the area is fenced, an arch or simple gap in a hedge or fence may be sufficient for your needs. This is also the case within the garden, where a variety of gaps and arches allow one to wander from one section to another without the hindrance of opening and shutting anything at all.

Obviously, where security is an important factor and you do not want people to have free access to (or through) the garden, you will be sure to need a well-designed door or gate which prevents this from happening. While a modest wooden gate or typically Victorian wrought-iron one may be quite adequate and perfectly in keeping with the style of your home and garden, if the gate is there to prevent people from entering, or peeping into, the garden you will need a more substantial design, with handles or locks which cannot be easily released from the outside.

The size of the gate will usually be determined by function. For instance, where there is a path, and a gate or door is provided for the exclusive use of pedestrians, the entrance will usually be in proportion to the width of this walkway. The height of any gate or door which is fitted will also match these proportions. Often gateways within the garden are narrow and low, although a more lofty and solid wooden door is undoubtedly a better option in a screen wall planned to hide an area from view. If the gate is to admit vehicles, it will need to be wide enough to do this comfortably. For security reasons you may want to consider those which are remote-controlled (see page 29).

Although there is something to be said for unusual portals which demand attention and make an architectural statement, this approach should be avoided by those with no design experience at all. Rather keep gates and fences simple. A safe rule of thumb is to ensure that the design complements the style of the house, perhaps duplicating features like arches and columns, or simply by framing the house in a sympathetic way.

Materials chosen should generally be consistent or analogous with those used for fences and walls. Timber and metal are probably the two most popular types of material and both may be combined successfully with most enclosures, from planted hedges to solid brick or block walls. Wooden gates usually create a more modest impression, while wrought iron can be as simple or elaborate as you wish.

Capping above an entrance adds character and style.

A modern wall and driveway gate painted white to fit the theme.

Pillars and piers

Often incorporated in walls for structural reasons, pillars and piers can be quite decorative features in themselves. Topped with orbs and spheres, finials, urns and other ornaments, they will add character and charm to any garden style. This is particularly useful when pillars are used as part of a design which incorporates metal- or latticework. You may even choose to decorate them with pots or ornate containers, using plants to create another dimension.

Of course, it is not necessary to embellish every pillar in the structure – many people prefer to limit the use of these embellishments to gateways and entrances (see page 27).

Niches, alcoves and arches

Primarily decorative features, niches, alcoves and arches are common in many period gardens. Even though some of the oldest walled gardens featured recesses which were used for storage, nowadays niches and alcoves are more commonly used to display statuary and sculpture, or simply to add interest. Plaques, wall-mounted sundials and even wall pots may all be mounted within these recesses. Whilst most traditional niches are probably oval or arched in shape, there is no reason why they should not be squared off.

Arches are commonly constructed to support gates and doorways in walls.

However, this is not always the case, and they may be included in the structure to frame a niche, plaque or even a water feature, in which case there will obviously be no access through the archway.

Some Mediterranean-style walls include arches as a design feature, either as points of entry or as openings above ground level in which to place potted plants. Where security is a factor, these arches may be secured with wrought-ironwork.

Planters

A favourite design feature for walls built with bricks, blocks or stone, planters give you the opportunity to soften the hard lines of any structure. They are specially suitable for the exterior of boundary walls and for smaller patios and courtyards where plants will be well contained and generally easier to tend than any established in adjacent beds.

The possible configurations are endless: a parallel low wall built alongside the main structure will create a continuous planter, while recessed compartments will create a more punctuated effect. In situations where a wall cuts across the corner of a property diagonally (some countries have legislation which limits the construction of walls at traffic intersections because of loss of visibility) it is sometimes possible to use the 'lost' piece of land by building

a low planter into the corner. On a patio, planters may be used to create a decorative and interesting stepped effect in the wall.

Paint

Undoubtedly a magical decorating tool for use both inside and outside the house, paint gives instant colour and verve to an exterior. Both walls and fences may be painted (presuming the material is suitable, see page 26) in a single hue or combination of shades, while the location of some structures offers the opportunity of an even more adventurous approach in the form of murals or trompe-l'oeil.

The decision to introduce colour will be an intensely personal one, which should be in keeping with the scheme employed for the house itself. Usually, the most appropriate approach is to match or harmonise the paint finish used on garden walls with the exterior of the house. However, wooden fences may, quite successfully, pick up contrasting accent hues. For instance, a bold blue picket fence might look quite odd around some houses, but if the style is right and the window frames and doors are painted in the same colour, it could look remarkable.

White paint is frequently and very successfully used for all kinds of enclosures and screens. This colour is particularly suitable for formal fencing, latticework screens and all kinds of rendered (plastered) walls.

Spikes set along the top of a garden wall will deter intruders.

An attactive yet reasonably solid automatic gate is a good option for larger properties.

The earliest walls and enclosures were erected for security or safety. In medieval times, solid walls were built for defence, to create an impregnable barrier to thwart the enemy. Early fences were constructed to protect crops from foraging animals or to stop wild animals from attacking stock.

Generally, walls are more secure than fences, but a substantial board fence or a sturdy metal one will also provide a barrier which will deter would-be intruders. Height is important though, as a low enclosure which can be scaled easily will not create an effective obstacle.

Many people believe that a solid enclosure is preferable for security, since potential intruders cannot see into the property – perhaps these walls are effective psychological deterrents.

However, once on the inside of a solid structure, burglars will be out of view of passers-by, and may well take advantage of the added privacy afforded by the solid wall or fence. It is necessary, therefore, to take additional steps such as effective lighting, an alarm system and perhaps burglar bars on the windows to protect your house and belongings.

Remember, too, that any boundary barrier is only as strong as its weakest link, and this is usually the entrance. Doors and gates (see page 27) should be high enough to prevent people from climbing over them, and they must be secure. Generally, it is a good idea to make them the same height as the perimeter enclosure. Furthermore, they should be kept closed and locked at all times: if they are not, anybody can walk in.

Remote control is a great advantage when it comes to opening and shutting entrances. Not only will this enable you to enter your property and close the gate again without leaving your car, but you can also open pedestrian access points this way. A two-way communication system will enable you to speak to visitors without having to open the door or gate; a viewer will allow you to see that person.

Some of the less attractive approaches to security involve the use of barbed wire, spikes and other hazardous materials. Not only do these look ugly, but they can be dangerous and have frequently resulted in legal action against the property owner. Furthermore, in some parts of the world use of these materials is restricted. Check with your local authority before installing something that is intended to cut, impale or give an electric shock to intruders.

Walls and fences come in many different types, from random stone and brick structures to timber palings, picket panels and wire-mesh fences. The classification of barriers and enclosures of all kinds is determined to a large extent by the materials which are used; however, the various categories also depend on the method of construction employed.

The decision about which type to use will depend on numerous factors. By now you will know where your fence or wall is to be sited and you will probably have some idea of the design you want. Before you make a final choice, consider all the options carefully. Apart from aesthetic considerations, evaluate all the practical aspects of the different types. Determine the cost of the materials required, ascertain how durable they will be, and establish the probable maintenance the finished structure will need. It is generally accepted that solid brick or stone walls are more durable than other types, but they are also more costly and take longer to construct than a simple wire enclosure or post-and-rail or picket fence. On the other hand, if timber fencing is to last indefinitely, the wood must be well maintained and repaired immediately there is any deterioration.

If you are going to erect the fence or build the wall yourself, make certain you have all the necessary skills before you start (see pages 40–45). If you are in any doubt about your capabilities, employ a professional to help you or opt for a different type of structure altogether.

WALLS

Although walls may be built in a vast range of styles, there are only a few different types, and these are generally categorised by the materials used for construction. Most walls are built with bricks or blocks made either from clay or concrete. Certain types of wall are best rendered (plastered), whilst others

Handsome wooden panels set neatly between sturdy pillars on a boundary.

Precast concrete units are bolted together to form a solid fence structure.

are intended to be left as they are. Other possible materials include natural stone, where this is available, and various types of timber.

Blocks

Versatile and generally cost-effective, blocks are frequently used to build garden walls. Even though some are large and bulky, most are hollow and reasonably easy to handle.

There are various types of blocks available in a wide range of sizes and finishes. Most are laid in the same way as ordinary bricks (see pages 44–45), and are equally suitable for the construction of decorative features, including flower boxes and archways. Various concrete modular blocks are useful for constructing retaining walls.

The most usual type of block is made from concrete, although adobe (mud) blocks can be found in the United States and clay blocks (maxi bricks) are manufactured in some parts of the world. Glass blocks are also available, although these are more commonly used inside the house.

Standard building blocks are generally quicker to lay than ordinary bricks, and the plain kinds are much cheaper per square metre.

Plain concrete blocks, which are normally hollow and relatively lightweight, will enable you to build a good, sturdy wall; however, they are not particularly attractive and may be faced with a decorative skin (which will obviously increase your costs) or rendered and then painted.

Screen blocks have pierced patterns which add a decorative touch and make them ideal for walls intended to form a partial partition. They can also be used quite effectively to create feature areas within solid structures.

To produce an attractive, regular pattern, these blocks are laid in a stack bond, with no overlaps. For this reason it is essential to construct supporting piers or pillars at regular intervals, which will give added strength and stability, and to include some horizontal wire reinforcement (brickforce) between courses.

Reconstituted (reconstructed) stone blocks are made from concrete which is coloured and moulded to create a textured 'stone' face. Available in numerous sizes (including jumper blocks which span two or more courses), they enable you to create walls which look as though they have been built with natural dressed stone.

Concrete modular blocks intended for the construction of retaining walls are available in a variety of designs. Some systems are interlinked, while others interlock on the horizontal and/or vertical plane. Most of these hollow units can be planted once the wall has been erected. Some are suitable only for light terrace walls rather than for more substantial gravity-retaining walls, which depend on their own mass for stability.

When using modular concrete blocks for a retaining wall, it is essential to follow the manufacturer's instructions. It may also be necessary to consult an engineer for more detailed specifications in terms of your site.

Adobe blocks are common in parts of the United States, particularly the south-west, where they have been made for centuries from the local mud. Nowadays these environmentally friendly blocks are stabilised with asphalt to make them stronger and impervious to water, and consequently are longer lasting. Inexpensive in the areas where they are made, adobe blocks are relatively heavy and cumbersome to work with. They are not available in other countries.

Clay blocks (sometimes referred to as maxi bricks) are manufactured in exactly the same way as ordinary clay bricks, but they are larger in size and can be laid more quickly, and with less mortar. Like non-face bricks, they are intended to be rendered.

Concrete blocks were used to build this pleasing wall.

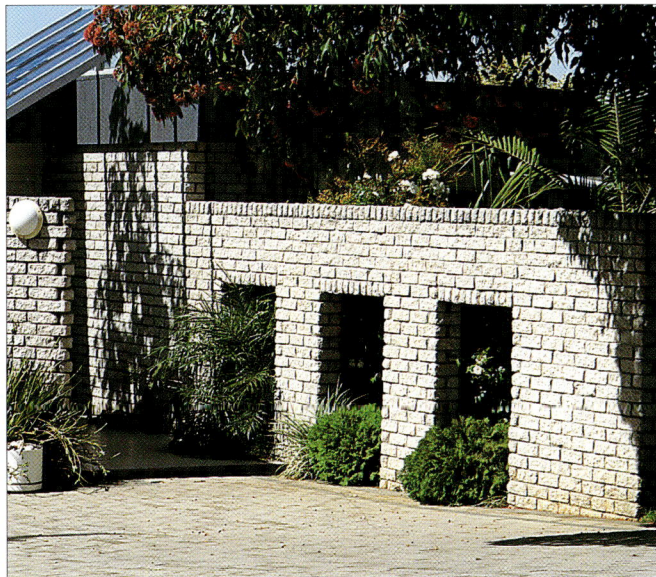

An attractive screen wall built from concrete facebricks.

Clay facebricks are a popular choice for garden boundary walls.

Glass blocks are manufactured so that they may be laid with mortar in the normal way. They are hollow and come in a variety of sizes and finishes. Even though they are more commonly used for walls within the house itself, they may be successfully incorporated in garden screen walls where some visibility is required.

Bricks
A readily available, universally acceptable material, brick is a popular choice for the garden. It is long lasting, versatile and blends well with virtually all architectural styles. Since bricks are relatively small in size and therefore easy to handle, it is also reasonably simple for most people to lay bricks single-handed, which increases their appeal for DIY builders.

Although the dimensions of different types of brick may vary slightly, their universally regular shape makes them easy to bond in neat patterns (a task which is considerably more difficult when building with a material like natural stone). A further advantage is that they may be laid effortlessly in both straight and curved lines, and can be used to develop a multitude of decorative features, including planters, niches and arches.

Manufactured in a wide range of colours and textures, both facebricks and common or non-face bricks, which are intended for rendering, are made from clay, concrete and calcium silicate. Some types are stronger than others, a factor which is particularly important in areas where severe frost, extreme climatic variations or constant sea mist and spray are experienced. Suppliers and local authorities will be able to give further advice.

While most builders use newly made bricks, some people prefer the option of second-hand bricks which are well-weathered and lend an instantly aged

and mellow character to the garden. These are not always easy to find although demolition or architectural salvage companies often have stocks.

Whatever you choose, it is important not to mix different types of brick in a single wall, unless each forms a separate skin (veneer). Concrete and clay bricks have a different rate of expansion and contraction which can lead to cracking if they are combined.

Facebricks (sometimes referred to as facing bricks) are attractive and durable. Clay facebricks are fired at a high temperature, making them strong and highly resistant to adverse weather conditions. There are numerous different types on the market, ranging from relatively smooth surfaces to rough rustic and rockface finishes. Colours, too, are varied, and you can usually find a hue which fits the general theme of an outdoor area. Concrete facebricks are also widely available and manufactured in a range of textures and colours.

Non-face bricks (non-facing bricks) are intended for general building work which is to be rendered (plastered). Since this type of brick is generally protected with rendered mortar, normal grades are not usually fired to the same temperature as facebricks. Non-face brick walls are sometimes left unrendered, to create a deliberate feeling of rusticity. If this is your aim, it is essential to check durability factors

Plants have been allowed to cascade over the edge of a dry stone retaining wall.

Common on sloping plots, retaining walls are invaluable for creating terraces and enlarging the functional area of any garden. They are also often essential where one property is higher than the adjacent one, or where it is necessary to cut into an embankment. Whilst it is quite acceptable to plant a slope (provided of course the gradient is not too steep), both activity and utility areas require a reasonably flat, level surface, and a retaining wall is often the answer.

As the name suggests, retaining walls are built to retain or restrain earth which would otherwise collapse. This means it is vital that the structure is able to resist the forces exerted by the retained material and any extra load which may be imposed on it. This includes everything from soil to buildings and even rain water.

Since even the lowest structure will have to hold a considerable volume of soil in place, drainage will be a vital consideration. If the earth behind any retaining wall becomes waterlogged,

the structure could collapse, irrespective of the method used to build it. If the wall is more than about 1.5 m high, you should always consult an engineer for advice or, possibly, plans. Unless the wall is less than 1 m to 1.2 m high, many local authorities will in any case require plans.

The layout of your house and garden, as well as the site itself, will determine where retaining walls (if any) are to be built, as well as the method of construction.

Various materials may be used, although the strongest and most suitable are probably limited to stone, concrete blocks (including specially designed modular retaining blocks) and clay bricks. Timber poles are sometimes used for very low walls, such as those found around flower beds, and reinforced concrete can be cast in situ to form some major, engineer-designed structures. These may be cantilevered, buttressed or, in the case of a gravity wall, built to such dimensions that it relies on its own mass for stability.

Apart from poles, the simplest type of

retaining wall is constructed with either interlinking or interlocking concrete blocks (see pages 61–63).

These are commonly laid so that they step backwards into the slope, although some designs create vertical walls and may incorporate steps, seating and flower boxes. Since these modular units are hollow, they are commonly filled with earth and then planted, to create what will eventually become a living wall.

The height of the wall will determine the type of foundations required. Low walls built with interlocking blocks may need no foundation other than well-compacted earth, but as a rule all masonry walls must be erected on proper concrete foundations. It is important that such walls should include weep holes or drainage pipes (which are sometimes perforated) at the base of the wall, and should be backfilled with free-draining material such as coarse aggregate to prevent soil from clogging the weep holes. Get professional advice for walls more than 1.5 m high.

Modular concrete retaining blocks.

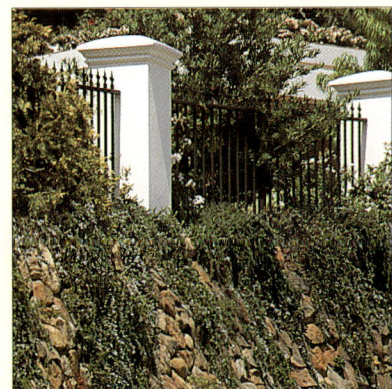

A timber fence runs along the top of a high retaining wall built from stone.

A combination of wall and fence types.

A smoothly rendered brick wall looks neat and attractive and blends with most houses.

Natural stone, found in the area, was used to build this retaining wall within the garden.

Stone

The natural tones and texture of stone are hard to beat. Whether you opt for a random method of laying the material or use dressed stone, cut to form regularly shaped blocks, stone will add charm and character to the garden. Your choice of stone will depend largely on what is available locally. In rocky country, you may be able to use stone found on site; otherwise visit any nearby quarries and see what they have to offer. Other suppliers may be listed in a classified telephone directory (Yellow Pages). If you require a specific type of stone, you may have to get it from another area and could be faced with costly transport charges.

You will find that stone suitable for building is available in a wide range of colours and surface textures. Some, like granite, are extremely tough, making the material durable but difficult to cut. Limestone and sandstone are probably the easiest types to cut and trim, but this can be a disadvantage, especially in very cold or wet climates. Since soft stone will absorb moisture, it is best to coat the finished surface with a good quality masonry sealer.

Stone surfaces are classified according to their finish: polished stone (not usually chosen for garden work) is very smooth; rockfaced (split-faced) stone is rough; while picked, axed and split stone (as well as several other types) has a finished appearance somewhere between the two. For the purposes of garden work it is sufficient to think in broad terms of either dressed stone or rubble walls.

Dressed stone is cut or trimmed and finished to some degree, so that it can be laid in a reasonably regular fashion. Ashlar, which is square-hewn and smoothly finished, creates an imposing effect, while squared rubble will look more informal. Both are laid in uniform courses much the same way as bricks or blocks.

The joints of a dressed stone wall are pointed in a similar way to brickwork, and may be finished so they are more or less flush with the surface or

with your supplier first. The characteristic white saltiness of efflorescence may add the bucolic charm you want, but if the walls are likely to crumble after a few years, you will most definitely want to use a better quality product or to consider rendering the surface instead.

Rendered (plastered) walls

Both blocks and bricks (see pages 31 and 32) may be rendered (plastered) with a mortar mix of cement, building sand, possibly lime, and water (see page 45). There are several finishes and textures which can be achieved, but your choice will largely depend on existing finishes which have been applied to the exterior of your house and outbuildings.

An even finish can be achieved by smoothing the mortar with a wooden float. Very rough finishes can be created by spattering the render, using a simple hand-operated appliance, while a fairly crude Spanish-plaster effect can be produced by indenting the surface with a float.

rusticated to create a sunken joint. Unfortunately it has become very expensive to use cut stone, and skilled craftsmen may be quite difficult to locate in many areas. Furthermore, handling large stones can be extremely slow and heavy work.

Rubble walls are built with uncut or rough-cut stone which is laid in a random fashion. Shapes are varied and so rows are not at all regular. To add stability to the structure, it is wise to lay a flattish course about every 300 mm.

Cheaper to build than a dressed stone (ashlar) wall, but just as much hard work and effort, a rubble wall is characteristic of the traditional cottage-style garden.

Pebble and flint walls are less common, but nonetheless attractive. The shape of the material is irregular, and its size small, so it will not produce a particularly stable structure if used on its own. For this reason, bricks are usually incorporated as a foundation, at corners and as a capping. Steel-grey flint is not available everywhere, but it is possible to use similar pebbles to create the characteristic effect.

Dry stone walls, built without any mortar, are particularly attractive in a rural situation. There is, however, an art to building a dry wall, and it can be an extremely time-consuming project.

Freestanding dry walls must be built so that they slope inwards from the foundation on both sides. This so-called 'batter' is accomplished by making the base of the wall wider than the top. To ensure that it is stable and well balanced, this type of structure incorporates regular bond- or tie-stones which extend through the wall, from one face to the other. The two faces are built with large, heavy stones, usually with a space between them which is filled with chips or smaller stones and pebbles. It is also possible to fill the gap and pack the stones with earth, an especially useful method if you want to plant the wall.

Various cappings may be used to finish a dry wall, including upended stones which may be laid in several traditional patterns. Or you can top the structure with soil and plant it with herbs or ground cover.

Although a retaining dry stone wall is similar in structure, it slopes backwards, in one direction, towards the earth it is holding in place (see page 33).

Concrete

Made by mixing cement, sand and a suitable aggregate (crushed stone or coarse gravel) together with water, concrete may be precast in panels and then erected between upright posts, or used to construct freestanding or retaining walls *in situ*.

Cast (poured) concrete may be used to construct a wall of almost any size or configuration and, if properly reinforced, will provide an exceedingly strong structure. This method is particularly useful for retaining walls (see page 33), but the structure should be designed by an engineer if it is to exceed a height of 1.5 m.

Precast concrete walls are usually factory-made and supplied in panels which are erected horizontally between precast posts. Reasonably versatile, the panels are made in a range of patterns and textures, including brick-faced, smooth and pebbled finishes. Although not especially attractive, they are relatively inexpensive and are well suited for enclosing properties.

A disadvantage of precast concrete walls is that nails cannot be hammered directly into the material and so it is difficult to train creepers and climbers over the structure. An obvious solution is to place a timber trellis in front of the wall and to allow plants to cover this.

Timber

Although timber is more commonly used for fencing (see pages 36–37), walls (stockades) of wood are suitable

An interesting, freestanding dry stone wall has a charm associated with the countryside.

Precast panels on a cast concrete base.

Timber fencing creates a good, solid screen around a suburban property.

A low post-and-rail fence made with poles that have been painted white.

for retaining soil. Since this material is likely to deteriorate more rapidly than masonry or concrete, sturdy logs, poles or railway sleepers (ties) are the most suitable choice. The timber should always be treated with a suitable preservative, and preferably coated with bitumen or some other suitable waterproofing compound.

FENCES

There are many different types of fences to choose from, some of which are more solid and substantial, as well as more secure, than others. Fences are often categorised by the construction material used, and this is how they are listed here. However, a combination of elements may be found in a single structure: wooden poles may be used to support wire mesh, or timber panels may be set between precast concrete posts.

Timber

Both hardwoods (from broadleafed tree species) and softwoods (from conifers) may be used for fencing, although it is the less expensive timbers which are normally used. Your choice will depend to some extent on the wood available in your area. At the same time, the most popular types and styles of fence are universal. Some fences are made from sawn and planed (dressed) timber, others from rough or machined poles. In some instances it is quite acceptable to use wood with the bark still on it – this really depends on the effect you wish to achieve. Generally, rough surfaces will give a rustic look, while a smoother, better-finished appearance tends to seem more sophisticated.

Regardless of the look you want to achieve and the type of fence you decide to build, a golden rule is to use only sound, durable timber. If you use inferior materials, the structure is likely to deteriorate, or even collapse, within a relatively short time.

It is usually sensible to choose timber that has been pressure-treated in the factory, since the average DIY products do not penetrate the wood thoroughly. However the heartwood (found towards the centre of the tree) of some hardwoods is naturally resistant to infestation, so in areas where this is affordable, it is a particularly good choice for fencing posts. Unfortunately these hardy, decay-resistant species (red cedar, redwood and cypress are probably the best known) are not always readily available in all parts of the world.

Paling (palisade) and pole fences are versatile and relatively simple to erect. They do, however, require a lot of timber and therefore can be expensive. Stakes may either be pushed into the ground or nailed to a timber frame which is erected first. If poles (or even railway sleepers) are used, they are generally set in a concrete foundation to create the impression of a stockade.

Panel fences may be built with various materials, including PVC, but timber is undoubtedly the most common option. Prefabricated panels are widely available and are set between some kind of pillar or post, usually made from either precast concrete, timber or even bricks and mortar. Although these upright posts obviously must be strong enough to support the panels, no horizontal framework is normally necessary.

Not only are these fences relatively quick to erect, but they are also economical, and will create effective windbreaks and a solid barrier wherever these are required.

Where timber is used for panel fences, it is generally less substantial in section than the wood used for either post-and-board or picket fences (see below). This does mean, though, that it can be easily interwoven to create an attractive basketweave effect if desired. Exterior-grade plywood is another material which is popular in some parts of the world. Nailed to a frame which is then fixed to the posts, this material forms a solid screen which provides maximum privacy. Lattice panels, on the other hand, create a shield which offers some visual access beyond.

Picket fences are a perennial favourite in numerous settings. Particularly popular for creating a period feel or country-cottage look, pickets are nailed to horizontal rails which in turn are fixed to upright wooden posts. The framework may be assembled *in situ*, and the pickets nailed on to complete the fence; alternatively, picket panels may be attached to the posts as illustrated on pages 48–51. Although the majority of picket fences have straight or angled picket tops, there are many other possibilities, including spear and arrow shapes and even various simple but very effective cut-out designs. While some of the more intricate patterns require reasonably competent carpentry skills, for most people it just means a little more time and effort. Or you may choose to craft the top of the posts and to keep the pickets plain.

Post-and-rail fences may be made with poles, sawn timber, or even with stout square posts and matching rails. The simplest and probably the most common design entails connecting a double row of horizontal rails to short upright posts, set in the ground at equal intervals. The wood you choose, as well as the method used to build the fence, will determine its character. Machined poles used for both post and rail look neat and may even be painted white. Some companies will supply the required lengths with pre-cut holes which enable one to simply slot the poles together. Alternatively, round upright posts may be combined with split-pole rails, which are nailed into the adjoining timber. If the bark is still attached to the wood, the fence will have a more rustic appearance.

Post-and-board fences are usually similar to post-and-rail designs, except that they use sawn planks or board rather than rails. The most typical type incorporates three boards attached horizontally to either sawn posts or wooden poles. Variations involve adding additional timber horizontally or incorporating diagonal slats.

Of course, timber posts and boards may also be used to create a solid 'close-boarded' structure, in which case the boards are positioned closely together when they are nailed to the posts. Alternatively, slats may be set in place to create a series of either horizontal or vertical louvres.

Hurdles and brush fencing are less usual options in many areas, but are attractive and ideal for privacy. Hurdles are hand-crafted using traditional methods which involve weaving lengths of green, pliable wood to form rustic barriers and arches. Brush fencing is held in place with wire stretched between poles.

Bamboo and reeds
Both bamboo and river reeds may be used to create an effective screen or fencing. Mature bamboo, which resembles thick poles when dry, may be set in place to form a closely abutting palisade, while younger plants or river reeds may be tacked or tied onto a post-and-rail framework. Alternatively, these materials may be assembled into panels and then erected against supporting posts.

Unfortunately, even though these materials are attractive and well suited to screens and fences, they are not always available commercially and may be difficult to source. If there is not a natural supply in your area, you may also find this an expensive option.

The most suitable reeds are the Spanish or Norfolk varieties depending on availability. They should be stripped of their tough outer growth and cut to size before they dry out and become hard and brittle; when the reeds are green and pliable they are easier to work with and less likely to crack.

Several types of bamboo may be used, depending on the look you want to achieve. Mature, woody stems may be used to create an open fence effect, while those with thinner, cane-like branches may be tied together in the same way as reeds and are generally better suited for panels. Like reeds, this plant material does tend to become brittle as it dries out, so if you are nailing it in place, it is advisable to drill pilot holes to prevent splitting.

Metal and wire
Various types of metal and wire fencing may be used between posts of metal, timber or masonry. While wire is probably the most inexpensive option, wrought-ironwork can be the most decorative. Another possiblity is chain, which may be strung between

Poles are ideal for an all-weather fence.

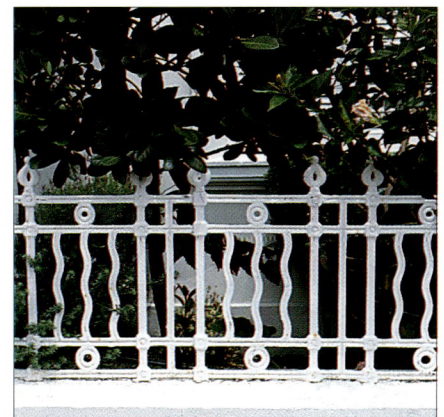
A decorative metal railing is set on a wall.

It takes considerably longer to create a hedge than to construct a fence or build a wall. However, hedges are an inexpensive option for both boundaries and internal screens and offer an attractive alternative in many situations. Used for screening and enclosing gardens for centuries, hedges provide privacy and, once established, create an effective windbreak. They also add interest, colour and texture to the garden, filtering sunlight and introducing an element of contrast.

A hedge effect created by planting.

A wide selection of plants is suitable for hedging purposes, and many of these species will encourage birds to visit the garden – an added bonus, especially in an urban environment.

It is possible to plant either an informal or a formal hedge. The former is really just a densely planted row of plants intended to create a barrier or screen. An informal hedge requires a relatively large space to succeed, and since a variety of plants are usually included, these will invariably grow at different rates.

Formal hedges are also created by growing plants close together, but here the same species is grouped for effect and the foliage trimmed regularly to create a neat shape. This cutting back also encourages growth and makes the hedge thick and bushy, especially at the base.

A common error when trying to establish a hedge is to opt for fast-growing plants. They will certainly cover the area quickly, but will invariably outgrow the framework you intended them to fill at an equally rapid rate. It may be frustrating to wait several seasons for a hedge to establish itself, but it is usually worth it.

Suitable plants need to be severely cut back when they are young and the growing tips should be removed frequently during the growing season. This is because it is essential to prevent plants becoming 'leggy', lower growth being vital to the overall effect. Once the shape and form of the hedge has been established, the only major effort necessary is regular trimming, the frequency depending on the species.

The type and size of hedge you decide to plant will depend entirely on its location and function. A boundary hedge may be allowed to grow quite high, whilst a pretty lavender border around a herb garden will be small by comparison.

There are certain plants which are considered traditional hedging species. These include yew, box and the deciduous beech. Myrtle is a useful plant for low hedges and various Eugenias are very suitable for boundaries. Climatic conditions and the general availablity of plants in your area will be a major factor to consider. Any competent nurseryman will be able to advise on the best hedging plants for your area.

posts; however, this will simpy define a boundary without offering some security or privacy and so is not considered in any detail.

Barbed wire, sold in single strand rolls, is most commonly used for farm fencing or between extension arms erected in industrial situations. Check with your local authority before using this material around your home as there are restrictions in some areas (see also page 29).

Wire-mesh fencing is practical and utilitarian, as well as being relatively inexpensive. Even though it is not particularly attractive on its own, many people choose it because it is affordable and is easily covered with climbing and twining plants.

The mesh is attached to horizontal straining wires stretched between upright posts and intermediate standards, made of either precast concrete, tubular metal or timber (which all must be concreted into the ground). Thinner metal risers or timber poles may be used as standards.

There are various configurations of mesh fencing available, including square welded mesh, hexagonal wire netting and diamond mesh (chain link), usually manufactured with either a clinched, open-ended or barbed top. Relatively lightweight chicken wire (poultry fencing) is another inexpensive option, although it is not generally suitable for perimeter boundaries, being better suited for barricades within the garden itself.

As a precaution against rust, it is important to choose mesh which has been galvanised or coated with PVC. The most common coating is green, but it is sometimes possible to buy black, white or even various primary-coloured materials.

Metal fencing comes in various guises including ornamental wrought iron, modern grille-work and lightweight aluminium. Also made from metal is special swimming pool fencing, commonly manufactured with a hoop top or attractive roll top and minimal horizontal supports to prevent children from being able to climb it.

Perhaps the most attractive metal fencing is the traditional wrought-iron type reminiscent of the Victorian era. Usually incorporated between pillars and above a low brick or stone wall, these designs are now also widely available in aluminium.

More modern designs may also be included within a wall design

Whilst some metal is coated with PVC, other types may be painted or, if the metal is galvanised, left bare.

Almost all types of metal fencing are best erected by professionals or specialist companies.

Normally designed to provide partial protection or privacy within the garden, screens are a useful landscaping tool. Like conventional walls and fences, they may be erected for many reasons: to separate activity areas, to hide rubbish bins, washing lines and other service areas from view, to provide some protection from the sun and to shield specific parts of the garden from the wind. Some types are useful for supporting plants, whilst others will enable you to create an illusion of solitude. With some imagination, it is even possible to use simple screens to create the effect of an outdoor living room.

Even though most types of fence (see pages 36–38), and even some walls, may be used for screening, many people prefer less substantial structures which allow a glimpse of what lies beyond, and do not block the light. The fact that they are essentially small in scale and size also increases the range of possibilities. For instance, whilst it would be foolhardy to use glass or polycarbonate panels to fence off an entire area, these materials may be successfully used as a short screen alongside a patio or pool. Similarly, properly treated canvas or awning material (shadecloth) may be fixed to a wooden framework to create a screen, or you may be lucky enough to find some old wrought-ironwork or decorative fencing which could be used to good effect. Elaborate latticework, or even a straightforward trellis, is also better confined to relatively short lengths.

Relatively lightweight structures, including latticework screens and trellis panels, may be used to create a period feel or to provide a climbing frame for plants. Made of thin laths of wood which cross one another vertically and horizontally, or diagonally in a regular, crisscross pattern, they will provide an attractive partition which does not block out too much sunlight.

Prefabricated trellis panels are usually available in various sizes. Alternatively, you can make your own structure, spacing the laths as close together or far apart as you wish. Latticework, which is predominantly a decorative feature, benefits from the addition of posts and finials, while trellis is planted.

Fencing, as already stated, is not always suitable for screening purposes, but a fairly low picket fence could be used

Several wooden screens shield areas of the garden and provide frames for plants.

very successfully in some instances, particularly if it is decoratively finished. Alternatively a bamboo palisade or pole fence might be an option. Where there is a need for a good windbreak or a structure to buffer noise, most solid timber fencing types (especially board and panel designs) could be used.

Walls are sometimes used for screening, particularly around entertainment patios or other activity areas which need some protection from the elements. However, consider the effects of wind before constructing a solid wall: staggered bricks or perforated screen (breeze) blocks are often a more practical option. For something different, glass bricks may be used on a small scale, or they may be combined with conventional building blocks.

Ultimately, your choice will depend on personal preference and lifestyle, the function your screen will fulfil and the site where it is to be constructed.

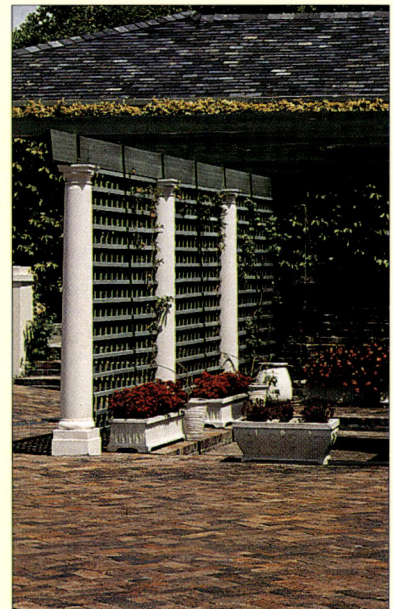
Latticework between precast pillars.

CONSTRUCTION PRINCIPLES

A club hammer is useful for knocking standards for wire-mesh fencing into the ground.

It is important to keep fencing straight and to ensure that all corners are at right-angles.

Careful planning and a thorough understanding of correct building methods are essential for anyone planning to tackle their own walls and fences. Whilst the basic principles are quite elementary, if you want a professional result it is necessary to practise the techniques involved. In addition, a newcomer to DIY will have to ensure that he or she is properly equipped with the correct tools.

There are only a handful of basic rules and these apply to all building methods, irrespective of the materials used: you need a reliable design, good quality materials, and the right tools for the job. But even more important is the need to keep all structures square, level and plumb.

BASIC PRINCIPLES

It should come as no surprise that essential building principles are based on common sense. After all, if a wall is not level, and the corners of a fence are not accurately angled, there will be a danger that these structures will collapse. Unless a wall or fence is curved, it will always be square, level and plumb. Even if a fence is to follow contours, the posts must be upright and straight; and if a wall is to be curved, both horizontal and vertical planes must still be kept level. Although this may be a little more difficult with a material like natural stone, these fundamental principles must be adhered to.

Square

For any structure to be absolutely square, the corners must form 90°. This means that foundations, the footings for pillars, brick courses and so on should all be checked for accuracy at frequent intervals during the building programme.

There are several ways of checking for square, the simplest being to use a tool made for this purpose. A steel builders' square is useful for setting out projects and for bricklaying, while a smaller combination or adjustable carpenters' square is ideal for any woodwork project.

The 3:4:5 method is an invaluable aid in ensuring that walls and fences have been correctly set out: measure 3 m and 4 m respectively out from a central point to form a right angle; then measure the distance between the endpoints of these two lines – it should equal 5 m. If it does not, adjust the angle of the two lines until you get 5 m; at this point, the angle will be 90˚.

Level and plumb

Although you may want to create a slight gradient for drainage purposes, most surfaces will need to be level. It is essential to check the levels regularly, from the foundations up. Poles and posts must be perfectly vertical and brickwork must be both level and plumb. If a wall begins to lean out of alignment, this must be rectified immediately.

The most common tool used for this purpose is an ordinary spirit level. When this is placed against any surface, the bubble in the vial should be centred. A line level, which is simply a spirit vial on a line, may be used to check the horizontal plane of brickwork. Many spirit levels have both horizontal and vertical vials and are invaluable aids for checking vertical planes (plumb).

A combination square (which also incorporates a spirit vial) is useful for ensuring that timber is properly aligned. Invaluable for setting out walls and fences on sloping ground, and for checking that posts and poles are the same height, a water level is also one of the cheapest tools available. The concept that water finds its own level is a simple one and the technique of using it is easy to master: all you need is a length of transparent tubing, or two short pieces of tubing inserted into either end of a length of garden hose. Once filled with water, the tubing is attached to a post or held by a helper at a given point, and the other end moved to the position you want to be the same level. Although not essential

A steel builders' square is invaluable for checking angles when setting out foundations.

Use a spirit level to ensure that all posts and upright poles are perfectly vertical.

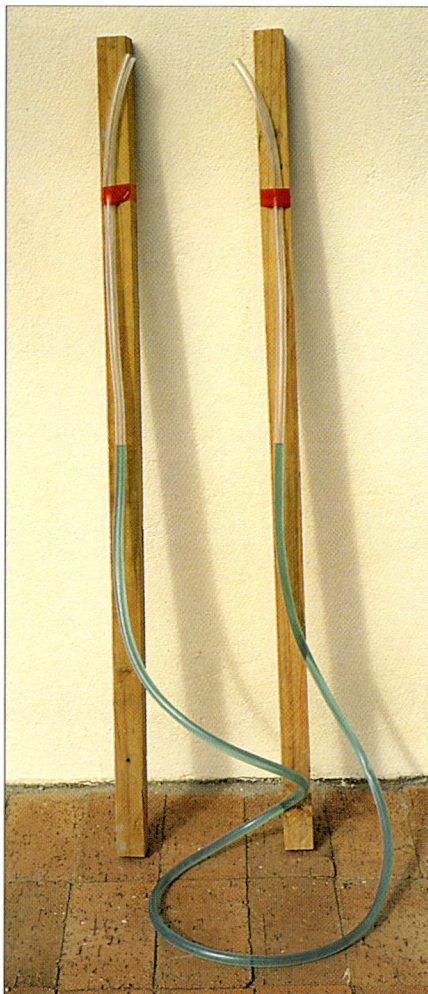
A homemade water level is invaluable.

Use a spanner to tighten nuts and bolts.

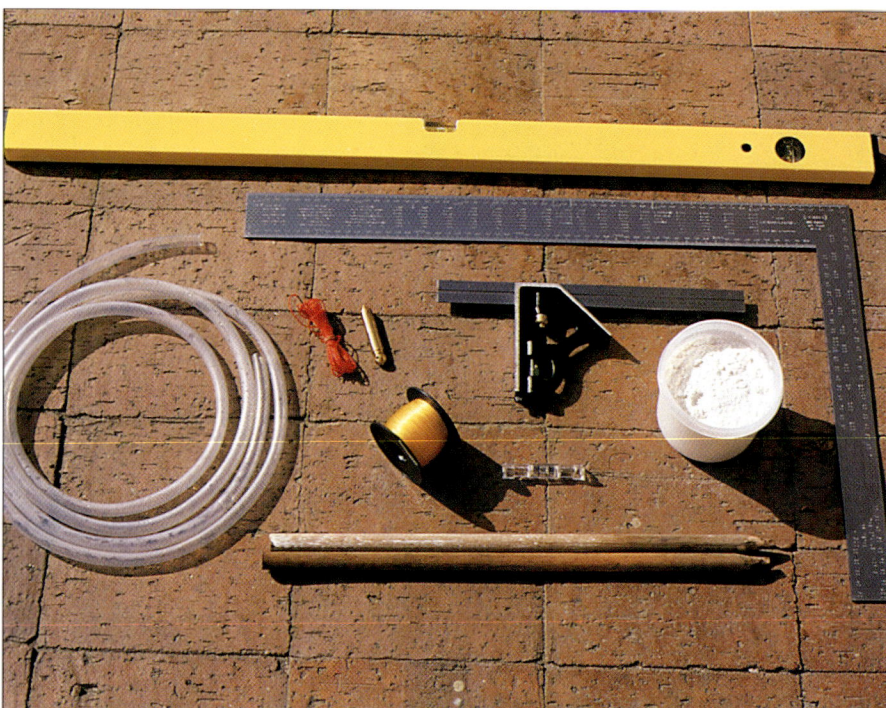
The essential tools required for setting out and ensuring all surfaces are level.

in the tool kit, a plumb bob may be used to check that brickwork is vertical. More commonly used as a final check, the simplest plumb bob is attached to a piece of string; more expensive ones have a built-in line reel.

THE TOOL KIT

It is not necessary to purchase an expensive tool kit to erect a fence or build a wall. In fact, a lot of DIY enthusiasts have most of the essential tools, including spades and shovels, a retractable tape measure, spirit level, screwdrivers, drill and builders' square (see page 40–41). If you do not have a spiral ratchet screwdriver, with different positions and a reverse action enabling you to remove screws easily, consider adding this to your tool kit.

For brickwork you will need a bricklaying trowel for spreading mortar, and a plasterer's wooden float if you are planning to render the surface. Both homemade corner blocks and metal line pins are invaluable aids for keeping brick courses straight and level. Although they are sometimes available commercially, corner blocks are simple to make from blocks of wood. Exact dimensions are not important, but you will need to create two L-shaped pieces of wood with a groove through the centre of each foot of the L. Once builders' line or string has been wound through the slots and around the feet, the blocks may be slotted onto the brickwork at either end, so that the string is in line with the next brick or block course.

Another useful tool, easily made, is a gauge rod: this is a straight-edged piece of timber marked off to indicate each brick course plus mortar joints of 10–15 mm.

A rubber mallet or a club hammer is useful (although not essential) for knocking blocks into place, as is a brick hammer or bolster chisel (used with a club hammer) for the rough cutting of bricks and blocks. You may also need an angle grinder in order to cut concrete blocks accurately.

For timber fencing you will need, as well as some of the above, a suitable handsaw or an electric saw. A general purpose bowsaw is useful for cutting poles, while a tenon saw is invaluable for trimming small pieces of wood. A jigsaw, which may be used to create curves and angles, is an ideal electric saw to buy, although a circular saw is a better choice if large pieces of timber are to be cut. Clamps are also a useful addition to your tool kit. Useful types include common G-clamps, corner clamps (useful when joining timber at right angles) and sash clamps (to hold long pieces of timber in place).

Spanners or wrenches will be required to tighten nuts and bolts on some types of fencing (see page 52), and fencing pliers or a wire strainer to tension a wire-mesh fence.

Power tools will make your job much easier. In addition to a saw, you will find that an electric (or even a battery-operated) drill is an indispensable aid for many projects. Ideally, invest in a machine that has adjustable speeds.

Although concrete may be mixed by hand, many people prefer to use a concrete mixer which may be electrically powered or driven by petrol or diesel. Available in various sizes, these machines may be hired.

While a portable work-bench is useful, a table or trestles may be used to assemble timber panels or pickets.

FOUNDATIONS

The importance of a solid foundation cannot be underestimated. While not all walls need to be laid on concrete, and not all fencing posts need to be embedded in a concrete footing, it is only the smaller and lower structures which may be erected or constructed without concrete.

The size, depth and type of footings or foundations will depend on the design of the wall or the kind of fencing you plan to erect, as well as soil conditions in your garden. Minimum dimensions will usually be specified in your local building regulations. If you are uncertain of the correct options, consult a professional.

The mass of any structure is spread over the width of the foundation. If the soil is unstable, it is usually necessary to make the foundations wider.

There are various kinds of footings and foundations in the building industry, but freestanding garden walls are almost always built on a strip foundation. For this you will need to excavate a trench for the concrete. If the ground slopes, the trench must be stepped down, so that each level is flat.

As a rule, the trench should be at least 100 mm deep for a wall no more than 800 mm high, and 150–200 mm for higher walls. The foundation must be wider than the brick- or blockwork; an easy way to calculate the width of the foundation is to add the width of the wall to double the depth of the foundation. For instance, if a 220 mm-wide one-brick wall is built on a 150 mm-deep foundation, the foundation should be 520 mm wide.

The footings for a freestanding brick pillar measuring about 400 mm x 400 mm must be at least 200 mm deep and 200 mm wider than the pillar on all sides. Precast concrete pillars may be set on fairly thin footings, whilst posts and poles will need to be embedded in the ground, preferably in concrete, to stabilise them.

A safe rule of thumb when estimating footings for posts of all materials is to allow for a depth which equals a quarter of the full length. This means that you should buy 1.6 m-long poles for a 1.2 m-high fence, and 2.65 m-long poles for a 2 m-high fence.

Ideally, posts should be encased in concrete. This does not mean that the entire footing needs to be filled with concrete, though; some people fill about half with hardcore (broken bricks, stones and so on) and then top the hole with concrete; others anchor the base of the post in concrete and then fill the top with soil.

If a concrete footing is not provided for poles, the soil around the poles must be well compacted. In this case, it is often best to bury a longer length to ensure it is properly anchored.

Where they are available, fence spikes are an option which simplifies the job. Manufactured in several sizes, the spikes are welded to a square metal socket designed to anchor posts securely. As these are driven into the ground with a heavy sledge hammer, it can be a little difficult ensuring they

Measure the width of the foundation and string a line as a guide before you dig the trench.

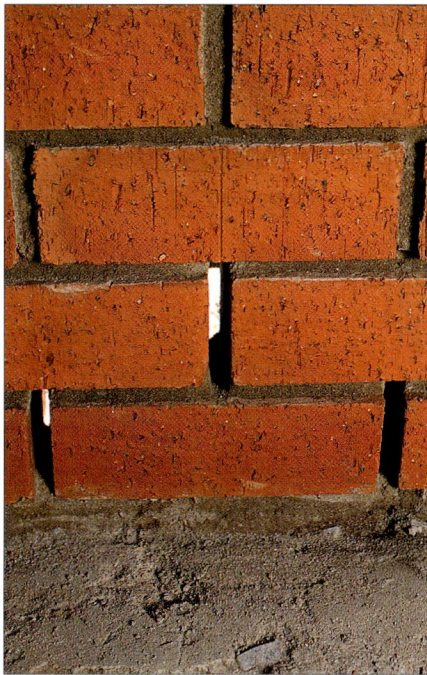

Stretcher bond brickwork with drainage.

Well-bonded reconstituted concrete blocks.

are absolutely vertical. Use an offcut of wood in the socket to check for plumb before you have hammered the fence spike right into the ground.

Concrete

Made by mixing together various quantities of cement, sand and crushed stone (aggregate) with water, concrete hardens as a result of a chemical reaction that occurs between the cement and the water. Although it gains most of its strength within the first 28 days of being laid, concrete in moist soil will continue to strengthen for several years.

Although there are various types of cement, ordinary Portland cement is most commonly used. Sold in sacks, it should be stored in a dry place where it will not get hard and lumpy.

The sand used for concrete should be reasonably coarse (or sharp) compared to the soft building sand used for mortar. Although some builder's merchants sell it in bags, it is usually more sensible to order in bulk, even though the smallest load most suppliers will deliver is 0.5 m³.

Crushed stone (aggregate) is sold in bags or delivered in bulk. Gradings vary, but 19–20 mm 'single-sized' stone is most commonly used.

Various concrete mixes are recommended, depending on local conditions and the type of work which is to be done. In areas where good quality crushed stone is available, a 1:3:6 mixture (cement:sand:stone) is quite adequate for lightly loaded footings and the foundations of garden walls. If a relatively inferior 19 mm crushed stone is used, a ratio of 1:4:4 is preferred. If a stronger mix is required, alter the ratio to 1:2½:3½. Remember that the more sand you include in the mix, the weaker the concrete will be.

Concrete is always mixed in batches, depending on how much you can place before it begins to set. Mix it on a clean, dry surface or in a wheelbarrow. Measure the dry materials out in the preferred ratio, using a suitable container (a clean 25 litre paint drum is a good option).

Mix together the cement and sand until the colour of the mixture is fairly uniform. Form a hollow in the middle, and then add a little water at a time (being careful not to make the mixture too sloppy), gradually mixing by shovelling the dry materials into the middle. When you have a workable consistency, add the crushed stone. If it seems dry, add a little more water.

When using a concrete mixer, it is advisable to load the crushed stone into the mixer first. This will help prevent a build-up of cement on the blades. Then add the cement, sand and enough water to blend it together.

It is vital that the concrete does not dry out before it is placed. Also, if the stone begins to settle, you will need to mix it again. Although the concrete should not be placed on saturated ground where water has pooled, it is good building practice to lightly wet the sub-base to prevent the soil from absorbing moisture from the concrete.

Unless the upper level of your foundation or footing will be above ground level for some reason, it is not necessary to construct formwork to hold the concrete in place. You can pour or shovel it into the excavated trench and then compact it well by tamping with the back of a shovel (or, for smaller jobs, even with the trowel). You can also use a straight-edged piece of wood to smooth the surface, using a chopping action to further compact it and expel air bubbles, and a sawing action to level it. Remember that where reinforcing is included, it is essential to compact the concrete thoroughly to minimise voids.

Concrete must be kept moist for it to cure, and ideally it should be left for five to seven days before building commences. In practice, though, most builders start brickwork the day after the foundations are complete.

BRICKLAYING

While the technique of laying bricks and blocks is well illustrated in the step-by-step instructions that follow, note that success lies in the basic principles previously mentioned: unless a wall is square, level and plumb, it will not look professional.

It is important to use a suitable mortar mix (see pages 46 and 48). The mortar is mixed in much the same way as concrete, but without the addition of stone (cement:sand in a 1:4 ratio, or weaker if required). You need clean builders' sand (preferably soft sand) for the mixture. Good quality building sand is evenly graded. Avoid sand with clay in it or any sand which contains salt or shell particles. Lime may be added to the mixture to improve workability, or use a proprietary plasticiser in the quantities recommended by the manufacturer. It is best to mix reasonably small batches of mortar, especially if you are not an experienced bricklayer.

Each course of bricks or blocks is bedded in mortar, while the end of every brick or block to be laid is 'buttered' by squashing the mortar onto it. Each one is pushed firmly into position and then gently tapped with the handle of the trowel to level it. If there is still a gap between bricks or blocks, this is filled afterwards with more mortar using a trowel. It pays to work neatly, and excess mortar should be scraped from the wall as you work.

Do not forget that you will need to check all your surfaces regularly with a spirit level to ensure they are level. Corner blocks and a line (see page 42) will help keep courses straight, and a gauge rod will enable you to check that mortar joints are even.

RENDERING (PLASTERING)
There are two reasons for rendering walls with mortar: aesthetics and to make them more weatherproof.

For a successful job, it is essential that the mortar sticks to the surface you are rendering. It must also cure without cracking. A newly built wall will usually be suitable for rendering; an old wall may need to be cleaned to ensure that it is free of dirt, dust and grime. Wet the surface just before work is to begin.

Before you start, you will need to estimate what quantities of cement and sand, and possibly lime, are required. A standard mixture comprises 50 kg cement, 25 kg lime and 250 kg of sand (1:½:5). Experts also recommend that the mortar used for block- or bricklaying should match that used to render the surface (see pages 54 and 58).

To help prevent cracking, avoid working in hot sun or strong wind. Mix small batches that can be used within an hour, and lay the mortar firmly on

the wall with a plasterer's trowel. The mixture should not be thicker than 15 mm, or thinner than 10 mm.

You will need to leave the mortar to set for about an hour before scraping the surface with a screed board or straight-edged piece of wood. Then wood float it to get a reasonably smooth surface. If you want a rough surface, this can be achieved by brushing with a block brush instead of scraping and floating.

If the wall is very smooth, and the mixture does not adhere at first, you may need to apply a spatterdash coat to roughen the surface. This is done by mixing a thick slurry of cement and sand in the ratio 1:2, which is then spattered unevenly onto the wall surface. It should be kept moist with plastic sheeting or sacking until it sets properly, and you can then continue to render the wall.

Make sure that the rendered surface does not dry out too quickly. Try to keep it damp for two or three days by spraying it gently with a hosepipe, being careful to use a fine mist which will not damage the surface.

DRAINAGE
It is important to ensure that walls and fences do not become waterlogged. This is especially important for a retaining wall, which can act as a dam for any water which builds up behind it.

The simplest solution is to leave some of the vertical joints in the first course unmortared to create weep holes. Alternatively, incorporate a 40 mm drain pipe in the base of the wall at 600 mm intervals.

To improve the flow of water to the drain pipes, backfill the area behind the wall with gravel or crushed stone. It may also be advisable (if, for instance, clay is a problem) to include perforated pipework and a layer of geotextile material to form a fin-shaped drain which will allow the water to flow freely.

To prevent the wall face becoming stained with dissolved minerals, insert a vertical polythene damp course against the wall before backfilling.

Stormwater drains may also be necessary at the upper level of a retaining wall to aid the discharge of surface water which could otherwise cause the collapse of the wall.

An effective, fin-shaped drain is created with perforated piping and geotextile material.

STEP-BY-STEP BUILDING METHODS

Armed with a thorough knowledge of correct building principles, you should be confident enough to tackle most fence and wall projects. Many of the basic techniques are covered on pages 40–45, while more specific information and detailed instructions are given in the step-by-step instructions which follow. These illustrated guidelines range from the erection of a straightforward wire-mesh fence (which requires minimal building skills) to the construction of a relatively ambitious concrete block wall. The intention is to demonstrate a range of skills which will enable you to undertake any of the plan projects on pages 64–73, or even to devise and construct your own fence or wall design and layout.

There are step-by-step instructions for two types of timber structure: a very basic lattice screen, and a rather unusual picket fence which demonstrates how to assemble a standard panel and could easily be adapted for any other panel fence. The picket fence guidelines also clearly illustrate how to set out any wall or fence structure and include a thorough description of the 3:4:5 method explained on page 41. The importance of keeping all posts vertical is also emphasised photographically.

While the step-by-step instructions for a wire-mesh fence are reasonably basic, they also detail how to tension the material correctly and how to use fencing pliers to neatly finish the job. Although the uprights used here are tubular galvanised metal poles, any type of suitable posts and standards may be used. Instructions are included in the box on page 52 for ordinary metal droppers and for timber poles, either of which may be incorporated.

In an effort to illustrate a good cross-section of wall types, the step-by-step instructions include a reasonably wide range of materials and possibilities. Additional information about bricks, blocks, foundations and mortar requirements is included, where relevant, in the introductory section to each set of guidelines. Again, the intention is that the instructions will enable you to tackle any type or design of wall you may wish to build.

Several possibilities are given in the plans on pages 64–73.

Basic bricklaying skills are illustrated in the step-by-step facebrick wall shown on pages 54–55. Facebricks were used here to build a one-brick (double skin) wall which includes a simple pillar which could be used to hang a gate. One would use the same techniques for all other brick types.

The reconstituted stone wall, also with pillars, illustrates how different-sized units are incorporated in a single structure, as well as how to lay capping along the top of a wall, while the concrete block wall features a rubbish bin compartment and a doorway. There are also step-by-step instructions for rendering (plastering) the concrete block wall.

The final set of instructions illustrates the basic methods used to construct retaining walls with concrete modular blocks and with smaller terrace blocks.

You could also build a retaining wall with bricks or concrete blocks and mortar, provided adequate steps are taken to ensure there is proper drainage (see page 45).

ESTIMATING QUANTITIES

BRICKS AND BLOCKS
To build a single (half-brick) wall use 55 bricks for 1 m²
To build a double (one-brick) wall use 110 bricks for 1 m²
To build a wall with 390 mm x 190 mm x 190 mm blocks use
 12½ blocks for 1 m², and 100 blocks for 8 m²
To build a wall with 290 mm x 290 mm x 90 mm/100 mm
 perforated screen blocks use 11 blocks for 1 m²
To build a wall with any other blocks divide the surface area of the
 wall by the area of one block

CONCRETE MIXES
Quantities based on using 19–20 mm crushed stone
For lightly loaded footings use
 1 cement + 3 sand + 6 aggregate, or
 1 cement + 4 sand + 4 crushed stone
For heavy-duty foundations use
 1 cement + 2½ sand + 3½ aggregate, or
 1 cement + 3 sand + 3 crushed stone

CONCRETE
For a 1:3:6 mix use 220 kg cement for 1 m³
For a 1:4:4 mix use 250 kg cement for 1 m³
For a 1:2½:3½ mix use 300 kg cement for 1 m³
For a 1:3:3 mix use 320 kg cement for 1 m³

MORTAR MIXES
For laying facebricks use 1 cement + ½ lime (optional) + 4 sand
For concrete blockwork and non-facebricks use
 1 cement + ½ lime (optional) + 6 sand
For rendering (plastering) use as for above, or
 1 cement + ½ lime + 5 sand

MORTAR
To build a single (half-brick) wall use 50 kg cement for 200 bricks
To build a double (one-brick) wall use 50 kg cement for 150 bricks
To build a wall with 390 mm x 190 mm x 190 mm blocks use
 32½ kg cement to lay 100 blocks

Assembling a simple lattice panel, consisting of laths of wood which crisscross one another vertically and horizontally, or diagonally, takes very basic carpentry skills which are limited to sawing the wood and possibly drilling holes for bolts. You may, of course, choose to make several panels, and to mount them to a series of upright posts in the same way as for the picket fence, illustrated on pages 48–51. Since these structures are intended to be relatively lightweight,

very slim timbers may be used. If, however, you intend nailing each piece where it intersects the next, you will need to opt for laths which are thick enough to accommodate the nails. Your choice will depend on the design and reason for building the screen: if it is to form a trellis for plants, the wood must be strong enough to support climbers and creepers; if it is simply going to block an unsightly view, you can use thinner wood, but you may want to place the slats closer together.

MATERIALS

This screen uses thin 2.2 m x 44 mm x 10 mm laths attached at 144 mm centres to a 2.06 m x 1.63 m frame made with 44 mm x 44 mm battens. The completed screen is bolted to fairly hefty 2.25 m x 96 mm x 70 mm upright posts, one of which is bolted to the wall. If your screen is freestanding, anchor the posts in a concrete footing (see pages 43–44): the posts should then be 2.75–3.45 m long. You need 8 x 100 mm and 54 x 25 mm wire nails.

1 Cut the wood for the framework and laths to size with a tenon saw. For this design, cut 15 x 44 mm x 10 mm laths to a length of 1.63 m and 10 to a length of 2.06 m. Trim the 44 mm x 44 mm battens to make 2 x 1.63 m and 2 x 1.97 m lengths.

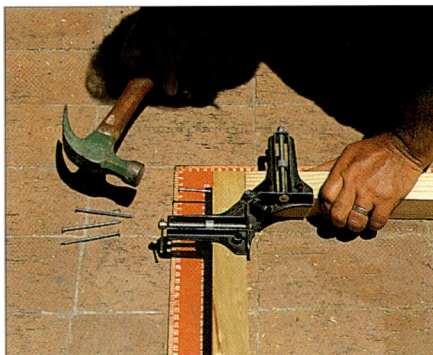

2 Assemble the lattice panel flat on the ground. Clamp the 44 mm x 44 mm lengths of timber at 90° with the longer lengths on the inside. Use a builder's square to check the angles. Nail together with two 100 mm-long wire nails at each angle.

3 Once the framework is complete, nail the 15 x 1.63 m horizontal laths into place at 100 mm intervals with 25 mm nails, placing a lath at each end to cover the frame. Nail on the 10 vertical laths, omitting the end lath on each side.

4 Bolt or concrete the upright posts into position, depending on the location you have chosen. Make sure they are correctly spaced and absolutely vertical. Position the latticework panel, using a spirit level to check for accuracy.

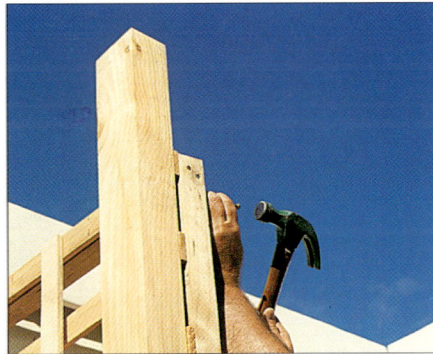

5 Now nail the panel to the upright posts, taking care not to shift it out of alignment. Alternatively, screw the panel into place, predrilling the holes. If the posts are a little longer than required, use a handsaw to cut the excess off the tops.

6 Finally, seal or paint the screen, or give it a coating of a penetrating oil dressing to preserve the wood. If you plan to grow plants over the screen, it is important to do this now, as the wood will be inaccessible once the plants have grown.

Picket fences are relatively simple to erect and yet, if they are imaginatively designed, they are one of the most attractive fencing possibilities available. Although they are traditionally quite low, picket fences may be built to any height. Similarly, while the typical kind features pickets that are fairly widely spaced, there is no reason why you should not attach them close together to gain privacy.

Made with posts and intermediate lengths of timber (or pickets) which are vertically attached to horizontal supports, these fences are sometimes sold in pre-assembled form.

If you are planning to make your own picket fence from scratch, it is essential to ensure that all the sections (or panels) between the posts are of equal length and that the pickets are all exactly the same size and height. The tops of the posts may be plain or decorative, and either sawn and planed timber or machined poles may be used, depending on the design.

The range of possibilities for pickets is endless, ranging from flat, rounded or pointed ends to intricate cut-outs or spear-shapes. The pickets shown in this step-by-step illustrate an ingenious method of creating the effect of a

triangular cut-out. No special carpentry skills are necessary, and the only tool you will need is a jigsaw.

MATERIALS

Sawn and planed timber is used for this 1.2 m-high picket fence. There is no need to use timber of exactly the same dimension as shown here, but choose something similar. Most timber merchants use nominal sizes when describing the material; these relate to the original dimensions of the timber. When it is sawn there is some wastage, and even more once it has been planed.

Fairly stocky 100 mm x 40 mm upright posts are used here, while the 2.4 m horizontal support beams are 45 mm x 45 mm. You could also use 38 mm x 38 mm battens. The 1.2 m-high pickets are 70 mm x 18 mm in size. These pickets are made from 2.4 m lengths of timber, which are sawn in half at the correct angle.

The spacing of the pickets depends upon personal choice. The ones shown here are attached in pairs, because of the design. The space between the pickets alternates between 30 mm and 70 mm. You can alter this spacing if you wish,

but remember that if you decrease it a greater number of pickets will be required for each panel.

FOOTINGS

Although the footings of a very low picket fence may be anchored directly in the ground, it is best to concrete them into place. The recommended ratio of cement:sand:crushed stone is 1:4:4. If you are using a really good quality crushed stone, you may alter this to 1:3:6. A stronger mix is not necessary for a fence of this height.

FIXING AND FASTENING

Galvanised nails should be used for all outdoor woodwork. Screws should either be galvanised or made of brass. Always choose nails and screws that will penetrate one piece of wood and go half to three-quarters of the way through the other.

Nails used to fix the slats to the support pieces are 50 mm long, while those used to nail the panels to the thicker posts are 75 mm long. Since a gate will be used often, it is best to use screws to fasten the timber; you need No. 6 (3.5 mm) x 35 mm-long screws for the Z-brace, and No. 6 (3.5 mm) x 16 mm screws for the hinges.

1 Mark out the position of the fence, hammering in pegs to indicate where the main supporting posts will be concreted into the ground. The distance between the posts will depend on the size of the picket panels (these are 2.4 m apart).

2 It is essential that you mark out the fence accurately. Measure the distance required between the pegs with a retractable steel rule, then string a line along the entire length to ensure that all the posts will be properly aligned.

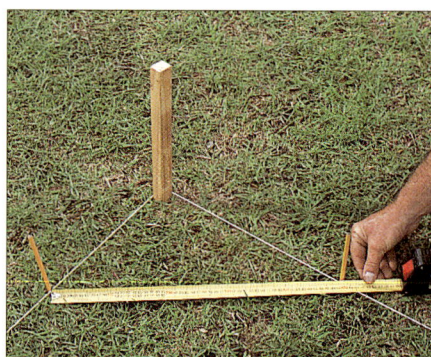

3 Make certain that all corners are at 90°. The best way to check this is to use the 3:4:5 method (see page 41): measure and mark 300 mm and 400 mm on each side of the corner; the distance between the two should be 500 mm.

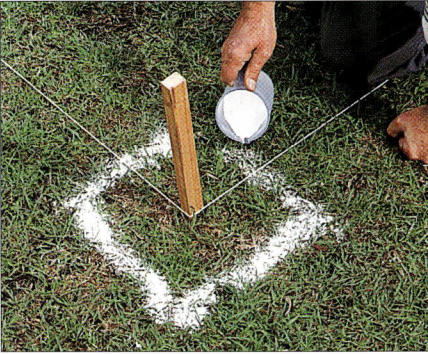

4 The wooden pegs mark the central position of each 400 mm x 400 mm footing. Since you will have to remove the pegs to excavate holes for the foundation footings, mark the area around each peg using cement, lime or even flour.

5 Remove the pegs and excavate each hole to a depth of about 400 mm, depending on the length of the posts. If the fence is to be erected in an area where there is established lawn, remove the sods of grass carefully so they can be re-used.

6 Use a steel tape to check that all the footings are the same depth as each other. Remember that each footing should be as deep as about a quarter of the total length of the posts, to ensure that the posts will be firmly anchored.

7 Timber which is to be buried in the ground should be given some extra protection, even if it has been previously treated. Coat the ends with creosote (although this is a toxic material) or with a bitumen waterproofing compound.

8 Now position all the upright posts in the footings, using battens or other suitable offcuts of timber to brace them firmly in place and keep them straight. Use a spirit level to ensure that each one of the posts is absolutely vertical.

9 You will need to make certain that the tops of all the posts are at the same height. Any longer ones will have to be trimmed, or dug deeper into the ground. Use a water level, and mark the top of the corner posts at the point where they are equal.

10 Tie a length of string tightly between each pair of corner posts at the height of the marks made in step 9. Use the string as a guide to mark this point on the other posts. Trim longer posts or dig deeper footings to make the tops of all posts level.

11 Now assemble the picket panels. Cut the tops of each picket to the required shape. These are to be cut at an angle, so use a carpenter's or combination square to mark an accurate cutting line, and cut all the tops at precisely the same angle.

12 Working on a portable workbench or on a secure pair of trestles, use a jigsaw to cut across the line you marked. Each picket is 1.2 m high from the tip to base, and you will need 20 for each panel. Hold the wood steady and cut firmly.

13 Make triangular side-cuts in the upper section of each picket for a cut-out effect. Make sure that the cuts are at the same angles and the same distance from the top. Cut out with a jigsaw. When a pair of pickets is placed together it will form a diamond.

14 Each of the panels is 2.4 m long and is made by nailing 19 of the 20 pickets to two horizontal lengths of timber. It is vital that each of these horizontal lengths is exactly the same: measure them all and cut off the excess with a jigsaw or tenon saw.

15 The first picket of each slat is not attached until the panels have been nailed to the upright posts. Before assembling the panel, measure and mark the position of the second picket, 100 mm from the end, and the position of the last picket, 70 mm in.

16 Place the two lengths of timber which will form the horizontal support beams for the pickets onto a working surface 800 mm apart, measuring this distance from the outer edge of each beam. Make sure they are equidistant along the full length.

17 Place the first picket across the two pieces of timber so that 200 mm extends above it and 200 mm below. Use a builder's square to make absolutely certain the picket meets the horizontal support beams at 90˚, or the fence will not be square.

18 Nail the picket onto the horizontal beams. Use two galvanised nails (that will not rust outdoors) top and bottom and make sure that they are long enough to go through the picket as well as three-quarters of the beam.

19 You will need to space the pickets accurately, and the best way to do this is with straight lengths of timber. Here each pair of pickets is spaced with a 30 mm-wide batten, and every second one with a 70 mm-wide plank the same width as a picket.

20 Once all 19 pickets have been nailed in place, fix the panel to the upright posts. The panel must be positioned so that it is absolutely straight and the horizontal timbers level. If the ground slopes, support that section of the base with wood.

21 Although it is not necessary to screw any of the panels into place, it is sensible to drill pilot holes to prevent the wood from splitting when you nail the panels to the posts. Make sure that the size of the drill bit is narrower than the nails.

22 Hammer one nail into each horizontal section at each end. Note that the bracing timbers are still in position and that the posts have not yet been concreted into the ground. This enables you to adjust the panels to keep them in a totally straight line.

23 The number of panels required will depend on the total length of your fence. Position and nail all the panels, remembering to use a spirit level to check each one. Then nail on the missing picket at the beginning of each of the panels.

24 Before you concrete the posts into the ground, make sure the panels are aligned and use a spirit level to double-check that each post is still vertical. If any of them have moved, adjust the bracing otherwise you will end up with a skew fence.

25 On a clean, dry surface or in a wheelbarrow, mix the concrete in the ratio 1:4:4 (cement:sand:stone) or stronger if you wish (see page 44). Slightly dampen the soil in the holes before adding the cement, to prevent moisture being absorbed from the soil.

26 The 900 mm-wide gate is made in much the same way as the panels, except that only 8 pickets are used and these are held together with a sturdy Z-brace. This is made with 110 mm x 22 mm timber screwed securely to the pickets.

27 You will need to use gate hinges to attach the gate securely to the upright posts. Each hinge is screwed to the Z-brace. Use a wood bit to drill the holes and then secure the hinge with either galvanised or brass screws which will not rust.

28 Before you attach the gate it is vital to ensure that it is properly positioned. As it will not touch the ground, you will have to prop it up on several offcuts of wood. If the ground slopes, you will need to use more pieces on one side.

29 Use your spirit level vertically to check that the gate is straight. Then check again, placing the tool on the horizontal sections of the Z-brace to make sure that it is level. It is important to check carefully, as if it is not level the gate will hang at an angle.

30 Mark the position of the hinges on the upright posts so that you can see where to drill holes in the posts. Remove the gate while drilling. Reposition it, then loosely position all 6 screws and tighten them gradually. Finally, fit a latch.

Wire mesh is the most inexpensive option when it comes to fencing. No complicated building skills are required, but it is essential to strain the wire correctly and to connect the mesh to the posts and straining wire neatly, using the proper tools.

If wire mesh is not properly strained, it will sag; all posts must be securely anchored in 600 mm-deep footings, filled at least halfway with concrete.

Intermediate standards can usually be set in 400 mm-deep footings.

Several types of corner and straining posts may be used (see box below). These are usually spaced up to 9 m apart, with standards set in the ground no less than every 3.5 m.

If there is a change in ground level along the length of the fence, an additional straining post will be required here.

MATERIALS
The step-by-step instructions show tubular metal posts (76 mm diameter at the corners and 48 mm in between). The PVC-coated 2.5 mm diamond (chainlink) mesh is strained with 3 mm wire, while thinner 2 mm wire is used to bind it to the post.

You will need 3 horizontal rows of straining wire for a 1.2 m-high fence, and 4 if it is 1.8 m high.

UPRIGHT SUPPORTS

Droppers (stakes)
Ordinary droppers are a reasonably cheap option, and are simply hammered into place. Thread binding wire through the holes and use fencing pliers to twist it around the straining wire.

Timber poles
Timber poles are easily included in a wire-mesh fence, even if metal corner posts are used. They are concreted into position. Hammer in 2–3 U-shaped fencing staples to connect the strainers to the poles.

Galvanised metal poles
These are concreted firmly into the ground. They are connected to the strainers with thinner straining wire. It is essential that holes for the wires are drilled before the posts are concreted into place.

1   Tubular metal corner and straining posts are usually assembled before they are concreted into place. Bolt the stays to the uprights using the correct spanners. If wooden posts and stays are used, these can be nailed together.

2   Before any posts are set in the ground, you will have to decide exactly where the fence is to be erected. Set out the line it is to follow and then mark out the position of all corner posts. Mark the footings and then excavate to the required depth.

3   Intermediate standards must be placed in line with the corner posts. Use the 3:4:5 method (see page 41) to ensure that the line you are following is at 90° to the first corner post, and then measure and mark the position of the other uprights.

4 Once the upright posts and stays are in place, check that the post is vertical. Fill the footings at least halfway with concrete and top them with soil. Leave the footings to set overnight and then attach the straining wires.

5 Insert suitable eye bolts (straining bolts) into the holes in the top of the corner posts, together with nuts and washers. Do not tighten the bolt completely; turn the nut gently until the bolt just appears through the back of the nut.

6 Measure enough of the straining wire to span the posts plus a little extra to enable you to wind it tightly to the posts at each end. Cut the wire with a pair of proper fencing pliers, using the correct slot to get a good, clean break.

7 Loop the wire through the eye of the straining bolt and use the groove in the front of the fencing pliers to hold it taut. Now secure the wire by twisting it back around itself, so that it does not slip back through the bolt when you start to strain the full length.

8 Tighten the nut with a spanner, using a screwdriver to stop the bolt from turning. Do not tighten either side completely; rather take up the slack gradually from both ends. It is best to tighten the bottom wire first before tightening those above it.

9 Using a screwdriver to help hold the bolt secure, use the specially designed underside of the fencing pliers (between the handles) to wind the wire neatly back around itself. Trim the excess with the cutting edge of the pliers, to create a neat finish.

10 Once the straining wires have been attached to the corner posts and tightly stretched, attach them to the intermediate standards. Do this by winding the wire neatly, as in step 9, but with a smaller gauge binding wire than previously used.

11 When these wires are secure, attach the wire mesh. Start at a corner, attaching one end to the top of the post. Wrap the binding wire several times around the post and through the mesh, then twist the ends with the pliers to tighten and neaten.

12 Finally, working along the full length of the fence, pull the wire mesh taut, and attach it firmly to the straining wires at regular intervals on all levels. Do this by looping the thinner binding wire around the diamond mesh and the horizontal straining wires.

All types of brick are suitable for garden walls (see page 32), but facebrick is a particularly good choice as it looks attractive and is easy to maintain. The basic technique of laying bricks is quite easy to master, provided the basic principles of construction are followed (see pages 40–45).

Both half-brick (built with a single skin of brickwork) and one-brick (which comprises a double skin) walls may be built in the garden – the choice will depend on both the length and height of the structure you are planning. Local building regulations contain minimum specifications, but all longish walls must always be supported by piers or pillars, and they should have regular expansion joints (see page 60, step 12) every 6–7 m.

Even though this 5 m-long wall is only about 800 mm high, it consists of a double skin and includes two stocky pillars to accommodate an entrance.

MATERIALS
Brick sizes are reasonably standard worldwide and so it is quite easy to work out how many you will need. First estimate the area of the proposed wall; for every square metre of double wall (like the one featured here) you will need about 110 bricks, and about 55 for a single wall. Quantities for pillars will depend on whether two, three or four bricks are used for each course.

The ratio of cement and sand used for the bricklaying mortar will depend on the type of wall you are building. For freestanding garden walls built with clay brick, a 1:4 cement:sand mixture is often recommended; for a more workable mortar, add builders' lime in the ratio of 2:1 cement:lime. This will result in a 1:½:4 cement:lime:sand mix. You will need about 50 kg cement for every 200 bricks in a half-brick (single) wall and every 150 bricks in a one-brick (double) wall.

If the wall is to be rendered, use a similar 1:4 cement:sand mixture – 50 kg will be enough for about 1 m².

FOUNDATIONS
A solid foundation is a prerequisite for all walls. Dimensions, however, depend on the design of the wall as well as on soil conditions in your garden. Minimum specifications for a low half-brick wall stipulate a strip foundation at least 300 mm wide and 100 mm deep. The foundation for a thicker wall will be wider and deeper (see page 33 and below).

Note that if your wall is to be higher than the one illustrated here, the foundations must be more substantial.

BONDING
It is essential to bond brickwork so that the units are 'tied' together to form a solid mass, and to ensure that the load of the materials is evenly distributed along the length of the entire structure. To do this the bricks are laid so that the joints do not coincide with one another; at the same time they create a regular, and quite attractive, pattern.

There are several types of accepted bond patterns, some of which are more popular than others. The most common, which is particularly simple for the beginner builder to lay, is known as stretcher bond. This has bricks laid in consecutive courses overlapping one another by half. In a single wall, half bricks are laid at the ends to allow for bonding; in a double wall, the end bricks may be laid across the width of the wall, as headers.

Other options include the particularly strong English bond, English garden wall bond, American bond and Flemish bond, all of which involve laying both stretchers and headers and so are only suitable for one-brick walls.

| 1 | Use pegs and line or string to mark out the area of the 300 mm-wide strip foundation. Remove the sods of grass and dig to the required depth, in this case about 110 mm. Mix the concrete (see page 44) and lay the foundation. |

| 2 | The foundation is always wider than the wall itself. When it has set (usually overnight), string a line along the length of the proposed structure to indicate the face of the wall and loose lay the first course of bricks, adjusting to avoid cutting. |

| 3 | Mark the position of the first few bricks and then mix mortar using the recommended ratio of cement and sand. Place a 'sausage' of mortar where the bricks are to be laid, flattening it slightly before bedding the first course in place. |

4 If pillars or piers are to be incorporated, it is a good idea to loose lay bricks (as in step 2) to determine exactly where they will be built. An additional 600 mm x 600 mm foundation must be excavated and concreted for these structures.

5 Lay the courses of the pillar in the same way as the wall, taking care to ensure that all four corners are at right-angles. Once the bricks are in place, use a builder's square to check the angles. Correct any inaccuracies at this stage.

6 It is usually wise to reinforce brick pillars. Either insert a metal rod into the foundation or, if it is a low wall, into wet mortar poured into the central cavity of the pillar. You may need to support the metal with battens while you work.

7 Once you have started work on the pillars, continue to lay the wall and pillar courses consecutively. It is essential that all the brick courses are absolutely level. Remember to use a spirit level to check both vertical and horizontal planes regularly.

8 Also keep checking all internal and external corners with a builder's square. If you are planning to fit a light on one or other pillar, insert conduiting alongside the reinforcing rod. This way, wires may be inserted by an electrician later.

9 An efficient bricklayer will 'butter' the end of each brick he or she is laying, but there will still be some gaps between some of the bricks. These may be filled by slotting additional mortar into the joint. Use the trowel to tap it into place.

10 It always pays to work neatly, especially if you are using facebricks which will not be rendered with mortar or painted. As you lay the bricks, it is inevitable that some mortar will ooze out of the joints: scrape any excess off with the trowel.

11 The best way to ensure that all brick courses are equal is to use a gauge rod – a straight-edged piece of wood marked off to indicate one brick plus a 10 mm mortar joint. Once the wall is complete, rake out the joints with a pointing tool.

12 If you need to cut clay bricks, you can do so reasonably easily with the chisel end of a brick hammer (as shown), or with a bolster (or brickset) and a heavy club hammer. It is not usually necessary to use an angle grinder or other power tool.

Reconstituted (reconstructed) stone blocks have become a very popular substitute for difficult-to-obtain natural stone. Not only do they look remarkably like the real thing, but they are made in a wide range of sizes. The beauty of many reconstituted stone walls lies in the interesting bonding patterns created by using different-sized blocks. Moulded from concrete and tinted with coloured pigments, their regular (and uniform) shape makes them relatively easy to lay.

MATERIALS

Many people prefer to mix a number of different sizes of stone blocks for interest, rather than using just one size. Suppliers will provide random quantities based on the overall area of the wall. To work out your quantities, you need to know the dimensions of all block sizes to be incorporated, and then decide what proportion of each will be used. This wall uses blocks of the following heights and proportions: 75 mm (11%), 100 mm (35%), 125 mm (38%) and 150 mm (16%), and lengths vary from 200 mm to 325 mm. Jumper blocks are used randomly, comprising 12% of the surface.

Requirements for foundations and mortar are the same as those in the concrete block wall on page 58.

BONDING

Mix sizes throughout the wall to create attractive bonding patterns. The blocks may be laid in straight layers or with extended jumper blocks

1 Start by marking out the foundation as shown on page 49 and excavate to the required depth. Hammer pegs into the ground to mark where the upper level of the concrete will come to. Then mix the concrete and place it in the trench.

2 Use a spade or trowel to tamp down the concrete. This will compact it and expel any air bubbles in the mixture. Smooth it out with the trowel or with a straight-edged piece of wood. Allow the mixture to set overnight before laying the blocks.

3 Use pegs to set up a builders' line which will accurately indicate the position of the front of the wall. Put a 'sausage' of mortar on the concrete and lay the first block against the line, using the handle of the trowel to knock it into place.

4 Continue with a bedding layer of mortar which should be about 100 mm wide and 10–12 mm thick. Flatten the mortar slightly with the trowel and then draw the trowel through the centre to make a slightly uneven furrow before laying blocks.

5 There are no rules to determine the order in which reconstituted stone blocks should be laid. By selecting a range of different sizes at random, you will create the effect of natural dressed stone wall. A jumper block is two or three courses high.

6 Lay all the blocks in the first course in position, leaving a gap of about 10 mm between blocks for the mortar joints. Then go back and fill all the spaces with mortar. It doesn't matter if the joints are slightly different widths – this will add authenticity.

7 Start the second course by spreading mortar on top of the first course. Bed each block in place, tamping it down to leave a joint 10 mm thick, and check that it is level. Use standard-height blocks next to the jumper blocks in the first course.

8 For a really good effect which will echo the solidity of stone, it is best to lay a double wall. Since different-sized blocks have been used for the wall, it is necessary to build the lower section to one height before constructing pillars.

9 Do not use too many different-sized blocks to build pillars. For ease of construction, use blocks of the same height for each course, choosing lengths that fit the dimensions of the structure. Use a trowel to scrape away excess mortar as you work.

10 Use your trowel to point or fill the joints between the blocks with mortar. Do not worry if any of the excess mortar falls into the central cavity; it is preferable to have a solid pillar, rather than one that is hollow in the middle (see step 13).

11 Even though reconstituted stone blocks are relatively irregular in shape and uneven in finish, it is essential to use a spirit level from time to time to check that both horizontal and vertical planes are straight and level (see page 41).

12 Use a piece of cut metal or a pointing trowel to scrape out the mortar joints neatly. As the two skins of this wall are laid about 60 mm apart, some of the joints in the sides of the pillars will be considerably thicker than those in the wall.

13 Before adding the capping, fill the gap between the two skins of the wall with mortar. Tamp it down well, then place a thick layer of mortar on top of the wall and level it out with a length of wood or the edge of your spirit level.

14 Reconstituted stone paving slabs are an ideal choice for the capping, since they match the colour and finish of the wall blocks. Place them on the mortar bed so they overhang the wall face slightly. Leave a 10 mm joint between the slabs.

15 Check the upper surface of the paving blocks with a spirit level and use a rubber mallet to gently tap any blocks which may be out of alignment. Use the trowel to fill the gaps between the pavers with mortar. Clean any excess from the surface.

Walls built from ordinary concrete blocks are sturdy, generally inexpensive and relatively quick to build since the units are larger than regular bricks, and usually hollow. They are available all over the world in a wide variety of sizes, and are used for many types of construction. Most freestanding garden walls are built with only one thickness of block; if added strength is required, these structures are simply reinforced (see below).

Although ordinary concrete building blocks are not particularly appealing on their own, they are an ideal material for garden walls. Furthermore, given a mortar rendering and a coat of paint, they can look very attractive indeed.

MATERIALS
The blocks used for this wall measure 390 mm x 190 mm x 190 mm and, like most concrete blocks, they are hollow. To build 8 m² of wall you will need 100 blocks of this size (12½ blocks per 1 m²). If larger blocks are used, it stands to reason that fewer blocks will be required.

It your blocks are a different size, calculate the surface area of your proposed wall and simply divide this by the area of one block (height x length). To avoid excessive cutting, it is best to base the overall dimensions of the wall on the blocks you plan to use.

The mortar mix used to lay the blocks will determine how much cement, sand and, possibly, lime will be required. Generally, a weaker mix is used for concrete blocks than for bricks and a ratio of 1:6 cement to sand is a common option. To lay 1 000 concrete blocks measuring 390 mm x 190 mm x 190 mm, you need 325 kg cement, 162.5 kg lime (if required) and 1.3 m³ sand.

The mortar rendering should be compatible with the mortar used to lay the blocks. If a 1:6 mixture is used, you can cover an area of 7 m² with 50 kg cement and 300 kg sand.

Cement, crushed stone (aggregate) and suitable sand will also be required for the foundations.

FEATURES
Various features may be incorporated into a block wall, including planters, a door or gate, an arch, letterbox and even a compartment to store rubbish bins out of sight. This wall includes an arched door, corner planter and, on the inside, a low seat and a rubbish bin compartment. It is essential to plan for these features, as you will have to dig additional foundations to accommodate them in terms of your design.

The planter is formed by building the wall across one of the corners and then continuing the straight lines of the structure two courses above ground level. The bin compartment is made by building a 600 mm-high wall to create three sides of a 600 mm x 600 mm box which sits at 90° to the boundary wall. You need formwork to create an opening on the boundary (see page 60, step 10); this can be fitted with a simple wooden door.

FOUNDATIONS
Solid concrete foundations are essential for all concrete block walls. The depth must support the mass of the structure and so is determined primarily by the height and width of the wall to be built. If hardcore is to be included under the concrete, you will have to further increase the depth of the trench to accommodate it. Remember that the foundation must be wider than the wall (see page 43).

Although the foundation for this block wall is 200 mm deep, the trench itself is about 300 mm deep, so that the first course is partially below ground.

REINFORCING
Very high concrete block walls, or those that are to retain soil, should be reinforced. Foundation reinforcing will usually be specified by an engineer, but there is no reason why you should not set it in place yourself. It involves laying a grid of steel in the trench before the concrete is poured, and does not require any special skills.

Vertical reinforcing may also be necessary, but since concrete blocks have a hollow core, this is simple to accommodate. Steel bars are set in the concrete foundation (as indicated in steps 3 and 7 on page 59) and the hollow core of the blocks placed over them during the laying process.

Another type of reinforcing which may be required involves laying a wire grid of brickforce, supplied in a roll, over the horizontal plane of some courses (usually every four or five courses). It is not necessary to lay it on every course and may, in fact, only be incorporated over openings left in the wall for doors or other features.

BONDING
Laying concrete blocks is very similar to bricklaying, only you may find that blocks are more cumbersome to work with. Just as brick courses must bond with one another, so too must the courses in a concrete block wall. Since the finished surface of a standard block wall will invariably be rendered, they are laid in a stretcher bond (rather than any other patterned bond), with each block overlapping the one below it by half a block.

Although screen (pierced) blocks are laid in the same way as ordinary concrete blocks, they can't be vertically reinforced and so a straightforward stack bond is normally used. This is why a screen block wall should always include pillars for extra strength.

CUTTING BLOCKS
It is not easy to cut blocks accurately with a brickhammer, though an uneven edge will not usually create problems if you are to render the surface. Use an angle grinder to produce a clean cut.

1 Set out the foundations accurately: hammer in pegs and then string a taut line between them. The dimensions of the foundations will depend on the design of the wall (including any features) and the size of the concrete blocks being used.

2 It is helpful to mark the area to be excavated with chalk, cement or flour so that the pegs can be removed before you dig the foundation trenches. The depth of the excavation will depend on the height and thickness of your wall.

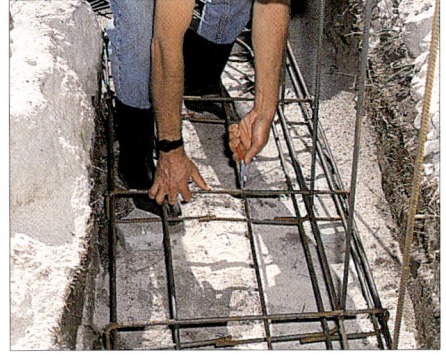

3 Reinforcing may be required for some garden walls, especially if they are relatively high. Check that the foundation floor is flat and level, before placing any reinforcing specified in the design. Wire the rods together to form a stable framework.

4 You will need to indicate the proposed position of the upper surface of the concrete foundations: knock metal or wooden pegs firmly into the ground at various intervals, allowing them to protrude to the required height, in this case 200 mm.

5 Mix the concrete by hand or in a motorised concrete mixer (see page 44). For large jobs, it is worth ordering ready-mix concrete to be delivered to the site in special trucks. Spread it out evenly in the foundation trench to the height of the pegs.

6 Build up the wall course by course in stretcher bond, checking regularly that the blocks are level and that all corners are truly square. Here a section of brickwork from the original patio is incorporated at the base of the wall.

7 If reinforcing rods are being used, centre the blocks over them and fill in the cavities with mortar. For extra strength, you can also incorporate brickforce in the mortar bed (see step 11). Use a builder's square to check the outside corner.

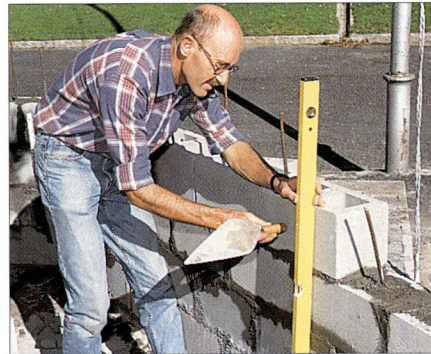

8 As you work, fill in the holes in the blocks with mortar to create a solid structure. Continue to lay the blocks in a stretcher bond pattern, so that each one overlaps the block in the course below by half. Check regularly with the spirit level.

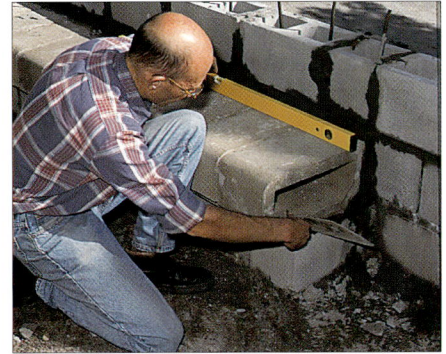

9 Any special features should be built into the wall as construction progresses. For a low seat, lay an additional course of blocks on the inside of the wall and top with terrace blocks laid on their sides; or lay two block courses and screed the surface.

10 For a rubbish bin compartment formwork is set in place to support the opening while building continues. Once the mortar is dry, the formwork is removed. Once the wall has been plastered, a door may be fitted to conceal the bin from sight.

11 In addition to foundation and vertical reinforcing, wire (brickforce) may be laid between some of the block courses to further strengthen the wall and minimise the risk of cracking. This is especially important over the opening for the bin.

12 It is essential to provide expansion joints every 6–7 metres to allow natural horizontal movement in the wall. Since these joints must extend the full height of the wall, blocks will have to be cut and half blocks used every second course.

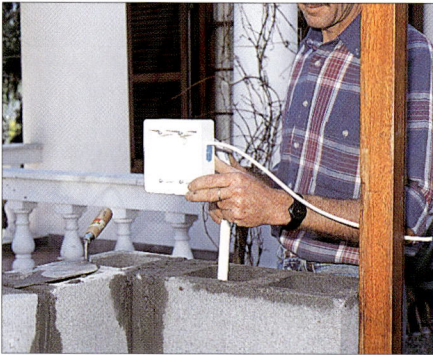

13 If lighting or a security system is to be incorporated into the wall, conduiting must be put in place during construction. You can do this yourself, but It is essential to ask an electrician to advise on the correct connections and to install the wiring.

14 If you want to include a door opening in the wall, build the frame into the blockwork as the wall rises. Use a braced prop to keep it vertical. Here its sill rests on a soldier course of bricks to form a neat step up to the higher level beyond the wall.

15 When the blockwork is complete and the mortar has set, mix cement and sand in the same ratio used for blocklaying (see page 58), adding lime if you wish. Put some of the mixture on a mortar board. Then use a plasterer's trowel to lay it on.

16 Cover the surface fairly roughly not forgetting the tops of the wall and bin box, applying pressure with the trowel to ensure the mortar sticks. Leave to set for about an hour. Then use a straight-edge to carefully scrape and smooth any excess mortar.

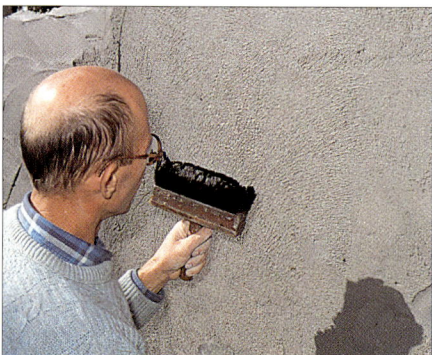

17 The finished rendering should now be 10–15 mm thick. Once you have scraped the wall, you can float the surface to smooth it out further. First splash a little water onto the surface with a wet paintbrush, working in fairly small areas at a time.

18 Use a wooden float to smooth the moistened surface. If you wish, you can use a steel float to get an even more uniform finish, but this is not normally necessary for a garden wall. Do not over-trowel, as this may cause surface cracks.

The simplest way to build a retaining wall is to use concrete modular blocks which interlock with one another to create a stable structure. These are manufactured in several shapes and sizes, from relatively lightweight, rectangular terrace blocks (see page 63) to much heavier units, most of which are plantable. Although there are obvious differences in the various designs, foundations, drainage requirements and basic method of construction remain the same. Mortar is not generally necessary unless extra reinforcing is specified by an engineer (see page 33).

The 200 mm-high blocks used here are shaped so that the convex curve of one block fits into the concave curve of the next. The rounded edge or the flat face may be used for the outer face. By simply turning the units very slightly it is possible to create a curved wall. This wall is 1.2 m high, and is stepped back gradually to create a plantable surface. It includes a seat, an open planter, and a totally vertical section. Steps can be included if the wall is to create a terrace.

FOUNDATION

The foundation must be properly prepared and level. Most low walls may be built on well-compacted earth or gravel, but a wall higher than 1.5 m or one built on poor ground needs a concrete foundation (see page 42). The top of the finished foundation should be at least 150 mm below ground level.

1 Decide on the design of your wall and then peg it out to show where the foundation trench will be located. Both the height of the wall and the angle at which the units are to be stepped back will determine the width of the foundation.

2 String a line along the length of the proposed wall, to indicate the location of the back of the finished structure. This is especially important if it is a boundary wall which must be accurately positioned. Then excavate a trench about 600 mm wide.

3 String a second line to show where the wall will start and then compact the soil with a punner. If a concrete foundation is required, remember that the trench will have to be at least 200 mm deeper to accommodate this material.

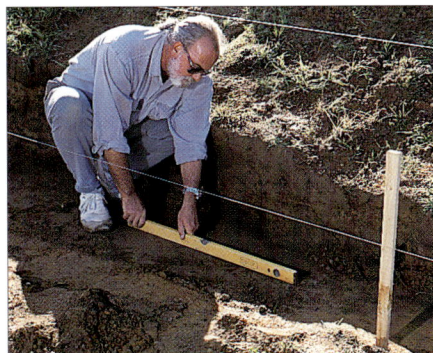

4 Use a spirit level to check that all foundations are absolutely level. If the ground slopes, you will usually be able to step the foundation by the height of one unit. This means you will need an extra course of blocks on the lower level.

5 Position the first block and make sure it is level. When building on a concrete foundation, use a small amount of mortar under each block of the bottom row to facilitate accurate levelling and to help lock the blocks in place.

6 Use pegs and a builder's line to ensure that the front of the wall is straight. If you are battling to get the first course level, put a little soil into each block and then manoeuvre them slightly so that the extra earth fills in gaps under the blocks.

7 Regularly check on levels and alignment, using a club hammer or rubber mallet to gently knock the blocks straight. If the first course is not laid correctly, and the blocks are not level, the rest of the wall will be thrown out of alignment.

8 Fill the blocks with top soil and backfill behind the blocks as each row is completed. Backfill material will depend on the design and height of the wall and the site. It is best to use a layer of free-draining river sand, especially at the base of the wall.

9 Most modular blocks are commonly laid in a stretcher bond pattern, although a stack bond may also be suitable, for instance if the wall is to be vertical. Where cutting is necessary, it is best to use an angle grinder or brick hammer.

10 This two-course high section of vertical wall has been designed to create a seating area. A backfill layer of crushed stone is incorporated for drainage and the second course of blocks backfilled with stone. This can be screeded with mortar if you wish.

11 Use soil to fill in over the crushed stone backfill and compact as before, using a punner or ramming tool. Note that it may be necessary to include a much deeper layer of coarse stone or sand. Consult an engineer if necessary.

12 The third course of blocks, which is laid above the surface of the seat, only just overlaps the second course, thus ensuring maximum width. The flat face of the unit is reversed to face outwards to create a comfortable backrest.

13 At the end of the seat, the blocks are reversed again and positioned to create a planter box. This entails compacting a shelf behind the blocks which have already been laid. It should be level with the upper surface of these blocks.

14 Continue to dry stack the blocks, stepping back and positioning according to your design plan. As each course progresses, it is helpful to place a row of blocks on their sides nearby so that you do not have to fetch individual units.

15 Concrete blocks at the ends of a retaining wall may be feathered out or curved inwards. Make certain all blocks are filled with top soil and the area directly behind the wall is backfilled and compacted. Watering the backfill will aid compaction.

Considerably smaller and lighter than the sturdy, rounded blocks used for the retaining wall on pages 61–62, these concrete terrace blocks are perfect for retaining soil within the garden itself. Various types are available, ranging from units which give an open checkerboard appearance to those with a closed vertical surface. All interlink or interlock for strength and stability. Like the larger retaining blocks, terrace blocks are generally plantable, which means you can cover the concrete structure with creepers, climbers or even small shrubs in a relatively short space of time.

The blocks used here measure 400 mm x 200 mm x 200 mm and are basically rectangular in shape. This particular design features a convex corner diagonally opposite a concave corner (to interlock with an adjoining block) and a right-angled corner diagonally opposite one that is cut out to form a matching angle (also for secure interlocking). Although they can be laid in various ways they are placed diagonally for this step-by-step sequence. Any similar block could be used in the same way, but since designs do vary, be sure to follow any special instructions offered by the particular manufacturer.

The wall featured here was laid beneath a timber deck to stabilise a sloping bank. Although the angle was not particularly steep, soil was frequently washed away in rainy weather. The wall is only a metre high and simple for an amateur to tackle.

While there are no special features incorporated here, the blocks could be laid on their sides to form either a seat (see step 9 on page 59) or to create a flight of steps leading to the top terrace. Note that if feature elements (like steps and seats) are included in your design, it is essential to fill the blocks with either a weak mortar mix or sand.

FOUNDATION

Although it is not necessary to throw a concrete foundation for a retaining wall of this height and constructed by this method, it is vital that the earth beneath the wall is stable and well compacted. If the soil is soft, it is essential to dig a foundation trench and to fill it with gravel or very fine (9.5 or 10 mm) crushed stone, which should also be compacted with a punner or ramming tool.

BACKFILL

In most instances, you can use the excavated soil to backfill a low terrace wall. If you have removed clay, however, you will need to bring in additional building sand, which allows the water to drain more freely. In this case, it would also be wise to backfill the first course or two with crushed stone or gravel to further aid drainage. Good quality soil must be used to fill blocks which will be planted.

1 Mark out the position of the terrace block wall and dig a trench about 200 mm deep and 600 mm wide. Compact well with a punner. Use a spirit level to check that the surface is flat.

2 Set up a line along the front of the trench by tying string around blocks at either end. Lay the blocks so that they interlock firmly for stability and the rounded corner is flush with the line.

3 Make sure that the blocks are level and fill behind them with gravel, sand or the excavated soil. If you plan to plant the wall, be sure to fill the blocks with good quality soil

4 The second row of blocks is laid over the first, but stepped back slightly to create pockets for planting. Use a spirit level regularly to ensure that the horizontal plane is level.

5 You will need to lay five courses for a 1 m-high wall. Backfill each course and all the blocks as you work. It is also best to compact the sand or soil behind the wall as it progresses.

6 There must be no voids behind the wall or in the blocks themselves. A good way to ensure that the soil is properly compacted is to hose the wall once it is complete.

This remarkably simple construction creates an attractive basketweave effect between timber poles. The ends of relatively thin horizontal slats, positioned close together, are nailed alternately to the front and the back of each pole. Left to weather naturally, the fence will soon develop a lovely rustic appeal. The materials listed are sufficient for one 2.3 m x 2.2 m panel, and presume you will be using a 1:4:4 concrete mix. Additional adjacent panels will, of course, require only one extra pole each.

MATERIALS

Footings for 2 poles
60 kg cement
245 kg sand
245 kg stone
hardcore and/or soil for fill

Fasteners
88 x 100 mm anodised
  wire nails

Fencing
2 x 3 m poles, 120 mm
  in diameter
22 x 2.2 m x 95 mm x
  15 mm slats (or similar)

1 Mark the position of the fence and peg out the footings at 1.98 m centres.
2 Dig 750 mm-deep footings, 750 mm x 750 mm in size.
3 Brace the poles in position and check that they are vertical.
4 Mix the concrete as described on page 44.
5 Pack the footings about two-thirds full with concrete. When the concrete has set, add enough soil to fill the holes completely. Alternatively, first put a 200 mm-deep layer of hardcore into each hole and then top up with concrete. Leave to set.
6 Before removing the bracing, nail the slats to the poles, alternately bringing one slat to the front of the pole, and then one to the back. Start from the bottom and use two nails at each end of the slats.

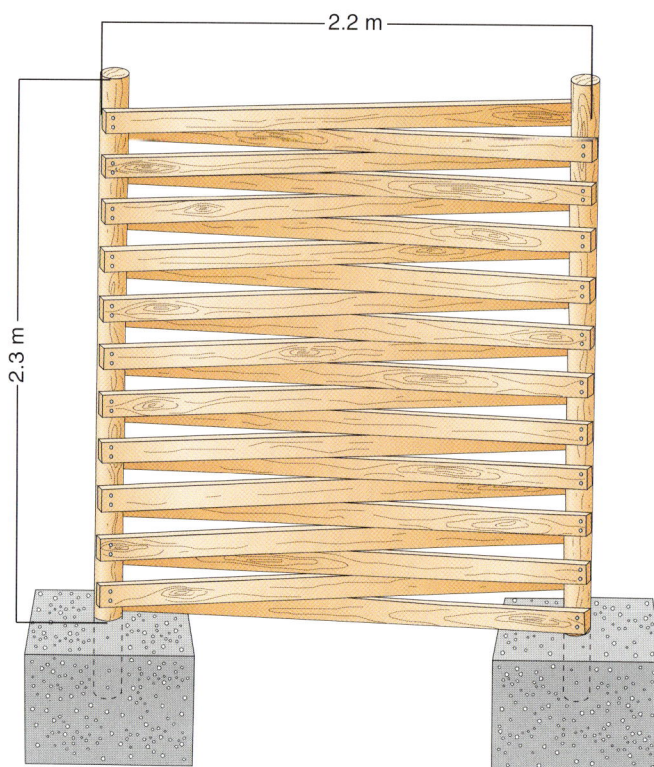

This attractive patio screen, made as shown in the step-by-step instructions on page 37, has been mounted on a low wall to shield the seating area from the neighbouring house. The screen is made by attaching 30 mm x 12 mm laths to a framework which is bolted to the wall and nailed to two supporting poles. Although the screen shown in the photograph is attached to the pergola beams, the plan allows for a freestanding screen. Materials for the 1.3 m-high wall are not included.

MATERIALS
Footings
50 kg cement
200 kg sand
200 kg stone

Panels
2 x 4 m machined poles,
  90 mm in diameter
2 x 4.25 m x 50 mm x
  32 mm lengths timber
  (or 2 shorter lengths
  joined with a lap joint)
1 x 2.3 m x 72 mm x 32 mm
  length timber

48 x 2 m x 30 mm x
  12 mm horizontal laths
52 x 1.8 m x 30 mm x
  12 mm vertical laths

Fasteners
2 x 100 mm masonry
  anchor bolts
2 x No. 8 (4.2 mm) x 50 mm
  brass screws
200 x 40 mm anodised
  wire nails
4 x 75 mm anodised
  wire nails
panel pins (optional)

1 Mark out 500 mm x 500 mm footings for the two poles at 4.16 m centres, and dig to a depth of 500 mm.
2 Position the poles in the footings and brace, making sure they are vertical.
3 Mix concrete in a cement:sand:stone ratio of 1:4:4 and pour into the holes. Allow the concrete to set.
4 Nail the 4.25 m lengths of timber to the top of the poles and 1.7 m down from the top respectively.
5 Position the 2.3 m-long central timber, allowing the overlap to extend at the bottom. Bolt it to the low wall, and screw to the framework.
6 Nail the horizontal laths into position, ensuring they are equally spaced.
7 Then nail the vertical laths into place, using panel pins at the joints for added stability if required.
8 Finish the screen with the paint or sealant of your choice.

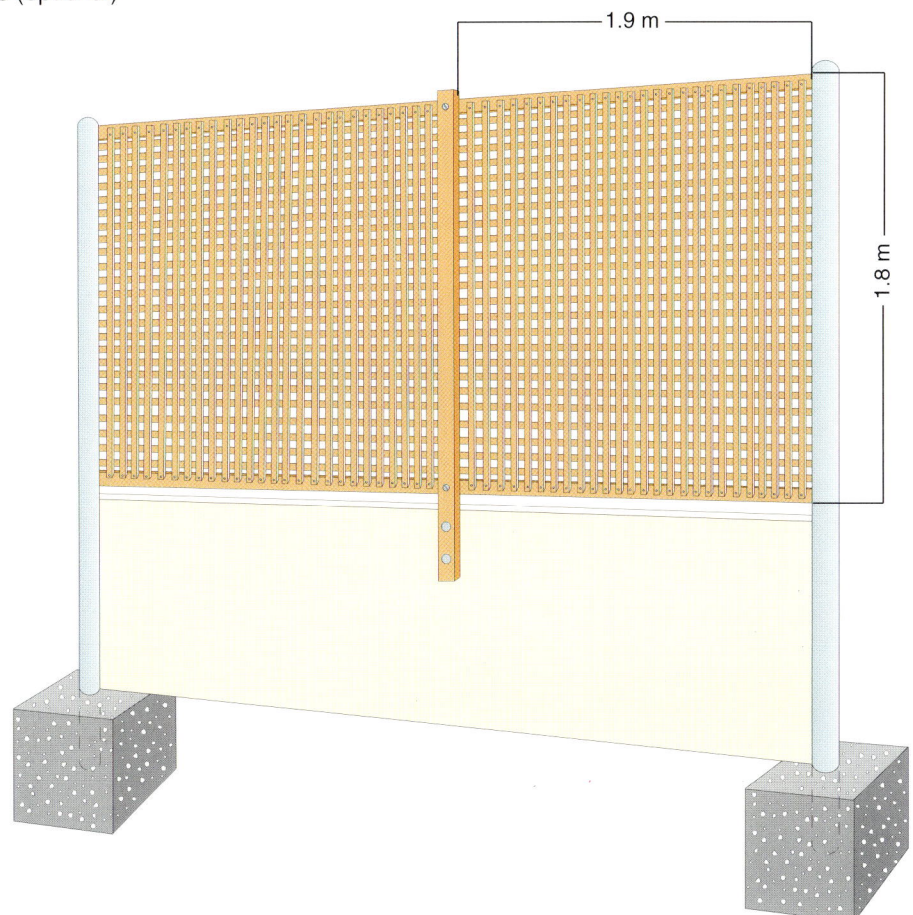

1.9 m

1.8 m

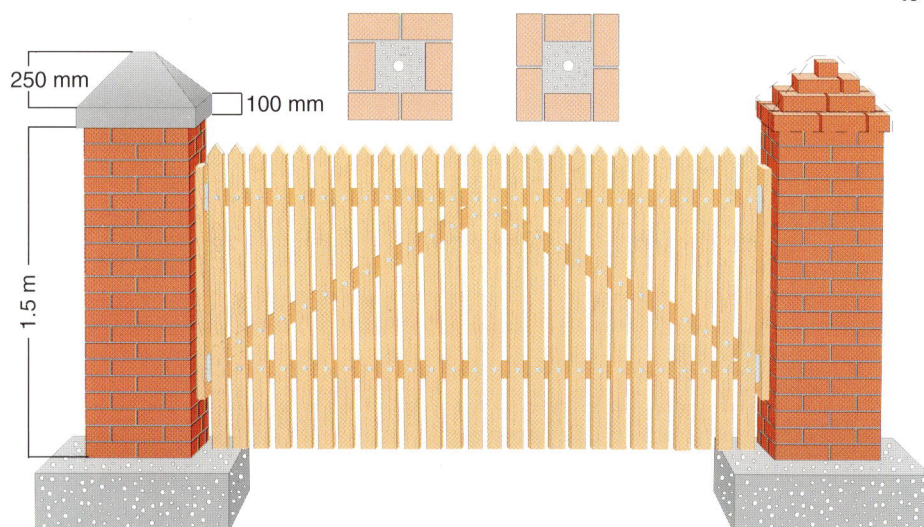

A plain picket fence and matching gate have been painted bright blue to add character and impact. Attached to stocky pillars, the 2.75 m-wide gateway is perfect for a driveway. (A single gate would be more useful in the garden.) The materials list will enable you to build the gate and pillars. You can make adjacent panels with 20 pickets attached to 2.1 m x 38 mm x 38 mm battens; attach these to 90 mm-diameter poles or planed timber posts as shown on pages 48–51.

MATERIALS

Foundations
100 kg cement
405 kg sand
405 kg stone

Pillars
264 bricks
100 kg cement
50 kg lime (optional)
395 kg sand
2 x 1.5 m reinforcing rods

Gate
2 x 1.05 m x 38 mm x
  38 mm battens

4 x 1.33 x 90 mm x 35 mm
  bracing timbers
2 x 1.5 x 90 mm x 35 mm
  bracing timbers
26 x 1.2 m x 70 mm x
  20 mm pickets, with
  tops cut to a point

Fasteners
4 x No 10 (4.9 mm) x 100 mm
  masonry anchor bolts
156 x No 6 (3.5 mm) x
  32 mm brass screws
4 x barrel hinges with
  screws
latch and screws

1 Peg out the position of the two pillars at 4 m centres.
2 Mark out the area for the two 900 mm x 900 mm foundation footings.
3 Dig the footings to a depth of 250 mm. Mix concrete in a 1:4:4 ratio of cement:sand:stone. Pour the concrete into the holes, compact, level and leave to set thoroughly.
4 Build the two pillars, alternating courses as shown in the illustration. Fill the central cavity with mortar as you work.

5 When you have laid about three courses, insert a reinforcing rod into the still-wet mortar of each pillar. The rods will extend to the top of each pillar. Brace with timber to stop them falling to one side.
6 When you have laid about 20 courses (more if the foundation was slightly below ground level), lay a slightly wider course of bricks to create a lip.
7 Form the capping by building each of the next three courses progressively smaller in dimension, to form a pyramid shape as shown in the illustration.
8 When the mortar has set, mix additional batches to render the surface, and fill in the gaps in the capping.
9 Allow the rendered mortar to dry thoroughly, then attach the battens to the inside surface of each pillar. Use two masonry anchor bolts on each side.
10 Now assemble the first half of the gate. Lay the two horizontal, 1.33 m lengths of the Z-brace 800 mm apart on a flat work surface and screw a picket to each end at 90°.
11 The diagonal, 1.5 m length of bracing must be cut at an angle at each end. Place it diagonally across the middle to form a Z and mark a cutting edge. Saw the ends neatly.
12 Slot the bracing in place. Drill through the bracing into the picket at the points where the pieces of wood meet, then screw in place.
13 Now position and secure the rest of the pickets in the same way, using a 35 mm spacer to ensure the gaps between them are even, and carefully lining up the base of each picket so that the bottom of the gate will be level.
14 Attach the gate to the battens with roll hinges, and fit the latch.
15 Repeat steps 10–14 for the other half of the gate.
16 Finish with the paint and/or sealant of your choice.

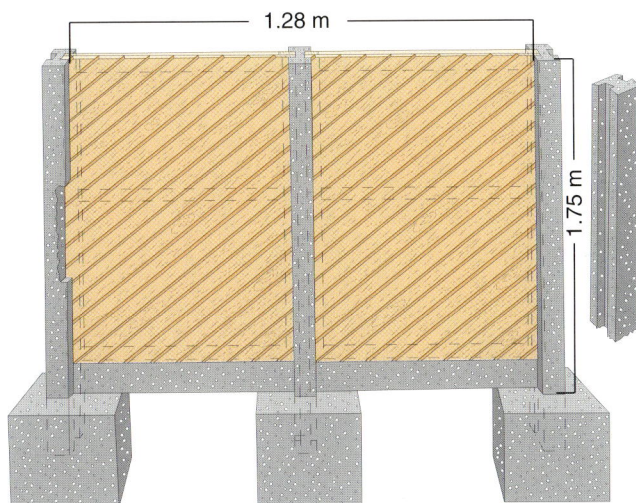

Attractive panels, made by attaching timber slats on the diagonal, are set between recessed, precast concrete posts, to create a good-looking fence which offers privacy and security. A narrow, precast concrete panel is slotted horizontally into place at the base of the timber panels. If precast materials are not available, this design may be adapted for timber posts or masonry pillars. In this case, build a low wall in place of the base panel or position the timber closer to the ground. While the illustration shows two adjacent panels, the materials are sufficient for one panel between two posts.

MATERIALS
Foundations
100 kg cement
405 kg sand
405 kg stone

Framework
2 x 2.35 m x 130 mm x 120 mm precast concrete posts, with 50 mm recesses in both sides
1 x 1.28 m x 200 mm x 45 mm precast concrete panel

Panel
2 x 1.48 m x 70 mm x 20 mm lengths timber
3 x 1.17 m x 70 mm x 20 mm lengths timber
24 x 70 mm x 15 mm slats to fit 2 m², cut to lengths from 300 mm to 1.95 m

Fasteners
144 x 25 mm anodised wire nails
6 x 100 mm anodised wire nails

1 Mark the positon of the proposed fence and peg out the footings at about 1.4 m centres.
2 Mark the 600 mm x 600 mm footings with chalk or flour.
3 Dig the footings to a depth of 600 mm.
4 Brace the posts in position with battens, making certain they are vertical, acccurately spaced and in a straight line. Concrete into position using a 1:4:4 mix.

5 Before the concrete sets, slide the base panel into position to ensure the posts are accurately spaced.
6 Check that the concrete is well compacted and leave to set overnight.
7 Working on a flat surface, position the five pieces of timber which will form the framework for each panel, placing the shorter lengths on the inside of the long pieces of timber.
8 Predrill three pilot holes in each 1.48 m-long piece of timber at the point where the shorter lengths are joined to it at right angles.
9 Join the framework together using the 100 mm-long nails.
10 Position one of the slats diagonally across the centre of the panel, and mark the cutting lines at the correct angles. Trim with a tenon saw.
11 Continue to mark and cut all the slats, ending with the shorter lengths.
12 Position the 24 slats across the framework, ensuring the gaps between them are even.
13 Nail the slats to the framework, using 25 mm-long nails at the top, bottom and middle, if necessary, of each slat.
14 Finally, slide the panel into the recesses in the posts (see illustration). If timber posts are used, nail or screw the panel into place. If you have built masonry pillars, bolt the framework to these before affixing the slats.

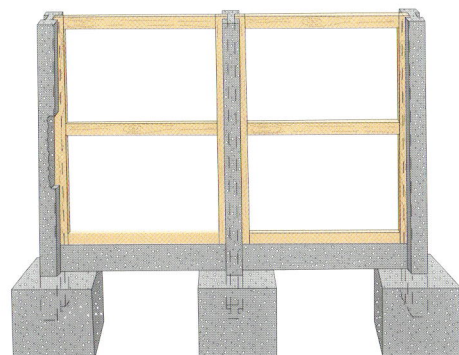

Machined poles are used ingeniously to create attractive fencing between rendered brick pillars. Holes are bored into the main uprights to accommodate the horizontal timbers, whilst the ends of the vertical poles are cut out in a slight V so that they can slot neatly into place. Planed pickets are affixed to the pillars to house the ends of the poles. The materials list specifies one approximately 4 m-long section of the fence only. It is not essential to use materials of identical dimensions; adjust the measurements on the plan to accommodate what is available.

MATERIALS
Foundation footings
115 kg cement
465 kg sand
465 kg stone

Pillars
200 bricks
75 kg cement
38 kg lime (optional)
300 kg sand

Fencing
6 x 1.6 m x 70 mm x 20 mm
  pickets
2 x 2.1 m upright poles,
  90 mm in diameter
10 x 1.65 m poles, 60 mm
  in diameter

2 x 1.12 m poles, 60 mm
  in diameter
5 x 1.08 m poles, 60 mm
  in diameter
6 x 500 mm poles, 60 mm
  in diameter

Fasteners
6 x No 8 (4.9 mm) x 75 mm
  coach screws with
  Rawl plugs or masonry
  anchor bolts
12 x No 6 (3.5 mm) x 50 mm
  countersunk screws
10 x 75 mm anodised
  wire nails
4 x 100 mm anodised
  wire nails

1 Set out the fence and mark out the position of all foundation footings.
2 Dig 500 mm x 500 mm x 500 mm footings for the poles, and 750 mm x 750 mm x 200 mm footings for the pillars.
3 Bore five shallow holes on either side of the upright posts as indicated in the illustration, using a router or wood chisel. Make sure that all the holes are accurately spaced to ensure that the horizontal poles will be parallel once slotted into position.

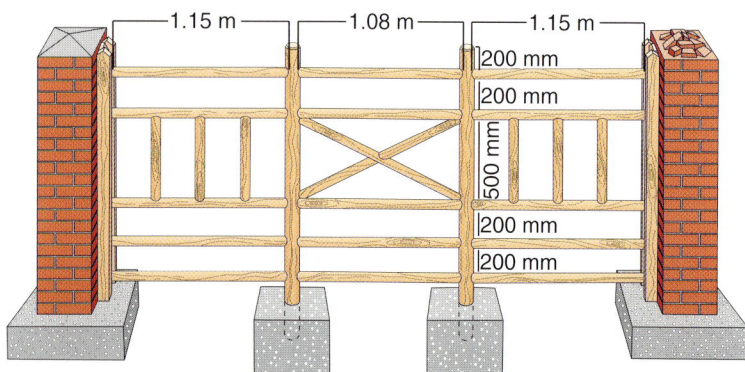

4 Brace the upright poles in position, using a spirit level to ensure that they are vertical, and check that the shallow holes are lined up correctly.
5 Mix concrete in a cement:sand:stone ratio of 1:4:4 and pour into all four footings. Make sure the concrete is well compacted and that tops of the pillar foundations are level.
6 Although the foundation for the pillars should set overnight, assemble the central panel of the fence while the concrete is still workable.
7 Starting from the bottom, slot the 1.08 m poles into place.
8 Cut curved blocks from the centre of each 1.12 m-long pole to enable you to create a lap joint.
9 Trim the ends of these crosspieces to fit the join between the vertical and horizontal posts, then slot into place and nail to the horizontal poles with the 100 mm-long nails.
10 Ensure the bracing is secure and that the upright poles are still vertical. Also ensure the concrete is well compacted.
11 When the remaining foundations have set, build the two brick pillars to a height of 1.6 m.
12 Once the mortar has set, mix another batch and render the pillars, creating a pointed capping if desired. Allow to set thoroughly before assembling the rest of the fence.
13 Use coach screws or masonry bolts to fix a picket to the inside surface of each pillar, ensuring they are centred.
14 Then position the remaining pickets at right angles to these, to form a casing to accommodate the end of the adjacent horizontal poles (see illustration). Fix these to the inside picket, using countersunk screws.
15 Slide the lower three 1.65 m horizontal poles into place on either side, nailing to picket casing.
16 Cut the ends of the 500 mm-long vertical poles to form a shallow V to enable you to brace them against the horizontal poles.
17 Evenly position three vertical poles on each side. Slide the next horizontal pole into position over the top of them.
18 Nail the last horizontal poles into place.
19 Finish with the sealant and/or paint of your choice.

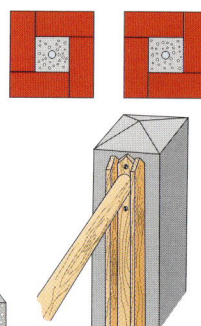

Lattice screen panels, made with thin, diagonal laths, have been mounted onto a low block wall between imposing pillars. The structure is angled at each end to give a curved effect. Precast concrete orbs fixed to the top of the pillars complete the design. The blocks may be rendered in the usual way, or simply smeared with mortar to give a lightly bagged finish. If the specified block sizes are not available in your area, adapt the plan and change the dimensions slightly. Materials are specified for one lattice panel only.

MATERIALS
Foundation
160 kg cement
650 kg (0.5 m³) sand
650 kg stone

Wall and pillars
330 x 290 mm x 90 mm x 90 mm concrete blocks
96 x 190 mm x 90 mm x 90 mm concrete blocks
300 kg cement
150 kg lime (optional)
0.9 m³ sand
5 x precast concrete orbs on 300 mm x 300 mm base

Lattice panel
4 x 1.2 m x 50 mm x 30 mm lengths timber
1 x 1.2 m x 70 mm x 30 mm cover strip
80 m x 45 mm x 10 mm laths, cut to length to fit frame

Fasteners
4 x 100 mm anodised wire nails
110 x 25 mm anodised wire nails
8 x 75 mm masonry anchor bolts

1 Mark out the position of the structure, allowing for a 500 mm wide foundation.
2 Dig the foundation trench to a depth of 200 mm.
3 Mix concrete in a cement:sand:stone ratio of 1:4:4 and place it in the trench. Level and compact as described on page 44.
4 When the concrete has set, mark the position of the five pillars at 1.52 m centres.
5 Build up the pillars and wall sections, laying the blocks for the pillars and walls consecutively.

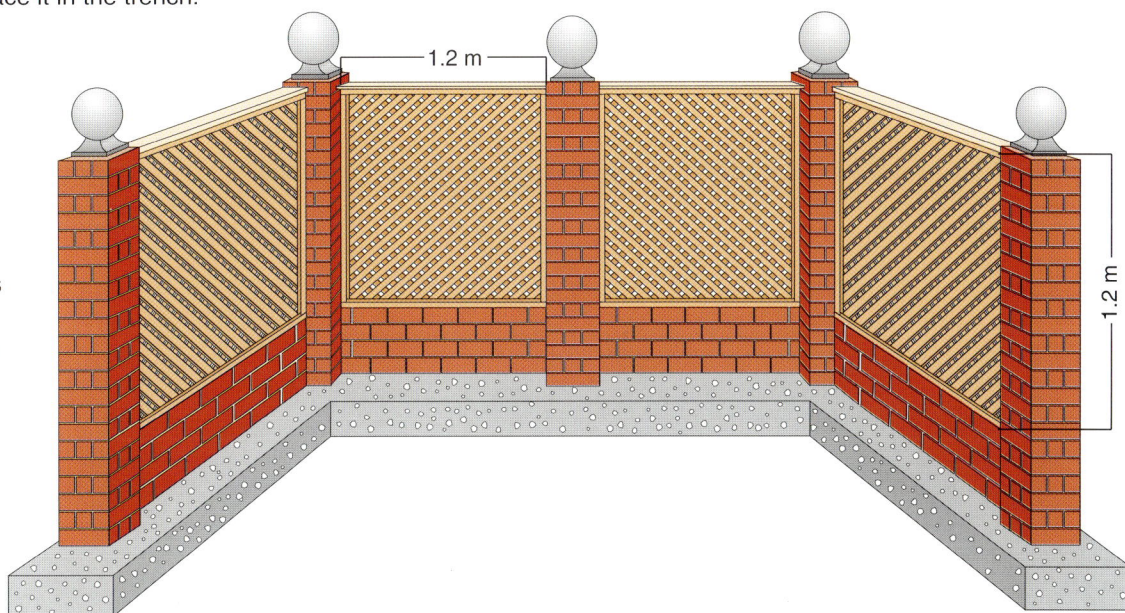

6 Lay an orb on top of each pillar, using a little of the mortar.
7 When the mortar has set, render the surface.
8 Position the framework for the lattice panel with the upright lengths on the inside. Use corner clamps to hold the timber at right angles and then nail the frame together with the 100 mm wire nails.
9 Cut the laths as you work, starting with the longest ones (about 1.8 m). As the laths are attached diagonally, cut each end at an angle to fit the frame.
10 Position the laths against the frame, allowing a gap of about 45 mm between each. Nail them to the frame, using the 25 mm wire nails.
11 Bolt the frame to the pillars, with the frame facing outwards.
12 Nail the cover strip to the top of the frame.
13 Finish with the sealant and/or paint of your choice.

Rustic timber panels combine beautifully with natural stone pillars. If natural stone is not available in your area, use reconstituted stone blocks. These 2 m-high pillars are 700 mm x 700 mm in size, and the low 10 m-long wall which supports the fencing is 500 mm x 500 mm. If reconstituted stone blocks are used, proportions may be smaller. The slats are cut from rustic timber with bark still attached; any sawn timber may be used.

MATERIALS
Foundations
570 kg cement
1.7 m³ sand
1.7 m³ stone

Wall
stones for 4.5 m³
mortar (amount will depend
  on size of stones used)

Fencing
4 x 1.6 m upright poles,
90 mm in diameter
3 x 3.2 m x 75 mm x 50 mm
  support beams
2 x 450 mm x 75 mm x
  50 mm support beams
105 x 1.4 m x 95 mm x
  22 mm slats

Fasteners
8 x 100 mm anodised
  wire nails
210 x 50 mm anodised
  wire nails

1 Set out the foundations, allowing a width of 750 mm for the wall and 1 m for the pillars.
2 Dig a 250 mm-deep trench for the foundations.
3 Mix the concrete in the ratio 1:4:4 and place in the trench.
4 Compact, level and allow to set overnight.
5 Build the pillars and the wall, allowing slightly larger stones to overlap the top of each pillar and so form a natural capping.
6 Set the upright poles vertically in the stonework to a depth of 500 mm, as indicated, to provide a support for the timber.
7 Use a spirit level to ensure the poles are vertical, and brace them in position while the mortar dries.
8 Use the longer nails to fix the horizontal supporting timbers to the upright poles.
9 Then nail the slats to these beams.

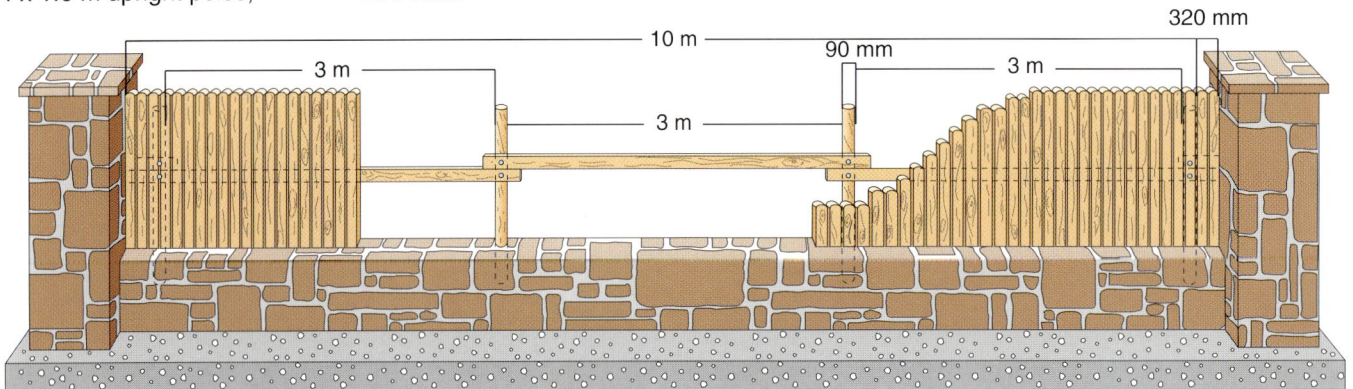

Clay screen (breeze) blocks have been attractively combined with facebrick pillars and a low, supporting one-brick wall along the boundary. Both the wall and top course of blocks, which is laid in the traditional stack bond, have been topped with a facebrick capping to create the effect of panels. This design is suitable for both flat and slightly sloping properties. Materials specified will enable you to build two pillars and an approximately 1.6 m-long section of pierced block wall, using facebricks and 150 mm x 150 mm x 110 mm blocks. If blocks in your area are a different size, simply adjust the overall measurement of the wall to fit.

MATERIALS
Foundations
65 kg cement
265 kg sand
265 kg stone

Wall
242 facebricks
60 x 150 mm x 150 mm x
  110 mm screen blocks
155 kg cement
630 kg sand
brickforce (reinforcing)

9 Lay the screen blocks in a stack bond, positioning them along the central line of the supporting wall.
10 Finish off by laying bricks on-edge along the top of the entire wall, including pillars. Since the blocks are not as wide as the supporting wall, neaten the base of the block portion with a little extra mortar if you wish.

1 Mark out the foundations, ensuring they are about 500 mm wide. The pillars will be at about 2 m centres.
2 Dig the foundation trench to a depth of 250 mm, stepping it down at each pillar if the ground slopes.
3 Mix the concrete in the ratio 1:4:4 and place in the trench, compacting and levelling in the usual way.
4 When the concrete has set, start laying the bricks.
5 Mix the mortar in a cement:sand ratio of 1:4, adding 25 kg lime to each 50 kg cement if you wish.
6 Lay three courses in a stretcher bond.
7 Top the section of wall between the two pillars with bricks laid on-edge to form a header course.
8 Start building up the pillars as shown. Place reinforcing over every third course.

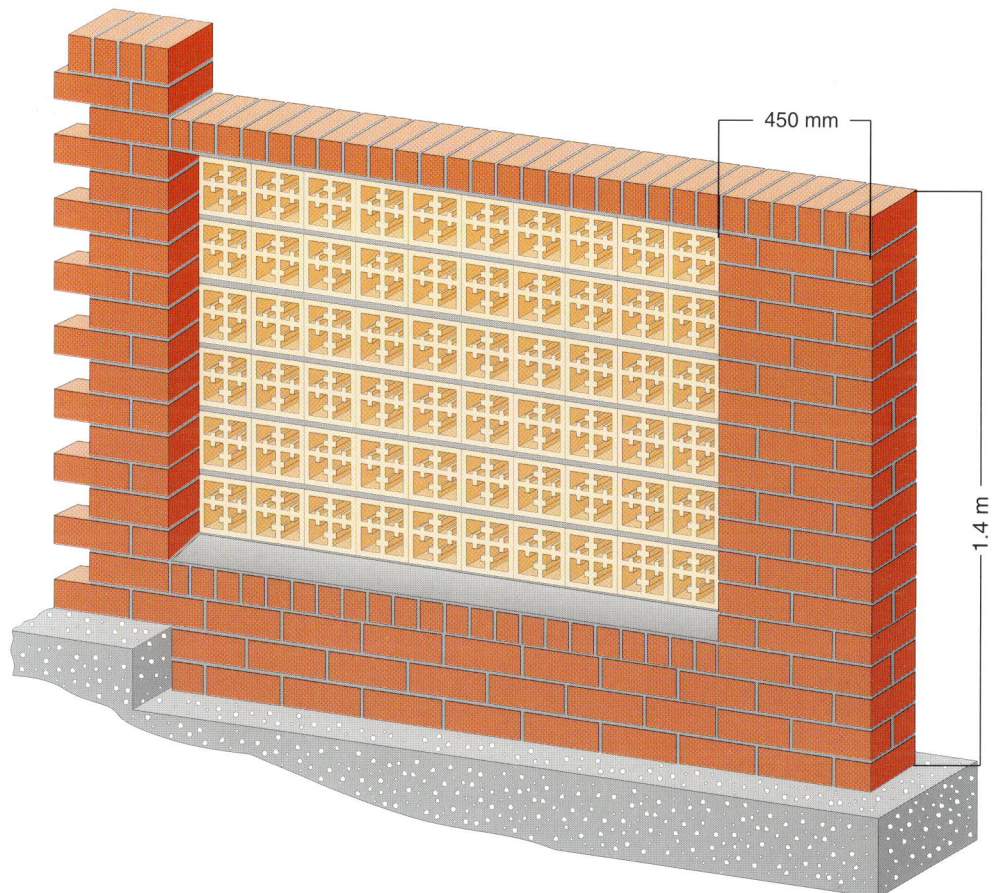

450 mm

1.4 m

Here a series of short walls laid at 90° to one another create a zigzag effect. To add interest, every second section of the wall is built slightly higher than the previous one. Constructed to screen the front entrance of a suburban house from the road, the wall is built with ordinary bricks in a stretcher bond and is then rendered and painted in the usual way. A flower bed in front of the wall adds colour and interest.

MATERIALS
Foundations
425 kg cement
1.3 m³ sand
1.3 m³ stone

Bricklaying
2 250 bricks
560 kg cement
260 kg lime (optional)
1.6 m³ sand
brickforce (reinforcing)

Mortar for rendering
260 kg cement
130 kg lime
0.8 m³ sand

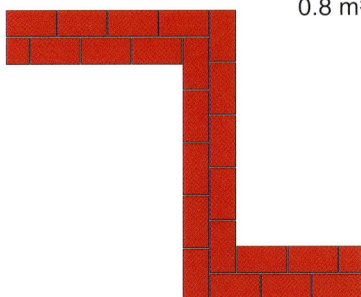

1 Peg out the wall foundation as shown on the plan, ensuring it is about 750 mm wide.
2 Dig out the trench to a depth of 250 mm.
3 Mix the concrete in a cement:sand:stone ratio of 1:4:4 and place in the trench, compacting well, and levelling with a straight-edged piece of wood.
4 When the concrete is well set, start laying the bricks in a stretcher bond. Leave a slight gap between the two skins of brickwork and lay reinforcing on top of every third course.
5 Step every second section of the wall up two courses, as indicated, so that the lowest section is 2 m (25 courses) above ground level, and the highest is 2.6 m (31 courses).
6 Allow the mortar to set, before rendering the surface as illustrated on page 60.

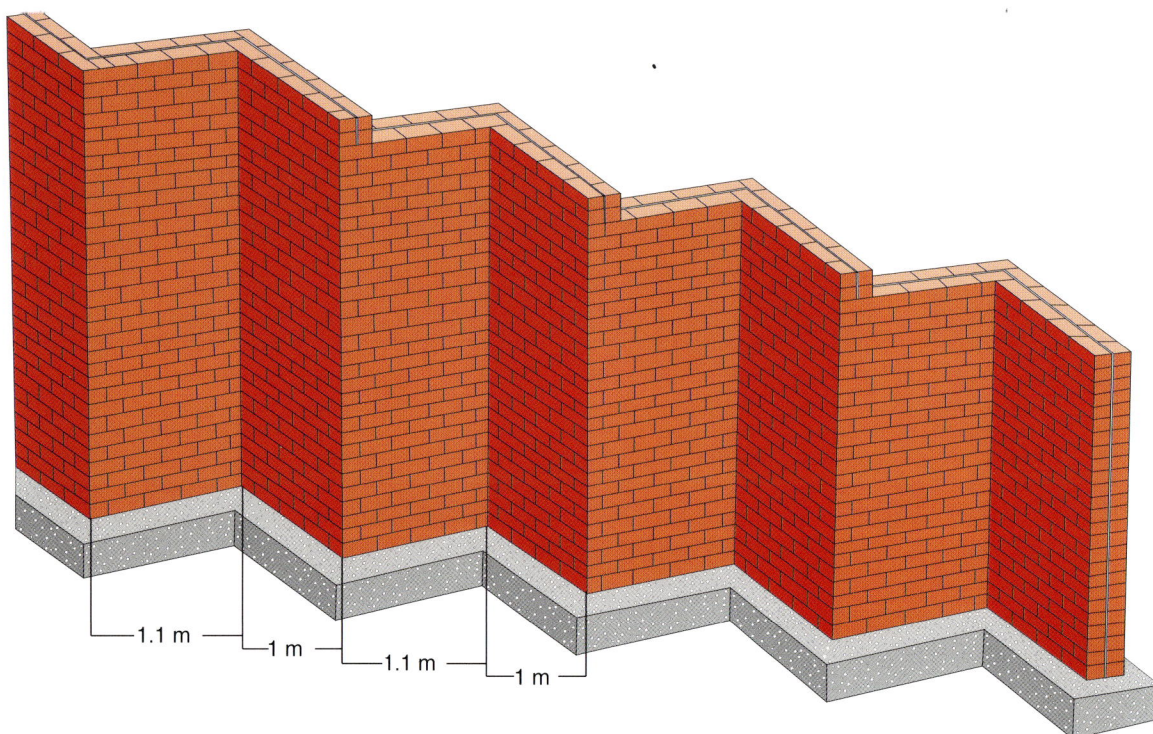

1.1 m   1 m   1.1 m   1 m

A sturdy boundary wall built with concrete blocks incorporates planters in alternate sections of the structure. The wall is constructed between attractive pillars, and the sections which back the planters are stepped back by 700 mm. As this design is imposing in effect, it is particularly well suited to a large property, but could be adapted for just about any location. Materials specified are sufficient for a 6.5 m-long section of wall, as illustrated in the plan.

MATERIALS
Foundations
365 kg cement
1.6 m³ sand
1.6 m³ stone

Blockwork
185 x 390 mm x 190 mm x
 190 mm concrete blocks
60 kg cement
30 kg lime (optional)

365 kg (0.3 m³) sand
brickforce (optional)

Mortar for rendering
150 kg cement
75 kg lime
0.7 m³ sand

1 Mark out the position of the wall as illustrated, with pillars at 3 m centres. Make sure the stepped-back sections are at right-angles to the pillars.
2 Mark the area of the foundations, allowing a width of 500 mm for the wall sections and 1 m x 1 m for the pillars.
3 Dig the foundation trenches to a depth of at least 250 mm.
4 Mix the concrete in a cement:sand:stone ratio of 1:4:4 and place it in the prepared trench. Ensure it is well compacted and level. Leave to set overnight.
5 Mix the mortar in a cement:sand ratio of 1:6, adding the lime if required.
6 Build the first four courses to form the base of the first pillar, using two full blocks as well as a third block split lengthwise in each course. This will make a solid, 800 mm-high base. Use two blocks per course for the rest of the pillar.

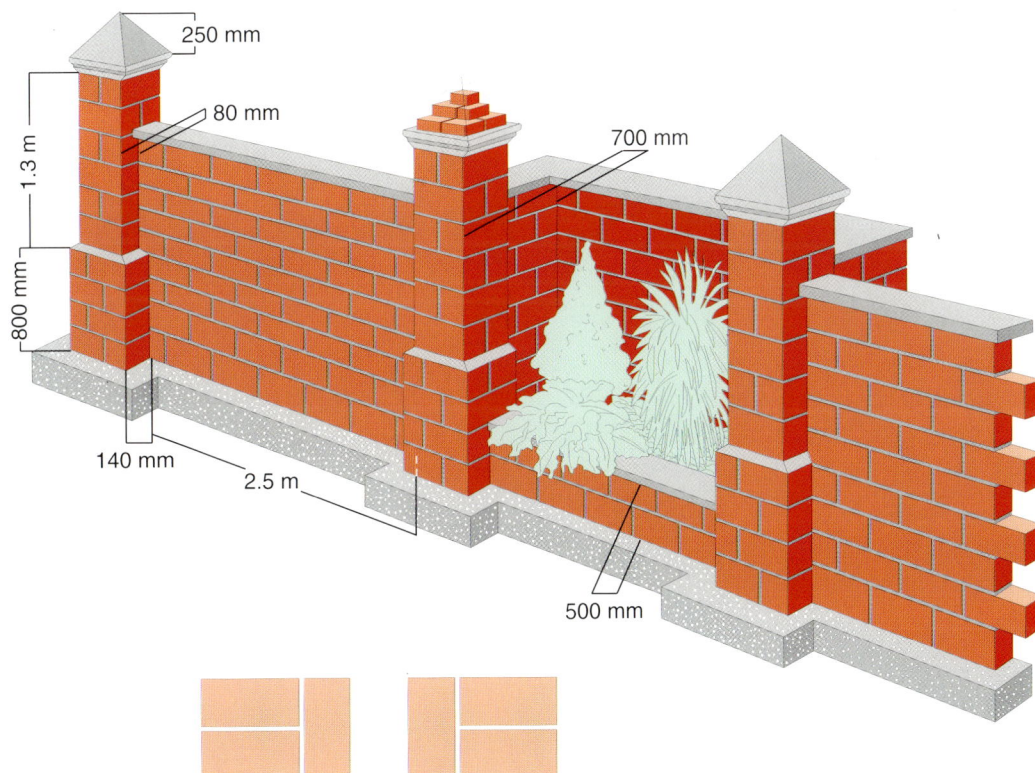

7 Build the wall sections in stretcher bond to a height of 8 courses, and the low planter wall to 2 courses. If 390 mm x 190 mm x 190 mm blocks are used, the wall will be about 200 mm thick once it has been rendered.
8 Use half blocks and broken blocks to build the capping on each pillar.
9 Once the mortar has set, render the surface, creating a lip on the top of the wall if you wish.
10 Ideally, keep the rendered surface damp for a few days before painting and planting.

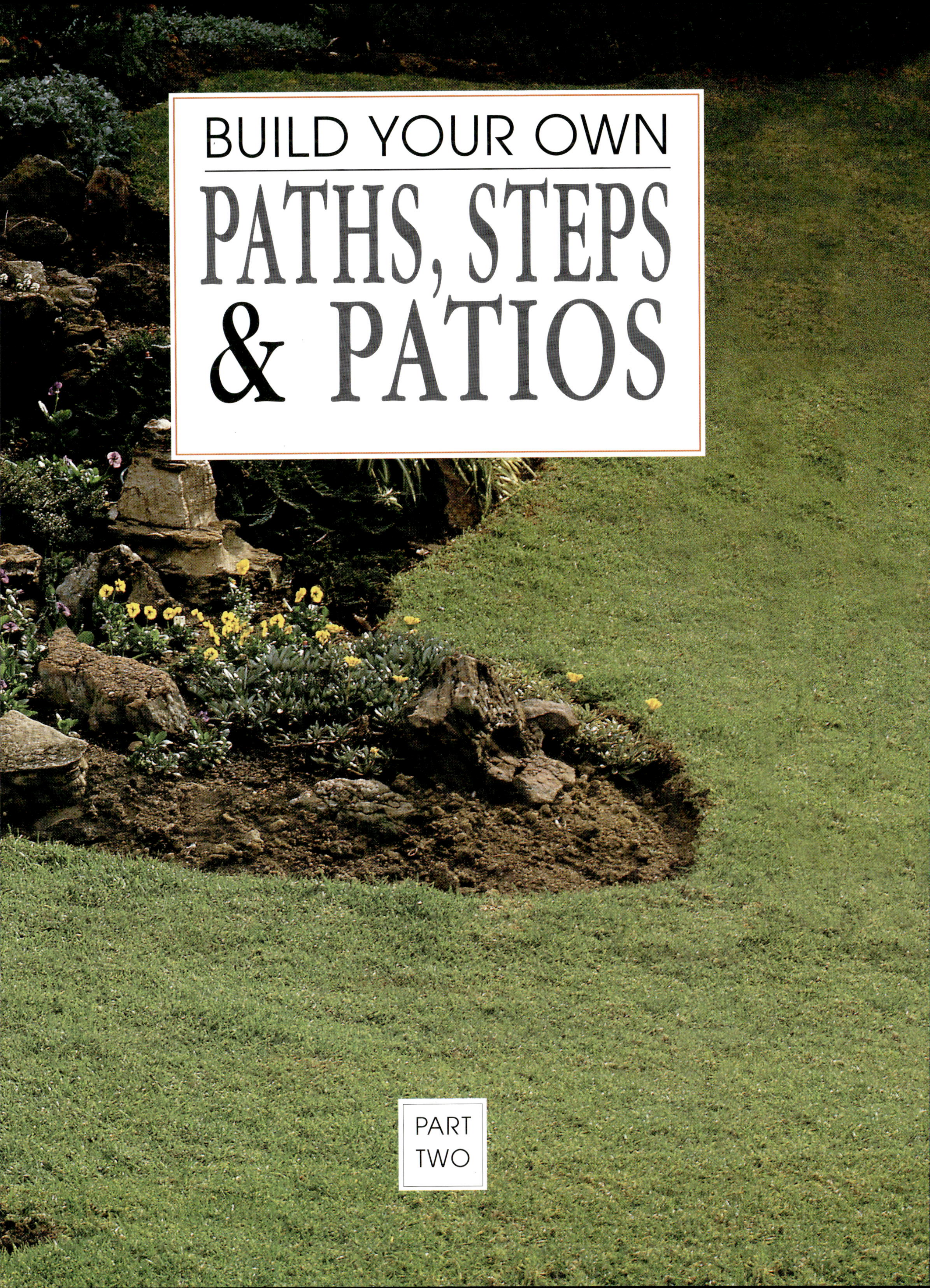

BUILD YOUR OWN

PATHS, STEPS & PATIOS

PART TWO

Paths, steps and patios are found in just about every garden, regardless of its size. Not only are they practical features, providing a solid and safe route for pedestrians and offering a place to sit outdoors, but they are also useful landscaping 'tools'. A wide range of materials may be used to construct them and to create an effective outdoor style that will suit your living environment, your tastes and your needs.

Functional factors usually come first, and irrespective of the type or size of your garden, designing any outdoor area is a creative challenge which demands patience and a practical approach. Paths, steps and patios are built from 'hard landscaping' materials such as bricks, stone and mortar, but they also rely on planting and other finishing touches to look attractive and enhance your outdoor scheme. Since gardens grow and constantly change with the seasons, it is essential to have a clearly defined idea before you begin to create a basic plan or alter an existing layout. Before you start either planting or removing established plants and cutting down trees to accommodate a new walkway, flight of steps or patio, consider all the options. You do not have to be a trained landscaper to succeed, but it does help to have a basic knowledge of plants as well as an appreciation of the various elements that can be combined with them.

For practical reasons, it is always best to tackle the permanent elements of a garden first, and to create a basic layout which will allow for expansion and development later. Once you have laid paths, driveways and patios, incorporating steps and terraces where necessary, and erected fences or walls, you can turn your attention to trees, shrubs and flowers. After all, if plants are to be included in a patio design, or perhaps grown between stepping stones or in planters on a garden stairway, it makes sense to complete all the messy structural work before you even start to prepare the soil for planting.

If, perhaps because of financial constraints, you cannot tackle all the building work now, it is usually quite possible to allow for later expansion and development of the plan (see page 80), but it is best to identify the position of future paths, steps, patios and so on at an early stage.

Apart from their practical functions, which include not only providing easy access and a stable place to walk but also linking or dividing different areas of the property, pathways also have an aesthetic role to play. Imaginatively laid out, they will add interest and charm to the garden, enticing one to follow the route that lies ahead, and they could provide visual and thematic continuity between various sections of the garden.

Whatever the size of your house and garden, the addition of a patio will extend your outdoor living space.

Natural rock forms a stepped path.

Cast concrete strips define the walkway next to a pretty brick-paved patio.

Originally, the patio was an inner courtyard which was open to the sky; today patios may be sheltered or open, and sited alongside the house or built as a separate feature within the garden itself. The design possibilities are almost endless, especially if you consider including additional features which could enhance the outdoor area. For those who enjoy entertaining and cooking outdoors, built-in seating and a brick barbecue are practical additions, while pergolas and screens provide increased shelter and privacy. Water features and planters soften the effect of hard materials and make the visual transition between the built surface and the garden itself less abrupt.

Most patios are built adjacent to the house. There are usually several positions in which you can build such a patio, leading from different rooms or parts of the house. Alternatively, you may prefer to locate a paved area for entertaining in the heart of the garden. This could be a sunken section surrounded by trees, or a terrace overlooking the garden.

Many patios are not built at the same level as the house or garden, and so it is often necessary to construct steps for easy access. While this practical function will always be paramount, steps can still be pleasing to the eye, especially if you include planters, pillars or flower beds on either side. Properly planned and imaginatively designed, they will be an attractive addition to any outdoor area.

This book will help you to plan and design a range of paths, steps and patios, and offers guidelines on how to site a patio and lay out your garden to best advantage. Practical details and aesthetic considerations are discussed, and there are many imaginative ideas and suggestions for new gardens, as well as for improving an existing layout.

Cost issues are examined and ways of quantifying various materials detailed. A wide range of materials is presented, helping to make your choice easier and more informed. There is advice on the relevant tools, and several construction methods are explained in detail.

The steps and porch have been tiled to create an authentic, period feel.

Clearly illustrated step-by-step instructions show the principles behind laying paths and constructing patios and steps, using a few basic building methods. There is also a selection of plans, each of which includes a detailed materials list. The designs use a variety of materials including concrete cast *in situ*, timber poles, railway sleepers, bricks and stone. The designs range from rustic steps and paths to stylish brick-paved patios with formal steps leading from them. All may be adapted to suit the requirements of your site. In some cases formal building plans will be necessary; you are advised to check with your local authority before putting the plan into action.

Whether you are an experienced do-it-yourselfer or a new home-owner with no building experience at all, *Build Your Own Paths, Steps and Patios* will arm you with a good balance of inspiration and technical know-how, putting you in a position to tackle a variety of projects or to oversee those which you prefer others to complete for you.

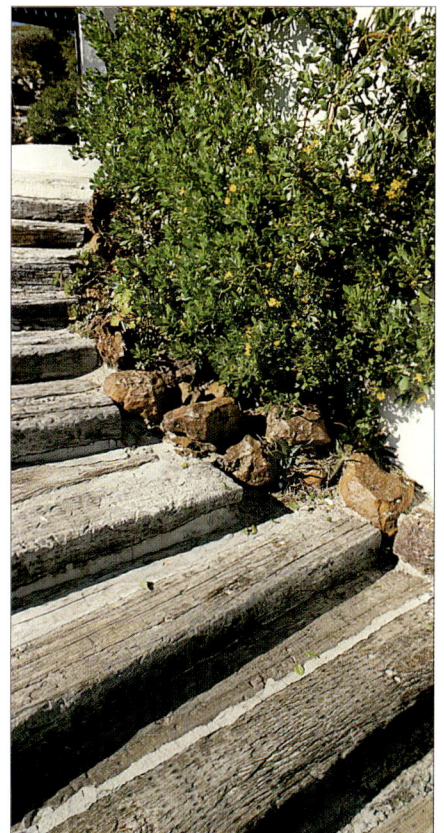

Railway sleepers used as steps.

Proper planning always pays off. If you know exactly what you want before you start building, particularly where you want to site the path, flight of steps or patio and what materials you will need for the project, you will save time and money in the end, and avoid the frustration which always accompanies a badly organised project.

The most obvious route for a path may be from the gate to the front door, but the biggest mistake could be to lay it out in a straight line that bisects a small front garden. Instead, the answer may be to move the gate, or to design a path that curves slightly around a natural feature such as a tree.

Start by identifying your needs and determining how these can best be accommodated in your garden scheme. For instance, should you establish a walkway from the front gate or parking area to the house? Is there a need for paths from the kitchen to service areas, or to a herb garden or vegetable patch? Are there sloping areas which would be easier to negotiate via steps of some sort? Do you want to increase outdoor living space by building a patio? Compare the various locations and layouts which may be suitable and then do a thorough costing to ensure that the plan is actually viable.

PREPARATION

If your house is new and building work has just been completed, the first step to take before you start laying out any paths, steps and patios is to ensure that all rubble has been removed. Earthworks may be necessary, and can include removal or relocation of large rocks and levelling of the ground. If rocks are to be moved or soil shifted, these tasks can be completed at the same time as the clean-up operation.

Regardless of the materials to be used, you should establish what kind of sub-base will be required and whether special steps will have to be taken to ensure that there is adequate drainage (see pages 101–102).

Foundations

A solid foundation is essential for this type of garden work. If the ground is stable and level, the site will simply need to be cleared and a bed of suitable sand (see page 97) used to cushion the bricks, blocks or paving slabs. However, you may need to compact or at least tamp the earth down firmly first, and if the ground is at all unstable, you should prepare a sub-base or in some cases a solid concrete foundation.

If ground conditions and soil are problematic, or if the property slopes steeply, measures ought to be taken to ensure that pathways, steps and patio floors do not subside. If you are not familiar with standard building practices, it is best to consult professionals for advice at this stage. Allow them to help you assess your site and recommend how to deal with it (see page 80).

FUNCTION

Paths, steps and patios are essentially permanent elements of the garden, and are part of the hard landscaping plan. Besides their most obvious functions, they also enable you to create a focal point for planting and

Simple brick steps lead to the front entrance of a house.

can be used to establish a particular theme in the garden. For this reason, it is essential to have a clear idea of what you want in the planning stages.

Patios

While patios are sometimes included in the plan of a house when it is built, many people add them on only once they have lived in a house for some time. The design and style of your house and garden will help to determine the best location for a patio and the materials which will be most suitable for its construction. But it is also essential to examine your needs closely and to consider the primary reasons for having a patio.

A likely motive will be to create an outdoor living area or place for entertaining guests. However, you may want a secluded patio where you can relax away from the hustle and bustle of the house. Perhaps you want somewhere to sunbathe, or a solid paved area where children can ride tricycles or push prams and carts within clear view of the house.

Once you have decided on the site of the patio, you can consider linking it to other outdoor areas by means of pathways and establish where these could be sited.

Paths, walkways and driveways

You may want a path leading from the parking area, carport or garage to the house, and invariably you will also need a pathway from the entrance of the property to the front door of the house. Additional walkways may well be necessary to provide easy access to areas or features within the garden – outbuildings, a swimming pool or pond, patio, herb garden or washing line, for instance. In the larger garden, pathways may also be used visually to divide the property by causing a break in the landscape, and by defining separate areas of interest or function. In the right environment, they may be built to flank lawned terraces or to create an attractive and useful border alongside flower beds.

Unless a garage is situated on the boundary, it is almost always essential

A change of materials from brick to slate demarcates a patio area.

Two strips of brick paving cut down costs on a long driveway.

Home improvements do not necessarily mean do-it-yourself projects. Some home-owners favour the hands-on approach – especially when it comes to gardens – while others prefer to supervise other people doing the work, or to consult professionals and contract specialists to do everything for them, from design to construction and even planting. The choice is yours.

If your house was designed by an architect, there is a good possibility that patios were included in the basic design, even if these were not initially built. Features such as driveways, swimming pools, patios and pergolas, and even garden walls are often drawn on building plans but only built at a later stage when additional finances are available. Steps may also be included in the plan, but it is unlikely that garden paths would be shown. Whether this is the case or not often has to do with the requirements of various local authorities. Some of the more obvious exceptions include substantial vertical walls, retaining walls, and long or steep external flights of steps, and in these instances, they may have to be built according to an engineer's specifications. A patio will often be indicated if the plans include a swimming pool, although this may not be necessary.

Check with your local building department and see what the authorities require. One concern is that no building exceeds your property's boundaries – in fact, some bylaws require that you keep within specified building lines which fall inside your property's boundaries. If you do need plans, an architect, designer, landscape architect or draughtsman will be able to help you.

Even if you are not required to have formal plans, you may want professional design assistance for paths, steps and patios once the house is complete. You could approach the architect who designed your house, although it usually makes better sense to engage the services of a landscape architect or even a landscaper with a lesser qualification. These people are garden specialists and will be able to assist with planting as well as construction plans and guidelines.

Landscapers may undertake garden brickwork, paving and so on, but it is best to enquire whether the person you are dealing with intends subcontracting the job or whether he or she has the resources to tackle the entire project. If not, you may be better advised simply to consult the landscaper concerned and employ a contractor or specialist company to do the building work for you. If you are prepared to liaise between the two, you are likely to save a substantial amount. In some areas, landscape contractors need a licence to do residential work.

The other possibility for those who are not keen to lay bricks or throw concrete is to employ subcontractors. These people range from experienced pavers to unskilled labourers. Artisans generally demand an hourly fee, while labourers charge a daily rate. Either way, negotiate the amount before work begins in order to avoid any misunderstandings later on.

Whether you use a highly qualified landscape architect, a building or paving contractor or subcontractors, make sure that you get references, preferably in writing, from previous clients, and check the quality of the work with at least some of the referees to ensure that you employ reliable and skilled people.

The only other professionals whom you may need to consult are land surveyors, specialist engineers and geotechnical experts. A land surveyor's report is useful if you are building on virgin land; an engineer's report will only be necessary if the site is a difficult one and you encounter large rocks or possibly clay. Make use of their services in the planning stages to save money later on.

Imprinting concrete to create a pattern is usually done by professionals.

Steep steps should be built by someone with considerable experience.

The treads of these neat rendered steps are paved to match the brick path.

A wooden walkway creates interest in a large garden.

to have a driveway. There must be enough room to open car doors so that passengers can get in and out, and ideally it should be designed so that there is enough space to turn a car. You may want to extend the driveway to include a forecourt or turning circle; furthermore, unless there is adequate street parking for a second car and guests' cars, you could even consider creating an extra parking bay or two if space is not at a premium.

Steps

Wherever there are changes in level, paths inevitably incorporate steps or ramps. Often it is also necessary to build steps leading up to entrances, providing access between terraces and linking parts of the garden on sloping ground, even where formal pathways have not been created. Not only will an outdoor stairway neaten a trampled slope, but it will also encourage one to explore further, in much the same way as a winding path that disappears from view does.

LAYOUT AND LOCATION

The site chosen for a patio will probably be determined by the function you would like this area to perform, together with ease of access to and from the house and the view from the site. Paths and walkways, on the other hand, are usually laid out to link specific areas, and steps are sited where changes in level make them necessary. Since the size, shape and topography of the property will also have a direct bearing on the plan, it is wise to plan everything carefully on paper first. It also helps to visualise the finished effect – wander around the garden and take note of both sunny and shady spots and the direction of prevailing winds, and remember that these will alter throughout the day and during the course of the year as the seasons change.

Consider all siting options carefully, and make an effort to see, for instance, which potential sites for a patio have a good view and which could lack privacy from neighbours. A patio located alongside the living room can become an outdoor sitting room in good weather, while one sited outside a bedroom is more likely to become a private retreat, especially if it is screened in some way. If the house is rectangular, a large area leading off several rooms may be the ideal plan; however, your lifestyle may require several smaller, more intimate areas instead. Only you can decide.

If you have a site plan of the property, or if you can get one from the local authorities, make a copy of it to draw on. Otherwise measure and mark out the boundaries as accurately as you can on a large sheet of graph paper, working to a scale of at least 1:200, and preferably 1:100. Show the position of the house and any outbuildings, as well as all other existing structures (pergolas, water gardens, arches, walls, fences and anything else which is immovable) and natural features (large rocks, established shrubs, bushes and trees, and any mounds or hollows). Make absolutely sure that you do not leave out anything substantial.

Now draw in the patio areas and any other structures or features you are planning. These should include everything from a swimming pool or tennis court to a planted kitchen garden or a children's play area. Also note service areas for hanging washing, storing dustbins, making compost and so on.

Then sketch in paths and walkways. These may, of course, be straight or winding, depending largely on whether there are any features they must detour around, the style of the garden and the effect you wish to create (see pages 85-88). The width will also be influenced by style, as well as function. A formal Victorian-style walk should be reasonably wide, whereas a rustic garden path can be quite narrow. A driveway will need to accommodate cars and passengers entering and leaving their vehicles, and sometimes a turning circle and a parking bay or two.

Wherever there is a change in level, between buildings or patios and the ground, steps are an obvious solution. If a path leads up a slope, you may

Two railway sleepers span a stream as part of a narrow, meandering pathway.

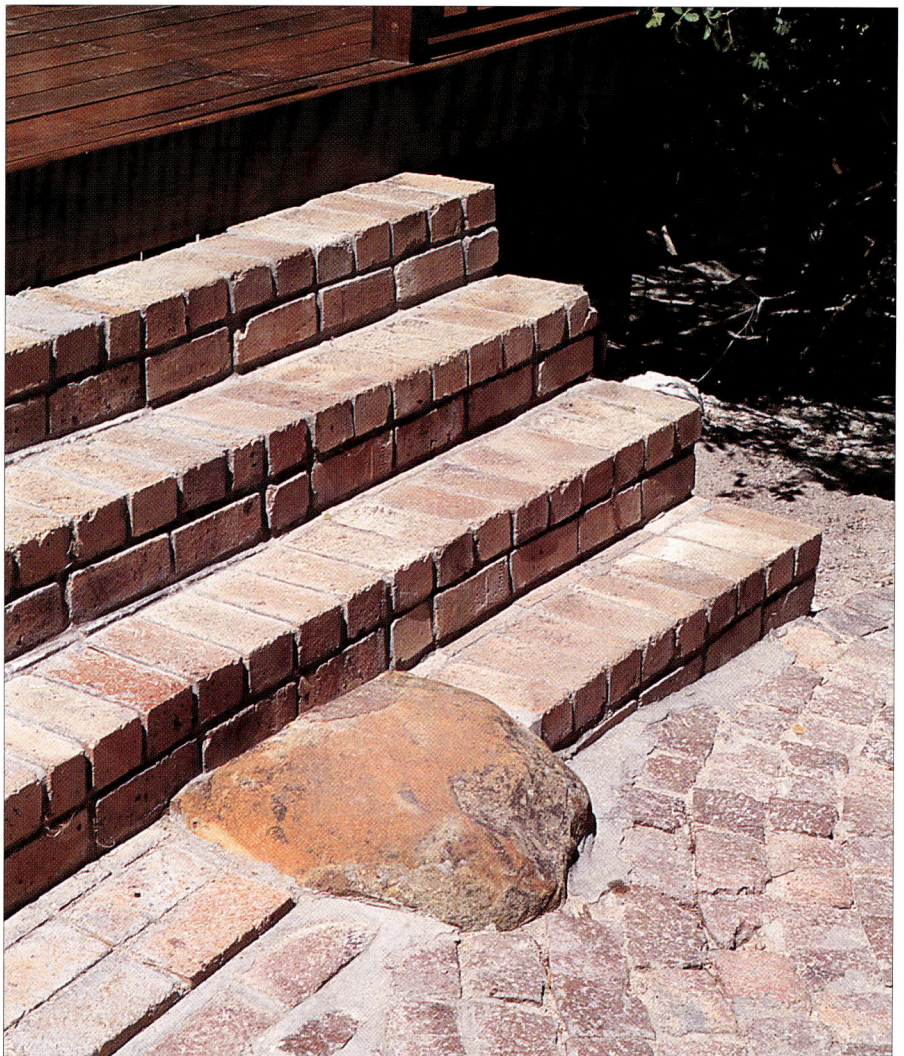

A large rock is retained as a feature at the bottom of these steps.

Open wooden steps lead up to the house from a timber walkway.

want to introduce stairs for visual interest as much as for practical reasons. Like footways, steps may be built in a straight line or they may be curved, depending on the site and any particular style you want to adopt (see pages 86-89). Dimensions should be in keeping with the pathways and entrances the steps lead to, but those constructed within the garden tend to be most effective when they are broad and gradual. A steep, narrow staircase can be an obstacle if one is taking a leisurely stroll about the garden, apart from which it can be dangerous in wet weather or at night.

MATERIAL OPTIONS
A wide variety of materials may be used to construct paths, steps and patios. These range from solid or precast concrete to sliced logs, from bricks and blocks to old railway sleepers. Some materials are more permanent than others, and each creates a different visual impression.

In many instances it is possible to combine various materials for effect as well as convenience. For example, a simple stepping-stone path, created with precast slabs or sliced tree trunks, may join up with conventional brick steps leading to a brick-paved patio. A cobbled pathway might meander from a substantial stairway built from concrete cast *in situ*, while a flagstone and ground-cover path could connect timber decking with a slate-tiled patio. However, take care not to mix too many different surface materials, as the effect could become disjointed rather than interesting.

What materials you eventually decide to use is largely a matter of personal choice, although it is always best to complement those used to construct existing features elsewhere in the garden such as planters, barbecues and garden walls, as well as the house itself.

The architectural style of the house and the materials used to create this style are also important considerations which should not be overlooked (see pages 86-90).

The full range of possibilities for outdoor surfaces is discussed on pages 87-91. You may find that there are several different surfacing materials which are suitable for your garden plan. Weigh up the advantages and disadvantages of each, taking into consideration cost factors, safety and ease of construction before making a decision.

COUNTING COSTS
It is always vital to cost a project accurately before embarking on the building programme. If you plan properly, you will be able to establish a budget which you can stay within. Inadequate planning often leads to delays and hitches which waste time as well as materials.

If you are going to do the work yourself, you will need to quantify materials and assess any additional costs. The main materials (paving bricks, concrete, precast paving slabs and so on) are just one part of the cost factor: it is also important to price everything else required for building, from cement, sand and stone to drainage pipes, conduiting, plants and lighting accessories. Once you have decided which construction methods you are going to use, examine your tool kit and make sure you have all the tools required. If you plan to hire any tools, make allowance for the fees involved.

Digging holes for foundations, mixing concrete and transporting heavy materials through the garden can be particularly arduous tasks. If you are likely to need assistance, include labour charges – even family members may demand remuneration!

Finally, itemise the various elements (basic construction cost, finishes, lighting, planting) and complete the project in phases if necessary.

Even if you are planning to call in professionals (perhaps to level the site before you start, or to pave the patio), it is vital to avoid expensive mistakes and unnecessary wastage.

A raised patio alongside the house.

An attractive patio designed to create an indoor-outdoor flow.

When designing patios and positioning paths, steps and driveways, it is essential to aim for unity and harmony. The type of walkway or sitting area you choose must suit the house and the garden, and their proportions should be in keeping with the property as a whole.

Designing a garden can be a daunting task, particularly if you are starting from scratch. It is also a time-consuming business which demands patience and persistence. Paths, steps and patios form a kind of skeleton within the garden, and along with boundary walls, buildings and any existing features, are all part of the basic design of any outdoor area. An understanding of the basic principles of design is therefore essential. You will also need to take local weather conditions and the microclimate of your garden into account, not only when planting, but also when choosing the materials for constructing any outdoor features. This does not mean that you have to be a horticulturist or landscape specialist to succeed; with enthusiasm and imagination, a tremendous amount can be achieved.

The first step is to put the basic plan on paper (see pages 81-82). This will give you a clear idea of how much land you have to work with, how the outdoor space is to be subdivided and where all the elements will be sited. The next phase is to consider the many design details which will enable you to create your outdoor haven.

Decide what effects you would like to create and what materials you should use in which areas. Ask yourself whether you are going to keep to a particular style and whether you want to achieve a particular visual theme. If there are problem areas (these may include embankments and steep slopes, rocks, marshy spots and so on), it is essential to decide at the outset whether special construction of terraces, decking, steps and any other features will be necessary.

Although plants are a vital part of the plan, at this stage it is simpler to think purely in terms of colour, size and shape rather than specific species.

When it comes to putting the plan into action, the main question will be what to do first and how to stagger the various stages of the project. There are always countless options, but the best solution is to tackle the job systematically. Just as structural alterations should be tackled before you begin decorating inside your house, any construction work in the garden should ideally be completed before planting gets under way.

You will want to establish a basic framework, but if you cannot afford to lay paths and build patios at this stage, mark the areas where these features will eventually be. Although you may decide to lay lawn or even plant flowers here for the time being, you will not want shrubs or trees to establish themselves where they will have to be removed later on.

THE BASICS

Paths and patios must be designed to suit the purpose they are to serve. It helps to think of the garden as a large outdoor room. Instead of carpeting, tiles and so on, you have a range of surfacing options from grass and gravel to brick paving, stone flagstones and concrete, some of which may also be used indoors. Inside you can introduce colour and texture with fabric and paint; outside, plants, flowers, and the materials chosen to surface your garden 'floor' will do this for you.

The way you decide to combine these elements will go a long way towards determining the ambience of the garden as a whole. You will need to decide whether you want the effect to be wildly colourful or quietly restful; whether you are going to aim for a cosy private patio which offers solitude, or an open outlook which is not blocked by screens and tall plants or intersected by walkways.

You may have decided to divide the outdoor space into a series of 'rooms' linked by paths. These may be quite distinct from one another, and different in design. There may even be various types of path. However, it is still important to aim for harmony and to establish an overall sense of balance and proportion. Remember that even a seemingly chaotic, wild garden, with rough gravel paths and informal seating areas, often needs to be carefully planned and laid out.

TYPE

The type of garden you plan to create (and the individual features you choose to make up the garden) will involve a basic design decision, namely whether you want it to be formal or informal, beautifully symmetrical or attractively irregular in character.

The rendering and painting of these steps adds style to the garden.

A path with an interesting blend of materials.

Gravel can be inexpensive, but effective.

The formal garden is generally characterised by straight lines, although circular paths may also be included in the scheme. Wide walkways, rigid planting and grand staircases are at home here, along with terraces and courtyards. Symmetry and balance are the two essential distinguishing features of the formal garden.

Paths and patios are made from similar materials, usually relatively sophisticated, and neatly finished off. Marble, for instance, was a favourite in the great classical gardens, but slate, brick and tile are equally appropriate.

Steps are usually built of brick, concrete or planed timber, often with pillars and balustrades on either side.

The informal garden contains design elements which are quite the opposite of those found in the formal garden. Here you find rustic materials and curved, irregular lines and forms. Herbaceous borders alongside paths, with plants spilling over the edges, are perfect, as are stepping stones which wander off around corners.

Materials chosen should be less contrived and tending towards rusticity. Gravel and slasto (slate crazy paving) paths are commonplace, while steps are often built with stone. If bricks or blocks are used, they should be laid to enhance the informal approach, and plants could also be encouraged to take root in the joints.

Of course, few things in life are as well defined as this, and in practice, many gardens include both formal and informal elements. This usually works best on a large property, where sections can easily be subdivided, but even in a reasonably small area, you could combine these two types and establish, for instance, an informal planted area with a winding pathway, which leads to a relatively formal patio built adjacent to the house.

THEME
Professional designers often choose to follow a theme. This can work well, but it is essential to ensure that paths, steps and areas intended for entertaining guests are appropriately designed and constructed. Style is an obvious theme option (see below), but is one which usually relies on the existing architecture of the house. For instance, a rustic cobbled path will not suit a clean-lined modern house, and a marble-topped patio could look quite out of place next to a brick cottage.

If you decide to focus on colour, you may want to use several shades of a chosen hue (a pink theme could range from deep cerise to soft powder-puff pink, while a blue theme could include lilac and purple tones) or you might prefer to mix colours. Perhaps your living room has been decorated in bold blues and yellows; if so, the obvious hues for a patio leading from this room will mirror the interior. This could change to yellow and orange along a linking pathway which disappears behind a screen wall or hedge into a herb garden. Here, the colours would be primarily yellow, orange and blue, without too much planning on your part. This does not mean that surface materials need to match; in fact it is probably more important to ensure that they complement established plants. There are always many possibilities, but a black slate patio could be very effective surrounded by blue and yellow flowers, while red brick shows up white blooms to good advantage.

Your theme may follow through the entire outdoor area, or it may be limited to one section only. Herbs and roses, for instance, are often planted in separate areas which are frequently bounded by paths.

SURFACE MATERIALS
The material chosen for your paths, steps, patio or driveway will depend on numerous factors including the specific role of each area, the type of garden you are planning and any style you may want to reproduce.

A selection of materials appropriate to some of the more popular style possibilities is given on pages 88-91 and 94-98. Consider these along with the other elements. For instance, a purely functional path leading to the

Steps and patios built from recycled bricks complement the Victorian style of the house.

Stepping stones lead through a small garden to a utility room.

When one is faced with a steeply sloping garden, the timber deck becomes an excellent alternative to the conventional paved patio. Not only does this form of construction enable home-owners to add outdoor living space to the house, but it also creates the opportunity to reclaim land which might otherwise be unusable. Where rocky ground cannot be easily flattened, or in areas where the soil gets soggy and waterlogged in wet weather, it is also a very useful option.

Decking has many other benefits and is certainly not for difficult sites only. Indeed, a timber deck raised just above the ground will provide an attractive, low-maintenance surface for year-round use in just about any garden. It may be built as an alternative to the conventional verandah, either at ground level or extended from an upper storey, or it may be erected around a swimming pool, spa or hot tub, a pond or even a tree house or play structure.

A garden which slopes slightly may be the ideal site for multilevel decking. This could create the feel of terracing, or it may simply produce a series of separate but adjacent areas for sitting, playing or entertaining. Designed so that each consecutive deck adjoins at an angle, multilevel decking can be a particularly impressive feature, and the slats produce an attractive pattern.

Sometimes timber decking is best used in conjunction with other paving or landscaping materials. A deck built alongside the house could lead down wooden steps to a brick-paved patio, or it could extend from an established patio beside the house, adding to the outdoor living space and possibly reclaiming a nearby slope.

Just as a patio will benefit from additional features, so too will a deck. An overhead structure of some kind will offer shade, while built-in seating, storage and perhaps even simple tables or worktops will immediately increase its usefulness. Railings will add detail and increase the safety of a deck, while screens (latticework is popular) will give you added privacy and shield the area from wind.

Although timber decking does suit most house styles, it is particularly appropriate for Japanese-style architecture and similar landscaping approaches; it also blends well with informal gardens.

Various methods are used for building decks, most of which will be within the capabilities of a competent handyman or DIY builder. Most are built with sturdy upright supports of timber or brick (which keep the decking above ground), and planed (milled) decking slats resting on an arrangement of beams, joists and ledgers.

The timber used to construct a deck will depend on which suitable types are sold in your area. Although not always available, and expensive in some places, Californian redwood is one of the traditional choices, since the heartwood in particular has a natural resistance to decay. Most decking woods should be pressure-treated before you buy them, and sealed and treated regularly to avoid infestation and rot, though some, like teak and balau, can simply be oiled or allowed to weather naturally. It is also important to use galvanised cleats, brackets and screws to avoid the problem of fittings rusting – not only is rust unsightly, it also weakens the structure.

An attractive deck built over a steep slope increases usable space.

A low-level deck in the garden is used for entertaining and alfresco meals.

Asphalt is a practical and relatively inexpensive surface for driveways.

A brick path between herbaceous borders.

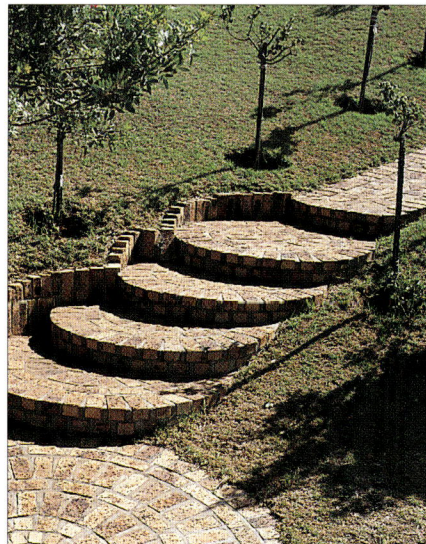

Bricks used to create flowing lines.

in some places as a surface material for paths. A major disadvantage is that the chips scatter easily, especially in high winds or when walked on. The visual effect of bark chips is similar to that of gravel, and they should only be used in informal parts of a garden.

Brick

Perhaps more than any other paving material, brick can be used in just about every possible type and style of garden. It has been used for centuries, and in some parts of the world brick paths estimated to be more than 4 000 years old are still in use today.

Made of concrete and clay, bricks and thinner pavers are available in a wide range of colours and may be laid in a multitude of patterns (see page 105) The most common configuration is probably running bond (a simple grid formation), and the strong-est, which is particularly suitable for driveways, is herringbone, laid either at right-angles or diagonally to the edge of the paving. Although a wall should never be built without the bricks inter-locking, a simple stack bond (jack-on-jack) pattern, which involves no overlapping of bricks, is quite acceptable for level paving. Circular patterns are also popular for patio and driveway surfaces. Interlocking pavers are perfect for any surface which will be driven on, while 'hard lawn systems', a relatively new range of products, comprise inter-locking paving blocks which, when laid, leave spaces for planting.

Bricks and paving blocks may be laid on sand or a solid concrete slab with sand or mortar between them.

Cobbles and setts

There is a certain fairytale romanticism about a narrow cobbled path, but it is important to consider practical factors before laying one in your own garden. The real thing consists of numerous rounded stones, often salvaged from river beds, pressed into mortar. They are not always easy to walk on and certainly not easy to balance chairs and tables on for patios.

A compromise, which is cheaper, though not always as natural in effect,

front door should be surfaced with a non-slip material; it should also take a short route and be well lit at night. On the other hand, a leisurely garden path leading to a bench with a view could be a little less practical, as it will probably be used less, especially in the rain and dark.

Asphalt

Ideal for driveways, asphalt is generally regarded as a low-cost material and is seldom considered suitable for either

paths or patio surfaces. Like tarmac, it is either rolled on by specialist contractors while hot, or applied cold. The cold-mix variety is aimed at the DIY market and is relatively simple to lay on a compacted sub-base. It is, however, not as hard-wearing as the material which is rolled while hot.

Bark chips

Suitable for play areas, as they allow a nice soft landing for children, and for mulching, bark chips are also favoured

Pretty brick steps topped with concrete treads.

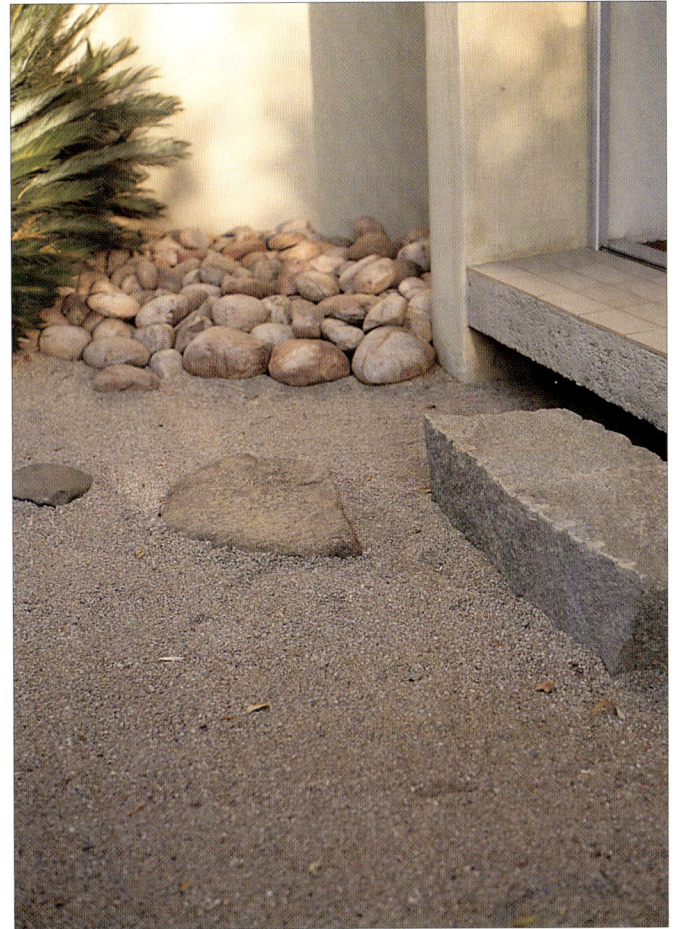
Fine gravel is combined with stone in the Japanese way.

is to use more regular reconstituted stone or concrete setts, manufactured in imitation of the original granite setts (which were cut from stone). Not as labour-intensive to lay as rounded cobbles, they are fairly regular in size and shape, and create a more even surface on which to walk.

Concrete

One of the least expensive and most unimaginatively used materials is concrete. Perhaps because it is considered 'cheap', people are generally uninventive when using it, yet simply by combining concrete with other materials and planting around it, it is possible to create patios, paths, steps and driveways which have a very special charm and character.

Concrete is available in numerous precast forms – rounded, square and rectangular slabs, kerbstones, reconstituted stone products, and even precast concrete sleepers may

all be used to great effect and can be laid in a number of ways. Square slabs can be used to create a chequer-board effect, alternating the concrete with herbs or a fragrant ground cover, rounded shapes may be laid as stepping-stone pathways, and precast kerbs may be used either to create steps or to raise a patio on a level piece of ground (see pages 108–111).

Concrete cast *in situ* is probably handled with even less sensitivity by the amateur builder. Sometimes, many square metres of ground are covered with the material and paths cast in long strips above the surface of the soil. Instead, concrete should be handled as a useful part of the design plan; age the finished surface if you like this effect and allow it to blend in with your environment.

Gravel

An inexpensive option, gravel is useful for paths and walkways in the garden.

It is also an acceptable material for level driveways and parking areas, and very effective when used in conjunction with paving slabs. As it is naturally loose, gravel may also be spread over flowerbeds or between the clipped hedges of ornamental parterres. It helps to control weed growth and conserve moisture in the soil too.

It is essential to compact the earth beneath this material thoroughly and to contain it with some sort of edging to prevent it from spilling into flowerbeds and spreading onto the adjacent grass or paving.

The type of gravel you use will depend on what is available in your area. Material sold for use as sub-base under driveways is suitable, otherwise you can ask for the smallest single-sized crushed stone. DIY concrete is usually made with 19 mm or 13.2 mm stone; you will need a much finer grade than this. If it is available in your area, pea gravel is a perfect choice.

Another possibility well suited for walkways is laterite, although it is not universally available. This material consists of a mixture of gravel and clay which is moistened with water and rolled to a smooth surface.

A few specialist companies offer pebble paving, which is made by bonding gravel-like stones in a special mixture of resin and cement; this is then applied over concrete to form a continuous surface.

Grass

Although grass eventually becomes worn down by constant foot traffic, it is sometimes the best choice for paths and walkways. Choose a hardy variety and be prepared to mow, feed and water it and generally to attend to its needs. Although people often neglect their lawns, grass should not really be regarded as a low-maintenance surface.

When it comes to patios, most people prefer, for practical reasons, to have a good, solid surface underfoot. Grass is, however, a reasonable temporary solution for some, and it can also be used as a more permanent material in combination with hard surfaces such as stepping stones.

Stone

Real stone slabs look wonderful in any garden, either as a patio or terrace surface, or as a pathway. They are also a good natural material to choose for steps, especially if they are sited alongside a stone wall. While steps may be built with slabs or with rocks (provided they have at least one flattish side), patios and walkways should be laid with flat, solid flagstones or as crazy paving.

Like other types of stone, slate is available in regular and irregular shapes and may be laid as tiles or as crazy paving. It is suitable for paths, patios and the treads of steps. The dark charcoal-grey reconstituted stone tiles which are available in some areas can look remarkably like slate.

As natural stone is often difficult to come by, reconstituted stone (made by casting and compressing concrete

in special moulds) is a good alternative. Sizes are varied and shapes usually reasonably regular, making them a good choice for the DIY builder.

Tiles

A wide variety of tiles may be used on patios. You may be able to continue a ceramic tile surface used in the interior of your home, but it is generally advisable to ensure that any area exposed or even partially exposed to the elements should be frost-proof and have a non-slip matt finish. Manufactured quarry tiles, handmade terracotta tiles, as well as those made from terrazzo (a mixture of coloured marble and stone chips bedded in mortar) are all popular options that are particularly well suited to the garden as their colours and textures blend in beautifully with those of nature.

If you are in any doubt as to whether a tile is suitable for your purposes, contact the manufacturer before buying the materials.

Timber

Apart from being the most common decking material, timber is often used for steps and sometimes to surface both paths and patios as well. Sliced tree trunks provide an inexpensive material for stepping-stone pathways, although they do become slippery, sometimes treacherously so, in wet weather. If you lay a large expanse of them, for instance a parking area, aim for a slightly uneven upper surface to give tyres a grip.

Old railway sleepers, often made from tough hardwoods, are also well suited for surfacing paths as well as small patios (if you can find enough to cover a large surface). They also make

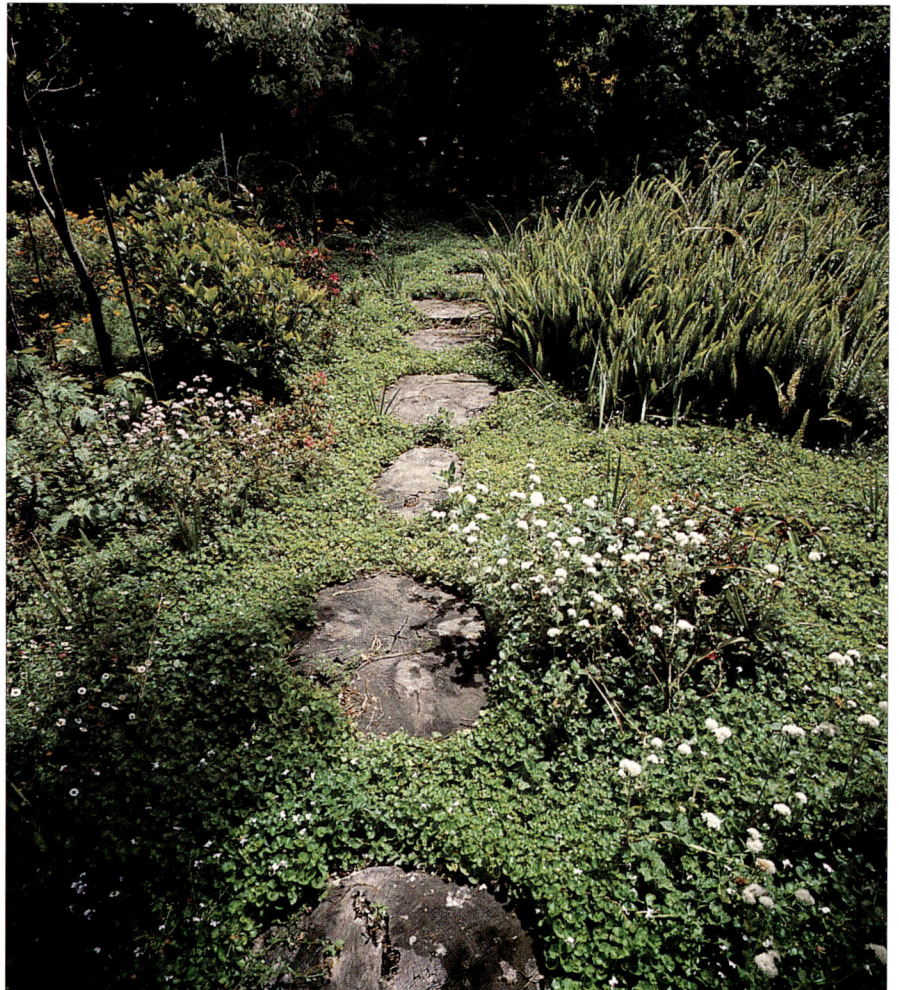

Sliced tree trunks in an informal, rambling garden.

very successful steps and may be used, together with other materials and plants, for attractive pathways. Debarked logs, which do not need to be perfectly rounded in shape, are also a good material for informal steps. Backfilled with earth and laid across the front of each tread, they will provide a good footing up a natural slope. When used for decking, timber is almost always sawn and planed (or dressed) to a good, smooth and attractive finish.

EDGINGS

Absolutely essential around most types of patio, edgings are also a necessity along the sides of pathways and walkways, and without them, driveways would inevitably collapse as cars ride over the edges. But an edging can also have aesthetic value. It is possible to be imaginative and creative while ensuring that paving bricks, slabs and so on are held in place, and loose materials prevented from spilling out onto adjacent surfaces.

If you have a Victorian-style garden, lay tiles on edge along pathways; if you prefer a more modern approach, a row of bricks may be laid at an angle to retain the surface material. Brick-paved paths and patios are usually edged with the same brick, laid at a slight angle for drainage, although precast concrete edgings (including special kerbstones) are also useful.

SCREENING AND SHELTER

Although not always strictly necessary, pergolas and overheads will offer some protection from the elements and increase the usefulness of any patio. Overhead structures could also be useful over walkways, particularly where they lead from a garage or parking bay, or link a gate to the front door.

Of course the roofing material of any pergola or overhead structure will determine the degree of shelter offered. Awning material (including shadecloth), canvas and timber will give some shade, but will not prevent you from getting wet. If the motivation for building a pergola over a patio or

walkway is to keep the area beneath it dry, then you will need to choose a more solid covering, like fibreglass, polycarbonate or even tiles, and the basic structure will therefore need to be more substantial to carry the weight of the roofing material.

Bricks set at an angle to form an edging.

Screening, on the other hand, is usually erected as a wind break or to make a patio more private. It can also be used to define or divide an area. Screen walls, plants climbing up trelliswork, or hedges alongside a pathway may be incorporated as

A pebble-paved surface edged in brick.

Once mature, plants grown over a pergola will offer shade from the sun.

design elements, defining the route as well as offering some protection.

Materials chosen for pergolas and screens should complement those used in the rest of the garden. Although materials may differ in appearance, the basic construction principles are similar for many of them.

LIGHTING

When it comes to garden lighting, the illumination of paths, steps, driveways and patios should be top of the list. Not only does lighting extend the usefulness of these outdoor areas, but it is essential for general safety and security as well. Steps can be particularly hazardous at night, and corners where intruders could lurk in the dark are potentially dangerous, especially in and near parking and entrance areas. If a patio is not illuminated at night, its usefulness will be severely limited. While you are taking the time and effort to construct such an area, it makes sense to ensure that you can use it after dark as well as during the day.

Lighting also adds to the decorative scheme outdoors. Used to highlight features alongside pathways and on patios, it lends character and charm to any garden.

Of course, the installation of electric lighting will usually involve enlisting the services of an electrician unless you can utilise existing plug points and light fittings. This is often an option when a patio is created alongside the house. Unless a floodlight attached to the house adequately illuminates a pathway or driveway, it is usually necessary to lay suitable waterproof cabling underground.

Although you may be able to lay the cables and fix the fittings yourself, it is essential to employ an authorised person to connect the wiring to the mains. Once underground wiring is in place, make sure that anyone working in the garden knows where it is, to prevent accidental damage with spades and other sharp tools.

It is worth noting that low-voltage lighting systems suitable for DIY installation are available in some

Well-lit stairs lead from the entrance to the house.

countries, and these have the added advantage of being much safer than standard installations.

Many lights and lamps are suitable for use outdoors, but it is essential that only sealed units are chosen. Although freestanding lamps and pillar-mounted fittings are useful alongside paths, it is best to aim for a good, general light on the patio. Wall-mounted lamps usually cast a warm glow over the entire area, while spotlights may be used to brighten a specific section of the patio, perhaps one used for alfresco eating. Uplighters are effective alongside steps, and floodlights will brighten a large area.

SEATING

Seating arrangements are found in most gardens. Some seats are fixed, others moveable, depending largely on function, where the furniture is

sited, and what it is made of. Although the patio is the most obvious place to sit outdoors, paths may lead to a spot with a good view or even to a particularly pretty part of the garden, and this is a good place to have a bench. If there is some sort of overhead shelter, an arbour or patio roof for instance, freestanding furniture is usually a practical option. If not, it may be preferable to consider built-in seats and tables, or even natural options like logs or planted earth banks.

On a patio, built-in seating can be a real boon; it can be left where it is in all weather conditions, all year round, and simply 'dressed' with cushions when you want to use it. There are various materials suitable for permanent designs, although brick and stone are probably the most usual and the most versatile. It is more cumbersome to cast concrete *in situ* than to lay bricks, but the latter can be an expensive option. Timber is another popular choice, but it is often better suited to decks than to patios.

Of course, some types of moveable furniture may also be left permanently in place. Ordinary precast concrete benches weather well. Left unpainted, they eventually become mossy and naturally aged; bear in mind that although this can look attractive, it can also reduce the practicality of the seat. If you prefer a slicker look, a coat of paint will do the trick. Metal designs are also suitable, especially hardy aluminium, which will not rust. Plastic tables and chairs may be left outside, but constant exposure to the elements does make many types brittle and they invariably deteriorate over a period of time.

PLANTING

The ultimate finishing touch for paths, steps and patios, plants can make all the difference. Flowering creepers and climbers will introduce colour on the patio, while hardy ground covers and small perennials will add interest to paths, steps and paving.

There are numerous ways in which to introduce plants. You may want to establish flowerbeds along the edge of a patio, build planters, or perhaps leave out sections of the paving and plant small shrubs in the spaces. Paths and steps may be flanked with shrubs, or you might consider sprinkling seed on paving laid without mortar and allowing the plants to grow in a spontaneous fashion.

Plants alternating with hard surfaces (see page 90) can be attractive, and this approach may be adapted to paths, steps and patios alike. Sweet-smelling ground covers like creeping thyme and pennyroyal are good choices.

It is essential to do a little homework before you plant and to make sure that the plants you choose will thrive in the environment in which you want to plant them. You will not always be able to imitate a look (perhaps seen in a book or magazine) with exactly the same plants. It is usually possible to find a species which may be substituted.

A precast concrete seat on an informal patio invites one to stop awhile.

A concrete lantern introduces a touch of Oriental style.

All building projects, no matter how simple, require a selection of tools and materials, as well as a fundamental knowledge of the basic construction principles involved. If you have undertaken DIY projects previously, you probably already have most or all of the necessary equipment in your tool bag, and you should be accustomed to much of the terminology used by builders. If not, it is essential to familiarise yourself with the basics and to ensure that you have all the items required before starting work.

MATERIALS

There is a fairly wide range of materials that are suitable for the construction of paths, steps and patios, and many of these materials are discussed on pages 87–91. A number of them are simply laid on the ground or on a base of soft sand, while others, including bricks, blocks, concrete and timber (if used for steps) demand specific construction skills (see pages 101–105).

Bricks and blocks

Bricks and blocks are available in a vast range, and all may be used to build paths, steps and patios. Clay, concrete and calcium silicate bricks and blocks are all perfectly suitable for the construction of steps and patio walls, while special pavers (which are made of clay or precast concrete in a range of colours) are often preferred for patios and pathways.

While there is a huge variety of block sizes, bricks are relatively standard in their dimensions, ranging from about 222-230 mm long by 106-112 mm wide, and about 70-76 mm thick, depending on where they are made. Facebricks, which are not meant to be rendered, are generally slightly thicker than stock bricks, which are usually rendered with mortar (see page 96). Paving bricks, which normally have a lightly textured

Bricks are a versatile material for building paths, steps and patios.

Concrete steps are coloured with pigment to enhance their appearance.

surface, are considerably thinner, and can be as little as 40 mm thick.

In addition to flat-sided pavers, concrete units are sometimes moulded into shapes which enable them to interlock. These are particularly suitable for driveways which will take reasonably heavy traffic or which are built on a slope.

In spite of minor differences in size, you can estimate quantities for building or paving based on the assumption that you will need 40-45 bricks or pavers to lay 1 m^2 of paving, 50-55 bricks to lay 1 m^2 of half-brick walling (one brick-width thick), and 110 to lay 1 m^2 of single-brick walling (two brick-widths or 222-230 mm thick).

Concrete and mortar

Both precast concrete and concrete cast *in situ* are immensely useful for the construction of paths, steps and patios. Concrete is also used on occasion to form the base slab for patios, particularly if they are to be tiled or topped with materials like crazy paving, slate or marble.

Mortar is used in most projects, for laying brick steps and for any stairway or patio walls, as well as for some types of paving. It is also used for screeding concrete slabs that are to be topped with tiles as well as for rendering some brick and block structures, including steps.

Reconstituted stone flags and precast concrete slabs are popular and practical options for patio floors. These materials are cast in the factory to a variety of specifications, and as they are simple to lay, they are particularly suitable for the DIY builder.

Interlocking blocks for terraces and retaining walls are a less usual but nonetheless versatile option for building steps. They are manufactured in a range of designs, although availability varies from place to place. The shape of each unit will also determine how it is used. Some types must be laid with the open surface uppermost, which means you will need to fill the block with soil or, preferably, concrete to create a level tread. Alternatively you may top the finished step with a precast tile or slab, or perhaps a simulated sleeper (see pages 108–111). It may be possible to lay modular units on their sides, creating a smooth, solid tread. If this is possible, it is wise to shovel mortar or soil into the hollow, central section of each one.

Concrete cast *in situ* is one of the most widely used materials for both paths and driveways. It is also a popular option for steps, and an essential material for patios that

Precast concrete slabs are easy to lay and are ideal for paths.

Interlocking terrace blocks are perfect for steps.

Circular concrete slabs with attractive planting.

Timber poles are used for risers and stringers, while the treads are simply filled with gravel.

require a solid sub-base. Made by combining cement, sand and crushed stone (or coarse gravel) with water, it is a versatile and economical material, but one which takes considerable time and effort to mix and lay.

There are several possibilities when it comes to purchasing concrete. You can buy the dry materials in bags, premixed and ready to be combined with water, or separately for mixing by hand or in a concrete mixer, or you can arrange to have it delivered ready for use. Ready-mixed concrete is only a feasible option if a large volume is required, and the premixed dry materials are not economical unless very small quantities are called for. For this reason, most DIY builders opt to buy all the necessary constituents individually and to mix them themselves.

You will need to use a concrete mix suitable for the project you plan to tackle. This will depend partly on the nature of the project, as well as on local conditions and the quality of the materials used. For instance, a 1:3:6 cement:sand:stone mix is suitable for most garden foundations, provided a relatively fine, well-graded aggregate is available; however, the crushed stone sold in many parts will result in concrete

which is too stony, and in this instance, a 1:4:4 mixture is preferred. For paths, steps and exposed slabs, a stronger 1:2:3 or 1:3:3 mix is recommended.

If concrete is ordered ready-mixed, you will need to give the suppliers details of your project so that they can determine the required strength of the concrete and thus the kind of mix they will need to prepare for you.

Mortar, made by mixing cement and sand with water, is used to bond bricks or blocks and give the structure, paved surface or edging maximum strength.

Just as cement, sand and crushed stone are mixed in different ratios for concrete, so too are the cement and sand used for mortar mixes. Generally, it is acceptable to use a 1:4 or even a 1:5 mortar mix for brickwork or paving with clay bricks. If concrete bricks or blocks are used, it is best to make up a weaker 1:6 mixture which is consistent with the building units used.

Cement is a very fine grey powder used to make both concrete and mortar, and as such is one of the most important ingredients in just about every building project. Several types are suitable, but ordinary Portland cement is used worldwide. It is sold in bags of 50 kg (and sometimes 25 kg, 40 kg or 45 kg).

Cement hardens when it is mixed with water, and it is this chemical reaction which gives concrete and mortar their strength. It is worth remembering that cement will not gain full strength if it dries out too quickly, so concrete and mortar should be kept damp while they set and cure.

Bear in mind, too, that unless cement is stored away from moisture, it is likely to form lumps and become unusable. Stack it in a dry place above the ground, and use it within two to three months. Discard any cement that has become lumpy or hard.

The quantity of cement needed for any project will, of course, depend on the strength of the mixture required.

Freestanding edgings must always be laid on mortar.

A patio being screeded with mortar before it is tiled.

When using a 1:4:4 ratio, you can base estimates on 4½-5 50 kg bags of cement being enough for each cubic metre of concrete; for a 1:3:6 mix, you will need four bags, six for a 1:3:3 mix and eight if the ratio is 1:2:3.

Sand is an important ingredient in mortar, both for bricklaying and for rendering brick and block surfaces, and it is invaluable as a bedding material beneath all types of paving. Furthermore, the properties of the sand used to make concrete will have a marked effect on the final product.

The best building sands are evenly graded with particles of various sizes, no bigger than 4.75 mm, and with 4-5% of the sand consisting of very fine material, sometimes referred to as fines. Poorly graded sand will produce concrete which is difficult to work with, while a lack of fines will result in a mixture which is hard to compact properly.

While the source of the sand you are using is not necessarily a reliable guide to its quality, it is worth knowing that natural river sand is generally clean and free of clay, and pit sands are usually well graded. Crusher sand, manufactured for building purposes from crushed rocks, should be of a suitable quality for concrete work, but crusher dust is too fine. Beach sand contains shell particles and salt, and unless it has been professionally washed, should not be used; mine-dump sand and fine, wind-blown sand from desert areas should be avoided.

In addition, the sand used for making concrete should be reasonably coarse ('sharp'), while that used for mortar and plaster should be softer, with more fines. When flexible paving is laid (see page 105), the sand used beneath the bricks should be coarser than that used to joint them; coarse river sand is suitable.

In some areas, suppliers add lime to sand and sell it as 'plaster sand' (as it is used to make mortar for plastering or rendering brickwork), 'mortar mix' or 'lime sand'. In this case, additional lime is not required (see below).

Sand is sold in bags of 50 kg (or sometimes 40 kg) by builders' suppliers and most hardware stores. If you want a large volume, it is best to order in bulk; the smallest quantity most merchants will deliver is half a cubic metre. Sand delivered in bulk will be dumped outside your house; if you live in a windy area, cover it as soon as possible with plastic sheeting to prevent it from being blown away.

Stone, the coarse aggregate in concrete, is screened to size specially for construction purposes. In some areas natural pebbles and pea gravel are available, otherwise you will have to use crushed stone, supplied in 'single sizes'. For DIY purposes, 19 mm (sometimes termed 20 mm) or smaller 13.2 mm stone is ideal. The smallest size commonly available is 9.5 mm (or 10 mm). While it is true that the smaller the stone, the easier it is to work with the concrete, you will need more cement for the concrete to gain the same strength, and this will also make it more costly. All quantities recommended here assume that you are using 19 mm stone.

Like sand, crushed stone is usually available from builders' suppliers and stores that stock DIY tools and materials. Alternatively, this material may also be delivered in bulk. Your choice will depend on what sort of quantity you require.

Lime is a useful ingredient which makes mortar more workable and aids water retention, and should always be included in the mix if the sand lacks sufficient very fine particles. Since it improves the plasticity and cohesiveness of the mortar, the addition of lime will make it easier to render a surface and will improve bonding between bricks and mortar. It will also help to prevent the rendered (or plastered) surface from cracking.

Available in 25 kg sacks from builders' suppliers and DIY stores, hydrated builders' lime should not be confused with agricultural lime, road lime or quicklime (calcium oxide), all of which should be avoided.

Plasticiser is a popular alternative to lime in some areas. Normally sold in a minimum quantity of 5 litres, it is mixed with the mortar according to the manufacturer's instructions – usually 50 ml to every 50 kg of cement.

Timber

Timber used to build pergolas and patio seating, decks and wooden steps, should be durable and structurally sound. Although you will be governed by what is available in your area, ensure that the timber has been treated and will withstand weathering.

While poles can be used to build rustic pergolas, sawn and planed timber is more commonly chosen for decks and steps. Both softwoods (from coniferous trees) and hardwoods (from broadleafed species) may be used, although some types will be more suitable than others, and some species more expensive. Wood is

A rustic approach with logs.

graded according to its strength and appearance; buying the best quality you can afford always pays off. If possible, avoid timber that bows or twists. Also be careful of splitting, and of large knots which may cause the timber to break.

Railway sleepers and sliced logs are both useful for pathways. Since any type of timber will tend to become slippery in wet weather, it is usually sensible to alternate the pieces of wood with other materials, or to plant ground cover plants in between them.

TOOLS

The basic toolkit required to construct a patio, path or simple garden stairway is within the means of most people. Although some power tools, for instance a drill and a saw, will make carpentry easier, most projects can be completed with hand tools. Larger items, including concrete mixers and compacting machines (which are useful for the more ambitious paving job) can be hired.

General items

Virtually every project you tackle will require a spade and perhaps a shovel, a hammer, wheelbarrow and tape

measure. Without these basic tools you will not be able to set out the area accurately or excavate it.

Tape measures are probably the first item in any toolkit. You will need a good quality retractable steel tape, ideally with a locking mechanism which makes it easier to handle if you are working single-handed. They come in various lengths; 8 m and 10 m are both useful lengths.

Pegs and line are used to set out paths, steps and patios. Although you can use proper builders' line (commonly used to ensure that brick courses are straight during bricklaying), ordinary string will suffice. Make pegs out of excess or reject timber.

Chalk is sold for setting out building sites, but it can be pricy. Instead you can use a little cement or even flour, which often works out the cheapest.

Spades and shovels are indispensable for all projects. You will need a spade to dig foundations and to prepare the sub-base for patios, as well as to level paths and excavate steps. A shovel, which has a slightly rounded shape (with either a curved or squared-off end), is better suited for shifting loose material as well as for mixing concrete and mortar.

Picks or mattocks are useful if you are excavating hard ground or removing large stones and rocks.

Wheelbarrows are essential for transporting materials on site and useful for mixing small quantities of concrete and mortar in. Invest in a proper builder's wheelbarrow, preferably with a pneumatic tyre, as flattish gardening wheelbarrows are not suitable for building work.

Hammers are the handyman's best friend. Officially part of the carpenter's toolkit, they are also used for knocking in pegs, extracting nails and assembling formwork for concretework and profiles for steps. In addition to an ordinary claw hammer, you will find that a hefty club hammer is useful for heavy-duty tasks (knocking in pegs or formwork). A brick hammer (which has a chisel end instead of a claw) is the answer when it comes to breaking bricks for bricklaying and paving, and a

Timber is a versatile material in the garden.

A builder's square is essential for accuracy.

A spade is an indispensable tool.

rubber mallet (essentially a hammer with a heavy, rubber-topped head) is invaluable for knocking paving bricks, blocks and slabs into place.

Tools for levelling and checking

Good building practice demands that brickwork is level and plumb, that paved surfaces are flat and that the corners of all structures or paving are square or set accurately at the correct angle. Certain inexpensive tools will help to ensure accuracy; some of them may even be made at home.

Spirit levels are used to check that both vertical and horizontal surfaces are level, no matter what materials you are using. Available in several lengths, they usually incorporate two spirit vials; if the bubble in the vial is centred, the surface is level. Although 1.2 m is a handy length, you will have to use it in conjunction with a straight-edged piece of timber if you are checking a patio or a long path. Alternatively, work with a line level, which comprises a vial indicator attached to a length of builder's line.

Water levels are simple home-made tools which work well over large areas and are invaluable when you are setting out a slope or when there is a need to establish points at the same height around a corner. They are also a useful aid in making a profile for steps (see page 106). All you need is a

A spirit level must be used throughout the building project.

length of transparent tubing (or a hose-pipe with a length of transparent tubing inserted at each end) filled with water. Working on the principle that water finds its own level, attach one end to a post or to brickwork so that the water is at a specific height (the datum level), then take the other end of the tube to another point whose height you wish to measure, taking care not to spill any. The level of the water here will be exactly the same height.

Squares are vital for checking right angles. Steel builder's squares are fairly bulky tools, but more accurate than a home-made square made from sawn timber assembled to form a right-angled triangle. They are marked off in metric and/or imperial measurements. Smaller combination squares (also used for carpentry) incorporate a spirit vial and are useful when you are working on a small scale, for example if you want to check that timber steps

A wooden float is used to smooth mortar.

A wooden pole may be used for compacting.

are square. Of course, you can use a home-made square to lay out a patio; to make one, cut three lengths of sawn wood in the ratio 3:4:5 (for instance 900 mm, 1.2 m and 1.5 m) and join them to form a triangle. Alternatively, use the 3:4:5 method, measuring and pegging to check for square (see page 101).

Tools for construction

When it comes to building, whether you are going to tackle bricklaying, concretework or paving, there are certain tools which you cannot be without. Others will merely simplify the task at hand.

Compactors are needed to flatten the sub-base for paving, to compress the backfill behind steps and in some cases to compact paving once it has been laid. While a mechanical vibrator (which may be hired for the project) is essential if there is fill (broken bricks, stones and so on) beneath a patio, it is usually sufficient to use a home-made punner or ramming tool. For small projects, even a thick pole will suffice. To make your own punner, set a post of some sort (a broom handle is perfect) in an empty 5 litre tin and fill the tin with concrete. Alternatively, weld a metal plate to a metal pole or affix a heavy block of wood to a post. If a mechanical plate vibrator is used

to level paving, care should be taken to avoid damage – a single pass of the compactor is usually sufficient, and going over the same area a few times may cause the pavers to crack.

Concrete mixers are useful for jobs which require a fair volume of concrete. Available in several sizes from hire shops, they may be powered by electricity, petrol or diesel.

Trowels, used for bricklaying, rendering brick and block surfaces and flattening small areas of concrete, are available in different shapes and sizes; which you use will depend on the application.

Mortarboards and screedboards are used by professional bricklayers to hold small quantities of mortar while they work. These are useful but not essential tools.

Floats, made from both wood and metal, are used to smooth the mortar used for rendering and for screeds laid over concrete.

Woodworking tools

These are necessary for constructing decks, timber steps and pergolas, and include drills (see below), hammers and a variety of saws and screwdrivers. Since both the formwork for *in situ* concrete and the profiles for steps are commonly made from wood, it is a good idea to include at least one

of each in your toolkit. There is a good range of hand saws commonly available. Useful saws include the general-purpose bowsaw, which is ideal for sawing logs, the stocky tenon saw, with a rectangular blade, which is perfect for cutting smaller sections of timber, the larger panel saw, and the hacksaw, which will cut through just about anything, including metal. You probably have screwdrivers already, but if not, consider investing in a spiral ratchet screwdriver which, with its variable positions and reverse action, not only simplifies the task of screwing in fasteners, but also allows you to remove them relatively easily.

Power tools

Although not an essential requirement for the average path, patio or step project, several power tools can make life easier. An electric saw in particular will enable you to cut timber with little effort, while a drill will simplify the insertion of bolts and screws. An angle grinder is invaluable for cutting thick tiles and bricks, while a block splitter or masonry saw is indispensable for cutting any precast concrete products.

Larger power tools, such as concrete mixers, compactors and vibrators, can usually be hired for a particular DIY project if necessary.

PRINCIPLES & TECHNIQUES

You will need only rudimentary skills to build straightforward steps or to lay an ordinary path or patio, but it is vital to have a thorough understanding of the principles which support good building practice. You will also have to master certain basic techniques if you plan to undertake the work yourself.

The basics

The one essential DIY rule is to keep everything you construct square, level and plumb. This means that bricks and blocks must be laid in straight lines or at right angles to one another, and their upper surface should be flat, while paving must be smooth and even. If you ignore the rules, walls, however low, may fall over and water will accumulate in uneven paving and on the treads of steps.

Square structures and paved areas have right-angled corners, so unless a patio is irregular in form, you will need to ensure that each corner measures exactly 90°. Although paths frequently curve, most steps are also 'square', that is, the treads and risers have right-angled corners and the steps are parallel to each other.

When setting out a square design, the simplest way to check that all corners are at right angles is to use the 3:4:5 method (unless you use a builder's square or make a square with timber – see page 100). Mark out the patio and then measure 3 m from the corner along one side, and 4 m from the same corner along the

adjacent side. Then measure the distance between the two points. If it is exactly 5 m, your patio is square; if not, adjust the layout until the sides of the structure measure 3 m, 4 m and 5 m. If your patio is smaller than 4 m long, or if you are checking for square in a confined space, simply use smaller measurements which are multiples of three, four and five (900 mm, 1.2 m and 1.5 m or 600 mm, 800 mm and 1 m, for instance).

Circular areas are not difficult to lay out – you will simply need to make yourself a large compass with pegs and a length of string. Knock one peg in at a central point, attach the string to it, then pull the string taut. Mark on the string the radius you wish the circle to be, then use it to find several points on the circumference, and mark them with pegs. Join up the points with a chalk or flour line.

Level and plumb are terms every builder is familiar with. The tools used to ensure that these principles are followed are detailed on pages 99–100, but the one you will use most often is a spirit level. This is used to check all horizontal surfaces (brick paving, slabs and the treads of steps) as well as vertical surfaces. Although all your upright surfaces, including patio walls

and the risers of steps, must be exactly vertical, paved areas and the treads of steps will usually slope very slightly to aid drainage (see below). If you are considering laying a ramp instead of steps, bear in mind that the gradient should not exceed 1:5 for a normal ramp or 1:12 for wheelchair access.

Drainage

Water is the life-blood of any garden, yet it can also undermine foundations and the entire landscaping framework, washing away plants and paving and causing substantial damage at times. Even if the soil is stable and the ground absolutely level, patios and paths must be constructed so that excess rainwater drains away from buildings and does not accumulate in pools on the surface.

Subsurface drainage must not be overlooked. Regardless of the materials used, the durability of garden paving and the structures that go with it will depend to a large extent on the stability of the ground beneath it. If the site is level and the soil drains naturally, you can lay most materials on a bed of sand without any additional subsurface drainage. If, however, there is a high clay content or marshy areas are evident in fine weather, it is advisable to lay a sub-base of

An angle grinder cuts bricks quickly.

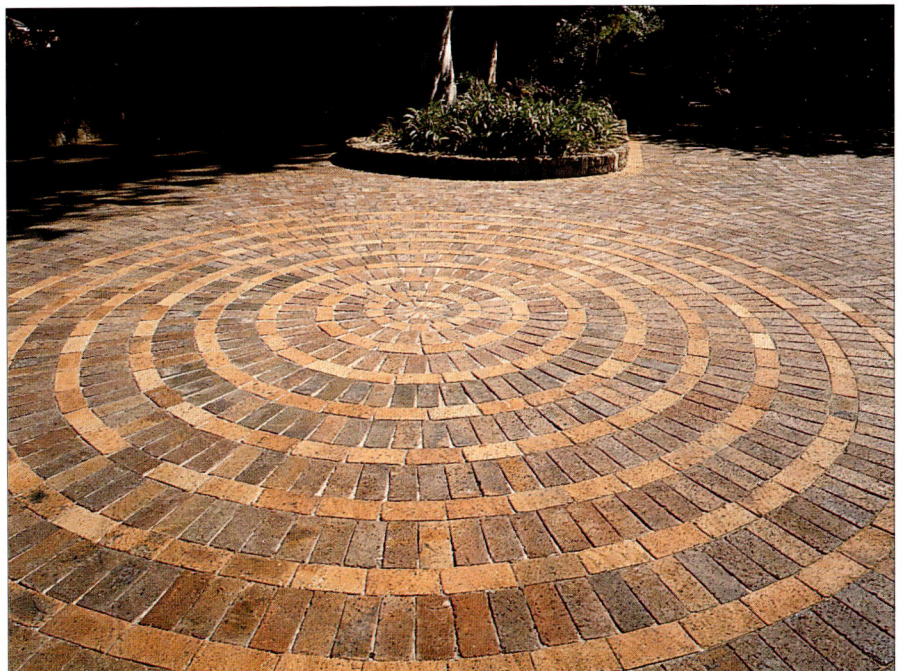

A circular paving pattern is an attractive option.

well-compacted hardcore or crushed stone under the surface. Perforated plastic pipe buried in this sub-base will help to draw off water to a surface channel or a soakaway. Alternatively, porous geosynthetic pipes (made from high-density polyethylene) wrapped in filter fabric (permeable polyester geotextiles) may be used. These may also be set in narrow trenches along the edges of paths,

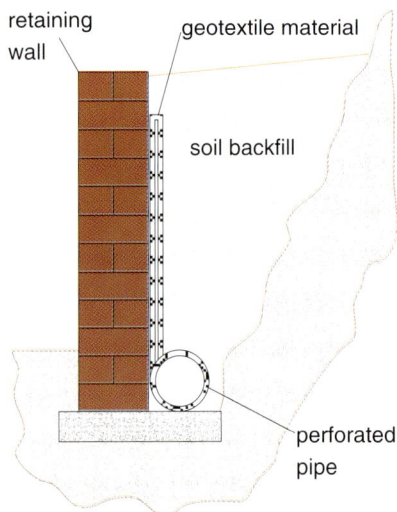

A fin drain behind a retaining wall.

driveways, patios and so on to create a very effective drainage system.

On sloping properties or where substantial drainage is necessary (behind a retaining wall, for instance), a vertical drain may be required. The most common type is made by setting pipework into a French drain filled with rubble and stone. This can involve substantial earthworks, and instead, a prefabricated fin drain may be installed if the materials are available. Lightweight and simple to install, this kind of drain is made by wrapping geotextile material (kept rigid by a layer of synthetic geonet) around geosynthetic pipework (see above), so that the fabric extends above the pipe to form a fin. Water is attracted to the highly absorbent fin, and flows down to the pipe, which directs it away from the base of the slope. It is ideal for the owner-builder to install as it obviates the need for cumbersome hardcore and stone and cuts down on both transport and labour costs.

Some form of drainage will also be needed behind most steps, unless they are very gradual and sited away from buildings and paved areas. In

most instances it is sufficient simply to backfill behind each riser with well-compacted crushed stone or gravel; if the steps are steep or involve a retaining wall, it may also be necessary to lead a pipe from a drain behind the structure to divert the water, or to use a fin drain.

Surface drainage is necessary to channel water away from buildings, and there should be a fall of about 1:40 or 1:50 across any patio, path, driveway or other paved area. With practice you will soon learn to judge just how off-centre the bubble in the spirit-level vial should be to achieve this run-off. To establish the correct gradient, attach a small block of wood under one end of a straight-edged piece of timber and place the spirit level on top; the bubble in the vial should be exactly centred. To achieve a gradient of 1:40, use a 25 mm block under a 1 m long straightedge; for 1:50, use a 20 mm block. It is also good building practice to set up a line as a guide following the angle of the straightedge. The finished surface of the patio should be below the inside floor level, and if there is a damp-proof course (DPC) in the walls, the patio floor should be at least 150 mm below the top of this. In cases where the interior floors are made of timber, the upper surface of paving, concrete and so on should be below the bottom of the floorboards.

If you want to divert rainwater underground, you will have to build a gully or lay a precast channel above the ground and direct this into a subsurface drainage system. You will not usually be permitted to drain surface water into an existing sewerage system, but you may be able to link up with a stormwater drain.

Often drainage is not an issue with garden paths; however, solid pathways (including those which are brick-paved or made from concrete laid *in situ*) should be fractionally lower on one side than the other to allow for a run-off, while the treads of steps should slope down to the front very slightly (no more than 1:100) to prevent puddles from forming.

It is essential to allow for drainage on all sites.

Pebbles are used to camouflage a drainage channel for rain water.

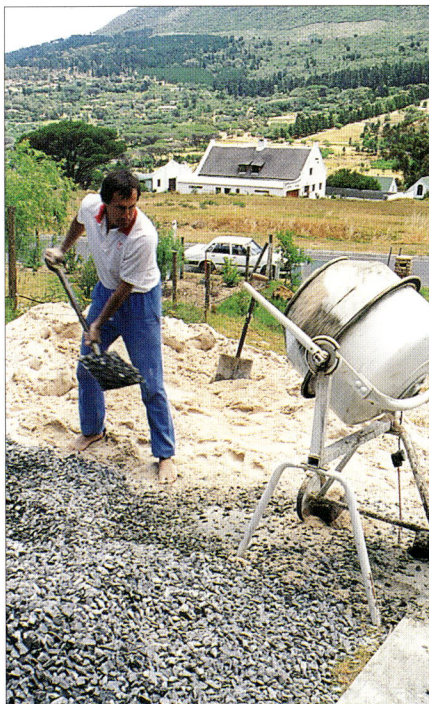

A concrete mixer simplifies the task.

Concretework

Working with concrete can be arduous, but the principles involved are not complicated. It is important to ensure that the proportions of cement, sand and crushed stone are correct and that you mix it properly with just the right quantity of water. Certain guidelines should also be followed when laying the concrete.

The proportions of cement, sand and stone (aggregate) used for concretework depend primarily on the use to which the concrete will be put. Generally there are three grades of concrete – low strength, medium strength and high strength – although the actual ratios of the dry materials used will sometimes vary depending on the quality of the materials available (see page 96). While low-strength concrete is commonly used for foundations and footings, a medium strength is preferred for garden footpaths, domestic driveways and steps, and for patio slabs that will be exposed to weathering. High-strength concrete is really only necessary for watertight walls and industrial situations, or driveways that will take very heavy traffic.

Mixing concrete is a laborious task. Even if you have a mechanical concrete mixer (see page 100), you will have to shovel the dry materials into the machine. Whether you are mixing by hand or by machine, you will also have to measure the materials in batches to ensure that the proportions used are accurate. Those recommended on page 97 specify quantities by volume, so use one strong, rigid container (a builder's bucket or a clean 25 litre paint tin) for measuring.

If you have a machine, load the stone with a little water first to prevent the mortar from building up on the blades, then load the sand and finally the cement and more water. When mixing by hand, combine the cement and sand first, either in a wheelbarrow or on a flat, dry surface. Do not mix them directly on the ground as soil, dead leaves and small twigs will almost inevitably get mixed in, and water may be absorbed from the mixture. Make a crater in the centre, then add water, shovelling the dry mixture from the edges to the centre. Once it is smooth, add the stone and continue shovelling. Aim for a firm, consistent mixture which is neither too runny nor too dry.

Formwork (shuttering) is essential if concrete is to be laid above ground level or if steps are to be built from concrete cast *in situ.* Various materials are suitable for this framework, including timber. Old wood may be used, provided it has reasonably straight edges and is rigid enough to bear the weight of the amount of concrete to be poured. For a curved path, you will need formwork which can be bent to shape. Hardboard (masonite) is ideal as it is reasonably flexible but strong enough to support the concrete. You will need to hold the shuttering in place with loose pegs, or nail it to flat stakes which can be

Stone steps laid on a concrete foundation alongside a concrete pond.

Creative use of bricks and crazy paving in an attractive courtyard.

motion to level the concrete to the height of the formwork. Make sure there are no gaps or hollows.

If you are planning to screed the surface of the concrete with mortar (for tiles, perhaps), the finish of your slab will not be important, but if the concrete itself forms the surface of the patio, path or treads of steps, you will want an even finish. Use a wooden float to smooth it or a stiff-bristled broom to create a rough texture. Alternatively, for a slip-proof finish, scatter fine crushed stone or pebbles on the wet surface and tamp lightly with a float or straightedge. When the concrete has almost set, spray with water and brush with a stiff broom to expose the aggregate.

When laying concrete over a fairly large area, you will need to create expansion joints to help prevent cracking. Do this by working in sections not larger than 3 m x 3 m, and laying alternate panels. When the first panels have set, fill in the remaining areas between them with more concrete.

Allow the concrete to set thoroughly before you remove any shuttering. Do not allow it to dry out too rapidly or it may well crack. In hot weather, cover it with sacking or plastic sheeting, or molsten lt now and then with water.

Brickwork and paving

Laying paving and building with bricks or blocks are skills which are easily mastered, but before you start to lay bricks, be sure that you can use a trowel correctly. Wherever you work with mortar, you will need this tool to butter the ends of bricks, and to make sure that they are laid evenly. Having done this, you will simply need to follow the basic principles and ensure that your work is square, level and plumb (see page 101).

Mortar is a material used in all bricklaying and some types of paving. Made from cement, sand and in some instances lime (see pages 96–97), it is mixed in the same way as concrete. First combine the dry materials on a clean, flat surface or in a wheelbarrow, then add water to them. Aim for a mixture which is thick and smooth

hammered into the ground (see pages 112–114). Whichever method is used, make sure that the pegs or stakes are on the outside of the formwork.

Laying or pouring concrete is much easier if you have help. Before you start, wet the ground to prevent the moisture in the concrete from being absorbed into the ground and possibly causing cracking. Either

shovel the mixture into the trench or formwork or pour it directly from the wheelbarrow. Chop into the concrete with your spade to allow trapped air to escape, and compact it roughly with the back of the spade or shovel. Then use a straight-edged plank to compact the concrete more thoroughly, using a chopping movement. As water comes to the surface, use a smoother sawing

but not watery, and only mix as much as you can use in a couple of hours. If the mortar gets hard, throw it away; adding water will weaken the mixture.

Bricklaying is one of those skills which improve with practice. The more bricks you lay, the easier it becomes. Whatever you are building, the techniques are exactly the same.

The first course of all walls (including the risers of steps) and most edgings around patios are bedded in wet mortar. Start by laying a 'sausage' of the mixture along the line where the bricks are to be laid. Use a bricklayer's trowel to create a furrow through the middle of the mortar, and place the first brick in position. The end of the next and subsequent bricks may be buttered, or you can use a trowel to fill in the gaps (which should be about 10 mm thick) once the bricks are in place on the bed of mortar. Use a spirit level to make sure that the first course is level; if bricks are not properly aligned, tap them firmly with the handle of the trowel. If necessary, lift the bricks and add or remove mortar.

The next course is laid in the same way, with a 10 mm wide joint and mortar separating the bricks. Stringing a builder's line along each course will help to keep the wall straight. You can keep the line in place with metal pegs, or wrap a builders' line around a pair of corner blocks (L-shaped blocks of wood with a slot and groove cut in each to accommodate the string) and hook the blocks onto the corners of the brickwork with the builders' line pulled taut.

An essential principle of good brickwork is bonding. If a wall or riser is laid so that the bricks don't bond and form a solid mass with an evenly distributed load, it will lack strength and stability. There are several different types, the most common being stretcher bond, where each brick overlaps the two below it by half.

Paving must always be laid so that the water drains off it effectively. This means that in most cases you will aim for an even slope with a gradient of no more than 1:40 (see page 102). In many instances, you will need to include some type of edging restraint.

The material chosen for your paved surface will to a large extent determine how it is laid. The basic choice is between setting slabs, bricks or blocks on a bed of sand and setting them in mortar. If bricks are used, they may be laid in any number of patterns, some of which bond particularly well and are therefore popular for driveways and surfaces intended for heavy foot traffic. A running bond (which is the horizontal equivalent of stretcher bond) is fairly common, as are both basketweave and herringbone patterns.

The simplest and least expensive form of brick paving is laid on sand. Known as flexible paving, it requires no mortar except for the edging, and sand is brushed into the joints. However, some people do lay bricks on sand and then brush either a very weak mixture of dry cement and sand or a slightly crumbly, moist mixture between the joints, then spray the surface with water.

Rigid paving is more time-consuming, and because mortar is required it is also more costly. However, this method is preferred for steps, as it is more stable. There are various methods of laying rigid paving, although all involve setting the bricks on a mortar bed. You can either butter the ends of the bricks as you lay them in place, or fill the joints later by brushing a dry cement and sand mix over them and then spraying the entire surface with water.

An unconventional bond pattern used for a path.

Herringbone pattern.

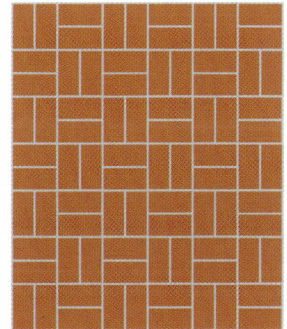

Basketweave pattern.

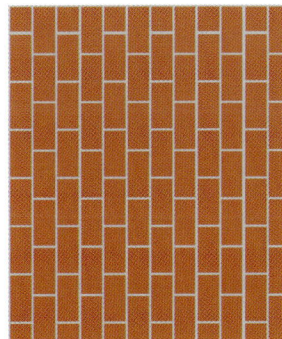

Running bond.

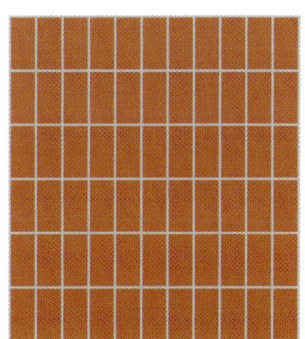

Stack bond or jack-on-jack.

STEP-BY-STEP BUILDING METHODS

Once you have a good understanding of the building principles involved and a thorough knowledge of the materials available and the tools to be used, you can get down to work. The step-by-step instructions which follow will guide you through several different building methods, suitable for a range of paths, steps and patios. Once you have mastered these, you should be well equipped to tackle any of the projects on pages 54-63, or to carry out a design of your own without any formal assistance.

The first building method shown here uses timber and will enable you to construct a simple flight of steps. You will need only a few tools and very basic carpentry skills.

A path, patio and steps, built from a range of precast concrete materials, may be adapted for virtually any loose-laid paving material; cut logs, stepping stones, railway sleepers and any other precast units may be substituted and used in a similar way. Here, the steps are built from modular blocks that are normally used to build retaining walls, while the path and patio are laid out with a combination of materials, all made from precast concrete. The 3:4:5 method of checking right-angled corners (see page 35) is shown in action, and the importance of keeping horizontal surfaces exactly level is clearly illustrated.

The principles of concretework are shown in detail in the step-by-step photographs, which follow through construction of steps and a pathway built from concrete cast *in situ*. Both straight and curved formwork (shuttering) are shown to illustrate how versatile this oft-maligned building material really is. The same method may be followed by anyone wishing to build a concrete patio slab; only the dimensions and the quantities of materials will vary. You would also have to lay out the area as shown in the step-by-step section on precast materials (pages 42-45).

Basic paving skills are illustrated in two step-by-step sections which show two methods of laying brick paving, as well as two different types of step. These may, of course, be combined in any way to suit your needs.

On pages 50 and 51 a brick patio and path are built on a bed of sand and a mixture of cement and sand is brushed into the joints; the steps shown here are built into a slope. On pages 52 and 53, the paving is laid on sand over a concrete slab, and the joints are filled with sand. The steps in this project are built up from the flat surface of the patio, linking this outside area with the house.

PLANNING STEPS

The secret of a successful flight of steps lies in the dimensions used for the treads and the risers. While indoor staircases may be quite steep, those in the garden usually rise much more gradually. The height of the riser is always less than the length of the horizontal tread, and often the longer the tread, the shallower the riser will be.

Two factors must be considered when determining the dimensions of the treads and risers – the depth of the slope and the materials to be used. For instance, if bricks are to be topped with a 500 mm x 500 mm paving slab, the combination will result in a tread of 500 mm and a riser of 80-100 mm or 115-120 mm, depending on whether the bricks are laid in the normal way or on edge.

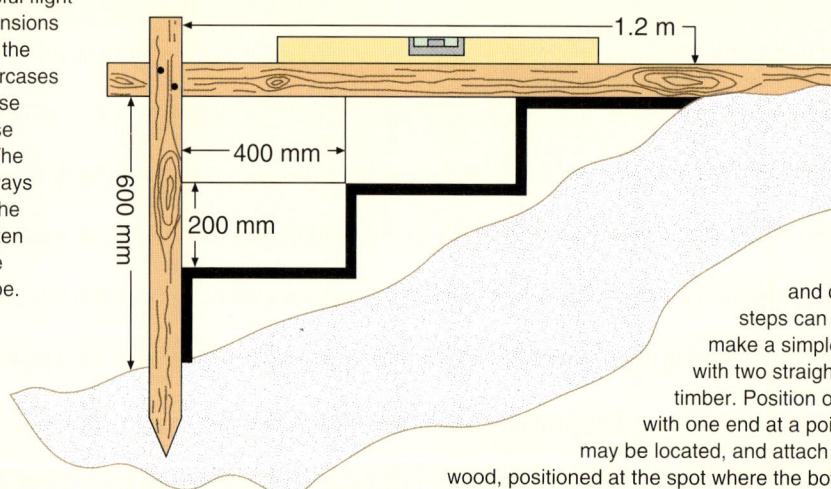

A simple profile may be used to determine the tread:riser ratio for steps.

To measure the slope and determine how many steps can be accommodated, make a simple profile (see illustration) with two straight-edged lengths of timber. Position one piece horizontally with one end at a point where the upper step may be located, and attach it to a vertical piece of wood, positioned at the spot where the bottom step will be. The total height of the staircase (indicated by the vertical length) will be a guide to the number of steps required, for instance, a 500 mm measurement would suit five shallow risers. If the horizontal length is 1.5 m, each tread will be 300 mm long. If you are not satisfied with the combination, try altering the position of the top or bottom step to suit your needs.

1.2 m

600 mm

400 mm

200 mm

Timber steps are useful not only for decks built above ground level, but also for spanning slopes in the garden and for providing access to places that are otherwise hard to reach.

There are many ways to build steps from wood; this project illustrates a very simple approach, with open risers.

If the steps lead to a verandah or a raised patio, you will need to attach a ledger or wall plate to the wall to support the stringers (the strips of wood on either side of the flight of steps).

MATERIALS

Any timber suitable for outdoor construction may be used for these steps. It must be sturdy enough to take the weight of people using it, and should be pretreated with a suitable preservative. Most types are pressure-treated in the factory and will only need to be coated with a sealant of some sort for protection from the weather, if possible before assembling the steps.

Softwood planks which measure 225 mm x 38 mm are used for the treads and the stringers, while 38 mm x 38 mm battens are used for the cleats, which support the treads.

To prevent rust, only galvanised or brass fasteners should be used; in this instance, 8 mm galvanised coach screws and 63 mm long No 8 (4.2 mm) countersunk brass screws.

The two stringers are set in concrete for stability. Presuming you are using a 1:4:4 mix, you will need 55 kg of cement and 225 kg each of sand and 19 mm crushed stone.

1 Determine the dimensions of the steps (see page 40), then cut the planks to size with an electric circular saw or a hand saw. Cut one end of each cleat off at an angle for a neater finish, ensuring that they are shorter than the stringers are wide.

2 You will also need to cut the ends of the stringers at an angle so that they can abut the deck fascia or ledger neatly. Paint the ends that are to be buried in the ground with bitumen or creosote to protect the wood from moisture.

3 Attach the cleats to the stringers at equal intervals (depending on the height and number of steps to be constructed), using a combination square to position them. Drill through both pieces of wood at either end of the cleats, then screw them together firmly.

4 Mark the position of the bottom step and dig a 200 mm x 300 mm footing, 200 mm deep, for each stringer. Position the two stringers and bolt them to the deck or ledger; alternatively, secure them with angle brackets and suitable screws.

5 Brace the stringers securely, using battens or other timber offcuts, and check that they are correctly aligned. Mix the concrete and fill the two holes, compacting it with the back of a spade or shovel. Allow to set overnight before proceeding.

6 The last step is to affix the planks to the cleats to form treads. Make sure that they are level, then drill through the upper surface of each tread into the supporting cleat. Screw the two timbers together, then fill all holes with a suitable wood filler.

Some of the prettiest paths, steps and patios are constructed using widely available precast concrete products, such as slabs, fake flagstones and imitation sleepers. There is a huge variety, and if the type shown here is not available in your area, substitute something similar, or adapt the design to suit your needs.

Irrespective of what you decide to use, preparation of the site will be exactly the same. Essentially, you will need to ensure that there is a solid sub-base, and then lay the slabs on a bed of sand. A certain amount of excavation may be necessary, and in some cases (particularly where the soil does not drain well) a layer of hardcore will have to be laid beneath an area to be paved.

The shape of your site will determine whether you build the steps, path or patio first. In this instance, it was sensible to start with the steps, as this made access up the slope easier during the rest of the building process. Since the path is slightly lower than the patio here, it was laid last. The simplicity of laying precast slabs and blocks on sand makes the entire operation very flexible, and mistakes are easy to rectify.

MATERIALS

Rounded precast concrete blocks, designed for the construction of modular retaining walls, are used to build these steps. In this case, the units are approximately 280 mm wide, 350 mm deep and 200 mm high. Designs vary from place to place, but the basic concept of interlocking units remains the same, and any type may be used. Since they are laid with the open side uppermost, the treads are topped with a precast imitation sleeper, giving the steps a neater and more attractive finish. Another option is to fill the blocks with a relatively weak concrete mix and screed the upper surface with mortar. Alternatively, look for modular terrace blocks which may be laid on their side, but remember that these should be filled with soil or concrete for stability.

The patio, which has a border of heavy concrete kerbstones, is laid using paving slabs made in three different sizes from reconstituted stone, which gives it a random finish and a pleasing, rustic feel. You could also use old railway sleepers or cut timber as an edging, and cut stone or ordinary precast concrete slabs for the floor. Stone chips are scattered between the slabs, both for effect and to level the patio surface. Otherwise you could plant a ground cover or low-growing, sweet-scented herbs to soften the look, or you may want to scatter seed amongst the chips to add colour and charm.

The same pavers are used for the path, alternating with a row of three imitation sleepers. Small pebbles may be used between the slabs and sleepers, and as for the patio, various low-growing plants are also an option.

1 The first step is to remove any vegetation from the area where the steps are to be located. If the ground is particularly hard or stony, you will need to use a pick to loosen the soil. Also remove any large rocks before you go any further.

2 Each step must be laid on level ground, so you will need to create rough steps in the embankment. Starting from the bottom, excavate an area of about 1 m x 1 m for the three-block-wide step, which will be 840 mm wide with a 350 mm tread.

3 Although a concrete foundation is not necessary, every step must be laid on well-compacted ground. A home-made punner is an invaluable and effective ramming tool; you can make one by concreting a pole or length of sawn timber into a tin.

4 It is also essential that each block is laid on a flat, even surface. Use a spirit level to check this, and scrape away soil if necessary. Place the tool on several spots, and draw it across the soil to make sure that the surface is level in all directions.

5 Place the first three blocks on the prepared surface, making sure that they interlock properly. The convex side of each block should fit snugly into the concave side of the next. The flat surface of each unit faces towards the front to create a flat riser.

6 Before filling the gap behind the blocks, it is essential to check that they are in fact completely level. A good way to get them level is to place a little soil in each hollow and then move them about so that the sand fills any voids and they sit firmly.

7 Do not rely on guesswork – use a spirit level to ensure that the blocks are level. If the bubble is not completely centred, put a little more sand in the hollow and move the block around a bit. If it seems too high, remove some of the sand.

8 Now fill the space behind the blocks with sand or soil. Never backfill with clay as this will prevent water from draining away effectively. Use a punner to flatten and compact the soil behind the first step thoroughly before preparing for the next one.

9 Follow the instructions given in steps 2-4, ensuring that the compacted ground behind the blocks is on the same level as the upper surface of the blocks. Place the next row of blocks so that the front edge overlaps the back of the first step.

10 Position and level the blocks as before, then fill them with soil or, if you wish, a weak concrete mixture. Fill the gap behind each step with sand or soil and compact each level in the same way until you get to the top of the slope.

11 Lay tiles or precast concrete sleepers (as shown here) over the tread of each step. These may be loose-laid or set on a little mortar to keep them in place. Plant a hardy ground cover in the soil at the back of the step to fill the gap.

12 Lay out the path from the top of the steps to the patio site. The path is 1 m wide because of the length of the sleepers used. Using a steel tape measure, ensure that the edges are parallel along the entire length; mark them with chalk or flour.

13 Although the patio is designed with cut-off corners, it is best to set out a full rectangle before laying the edging kerbstones in place. Use the 3:4:5 method (see page 35), measuring 5 m across the diagonal to ensure that the corners are square.

14 Prepare the surface of the path and the patio before you begin laying any of the slabs or stones. The amount of soil you excavate will depend on the thickness of the precast slabs as well as on the natural slope of the ground.

15 Make sure that the base is flat and even, with a slight slope for drainage. Use a spirit level across the path to check that you are not removing too much soil. Although the slabs are to be laid on sand, this should not be used to rectify levels.

16 Build the patio before you lay the pathway. First get the area where the patio is to be built level. As the patio is to be raised above the level of the path, it is not necessary to excavate the soil unless it slopes. Throw any excess soil into the centre.

17 To avoid unnecessary digging, it may be possible to fill in slightly in places, building up the level of the ground. Since the area of the patio covers more than 9 m^2, you will need to set the spirit level on a long, straight-edged piece of timber.

18 You will also need to check the level of the sub-base, diagonally across the surface from corner to corner. Place the straightedge and spirit level on bricks to help establish accurately how much soil must be removed from any particular place.

19 Once you are certain that the entire area is flat and level (or slopes for drainage if necessary), you can put the edging in place. Hefty precast concrete kerbstones are used here. Use a steel builder's square to ensure that the corners are at 90°.

20 Position all the kerbstones as shown. If the ground is stable, fill the space within the kerbstones with sand or soil, otherwise first half-fill the area with hardcore of crushed stone and gravel to aid drainage, then top with sand or soil.

21 The hardcore and all sand and soil used as fill must be well compacted before the sand bed is laid. You can use a home-made punner, although a mechanical compacting machine is useful for large areas as it takes less time and is more thorough.

22 The finished level of this sub-base should be below the top of the kerbstones, leaving enough room for a 25-50 mm bed of sand and the paving slabs, which in this case are about 50 mm thick. Cover the surface with soft building sand, the rake it.

23 The sand must be level before you start laying the slabs. Hose it lightly to aid compaction, then drag a straight-edged piece of wood across the sand, smoothing and levelling it. You will also need to check with a spirit level to ensure that it is level.

24 Start laying the slabs from one of the corners, leaving a small gap between each one. There is no particular pattern to follow; simply place them in an attractive fashion, using a good mix of the three sizes at all times. Use a spirit level to check alignment.

25 If you are not happy with the way the pavers are laid, change them now rather than later. When they are all in place, spread sand over the surface and brush it into the gaps with a stiff-bristled broom, then hose down the area lightly to compact the fill.

26 Spread pebbles or stone chips over the surface, then brush them into the gaps over the sand. Once the stones have settled, you can add more if and where you think it is needed, or you can sow seeds among the stones for an informal effect.

27 The path is laid in much the same way as the patio, but without an edging. Leave space for a step between the kerbstones and where you are to lay the first sleeper. Spread sand along the excavated path, smoothing it out with a spirit level.

28 Position the imitation sleepers across the path, about 30 mm apart. They are usually slightly irregular in thickness, as are timber sleepers, and it is sometimes difficult to get the upper surface flat. Remove a little of the sand bed if necessary.

29 Leave a gap of 30-150 mm, depending on the curve of the path, and then lay a group of pavers. All the gaps may be planted once the pathway is complete. As plants become established, they will soften the path and give it a pretty, countrified feel.

30 Continue laying sets of sleepers and slabs alternately, until the path is complete. Then build up the step to the patio. Having left a natural step, all you do now is spread a layer of sand over the slightly elevated surface and level it before laying the sleepers.

31 Lay two sleepers close together to form a step up to the patio. If they are slightly unstable, insert three pegs at the front of the two sleepers to hold them securely in place, knocking them in so that they do not protrude above the upper surface of the step.

Concrete cast *in situ* is an economical and extremely versatile material for paths, steps and patio slabs. The process is described in some detail on pages 29-30 and 37-38 along with suggested proportions for appropriate cement, sand and stone mixes.

One of the advantages of *in situ* concrete is its versatility – you can leave it as it is or top it with paving bricks, slabs or tiles to create a more sophisticated finish.

Concrete can also be pigmented or screeded with pigmented mortar. Pigment powders are available in several colours, including red, green and ochre. A simple way to apply it is to mix about 500 g of the powder with about a kilogram of cement (or a larger quantity in the same proportion) and sufficient water to make a paste. Trowel this onto the surface and smooth it with a wooden float or steel plasterer's trowel. A little of the colour will wash out with time, but a slightly mottled surface can be quite attractive.

Alternatively, you can colour the concrete or the screed, but you will need large quantities of pigment to get any colour intensity. If you do wish to colour the concrete, you will need to add 5-15 kg of pigment per cubic metre of concrete; if you colour the mortar for the screed, add 8-25 kg of pigment to each cubic metre of concrete, depending on the intensity of the colour you are aiming for. Another rather simpler method is to sprinkle the dry pigment onto the wet screed or concrete and then work it in well with a plasterer's trowel. For this method you will need 150-250 g of powder per square metre.

If you prefer to leave the concrete its usual grey colour, it can be artificially aged by brushing on a little yoghurt to encourage moss and lichen to grow. Take care, though, as a mossy walkway is potentially dangerous, so only treat risers and areas of a patio which will not take heavy foot traffic.

Another interesting innovation is imprinted concrete, which creates the effect of cobbles, stone or bricks. Special equipment is required to create the imprint, so it is generally laid by contractors.

FORMWORK (SHUTTERING)

When casting concrete yourself, you will have to erect formwork for any structure which is to extend above ground. This applies to all staircases, but not necessarily to paths or slabs that are built with their upper surface at ground level.

Both the curved path and the steps featured here were built with shuttering. Ordinary softwood planks were used in the construction of the five 600 mm wide steps, while pliable hardboard (masonite) was used for the pathway.

The height of the risers and depth of the treads will depend on the slope of your garden. In this case they are 140 mm high and 350 mm deep. Refer to the instructions on page 40 and adapt the measurements to suit your requirements.

MATERIALS

The mix used for this step-by-step project is of medium strength, and suitable for paths, steps and slabs that are exposed to weathering. The ratio used is 1:3:3 by weight, which means that each 50 kg bag of cement is combined with 115 litres (about 155 kg) each of sand and 19 mm crushed stone. If a smaller 13.2 mm or 9.5 mm stone is used, the ratio should be altered to 1:3:2.

Instructions are included here for mixing by hand. If you are going to use a concrete mixer, follow the guidelines given on page 103.

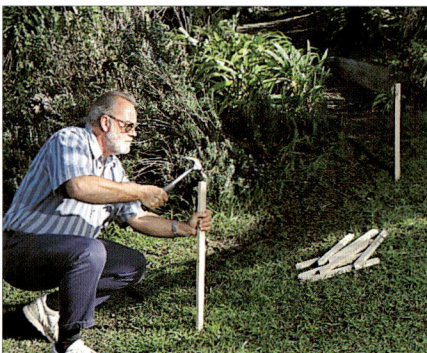

1 Assemble a simple profile to establish how many steps will fit the slope of your garden (see page 40). Decide more or less where you would like the steps to begin and end, and knock a peg into the ground at the top point and a longer post at the bottom.

2 Set a straight-edged piece of timber at the base of the peg and mark the point where it meets the post positioned on the lower part of the slope. For accuracy, it is essential that the straightedge remain level, so use a spirit level to check this.

3 Measure the distance from the ground to the mark on the post, i.e. the total change in level. Then measure the distance between the post and the peg to establish the depth of the slope. Use these figures to decide how many steps to build.

4 Peg out the remaining corners of the stairway. The two new pegs should be 600 mm away from the peg and post already in the ground. Check that the outside corners are at 90°, using a steel measuring tape and the 3:4:5 method (see page 35).

5 Stake out all five steps, spacing them as required. The pegs are positioned at 380 mm intervals, and the steps themselves will be 350 mm deep and 140 mm high when complete. Use flour, chalk or cement to mark the position of the treads on the ground.

6 Before excavating excess soil, remove any turfs of grass which may be re-used somewhere else in the garden. It is not necessary to dig out all the soil; if you dig carefully, you can create a rough stairway which will be a good guide for the formwork.

7 The wood you use for the formwork must be straight, not bowed or warped, although it need not be new or clean. It is important to cut the upper edges neatly and absolutely straight as the concrete will be levelled off against the top edge of the wood.

8 The formwork must also conform to the dimensions of the treads and risers. Measure each piece and then nail all the pieces together, using a combination square for accuracy. If you cut the ends to form a point, it will be easier to knock them into the ground.

9 Position the formwork along the sides of the excavated staircase and knock it firmly into the ground with a club hammer. Ensure that the horizontal surfaces of the formwork remain level by checking them with a spirit level.

10 Since the formwork will be your guide for levelling the surface of the concrete, which will form the tread of the step, use a spirit level across the width of the steps to check that the sides are level with one another. Adjust if necessary.

11 It is also vital that the two pieces of formwork stand perfectly vertical. There should be a very slight slope from the back of each tread down to the front. Check all planes with a spirit level before you begin to mix the concrete.

12 Once the sides of the formwork are straight and secure, nail boards between them to contain the concrete which will form each of the risers. If there are any gaps at the sides, they will also have to be closed off with timber.

13 Now compact the sub-base of the steps with a punner or heavy post. If a layer of hardcore or crushed stone is to be included in the structure, it must be placed below the level of the formwork, or the loose material will be exposed once the formwork is removed.

14 Once all the formwork is in place you can mix the concrete. Choose a clean, dry, flat surface which will not result in moisture being absorbed from the mixture into the ground. Measure out the sand first and tip it out onto the mixing surface.

15 Now measure out the cement using the same container to ensure that the proportions are correct – the ratio of cement:sand should be 1:3. Then mix the cement and sand with a spade or shovel until you achieve a consistent colour.

16 Make a small crater in the centre of the dry mixture and add water slowly. There is no need to measure the water, but it is important not to add too much or the concrete will be too runny. Rather work gradually and add a little more once you have mixed it in.

17 Shovel the dry materials from the outside of the crater into the centre. Take care that the water does not run out as you are mixing. Aim for a pliable mixture which is neither too watery nor too stiff. Add more water, a little at a time, if necessary.

18 Add the crushed stone to the mixture last. Measure it out in the container used for the cement and sand (see page 46 for proportions) then spread it evenly over the surface of the wet mixture. Continue to shovel until all materials are thoroughly combined.

19 Before you pour the concrete into the formwork, moisten the bare earth. This will prevent water from being absorbed from the concrete into the earth. Transport the wet concrete in a builder's wheelbarrow and then shovel it with a spade, filling each step.

20 Cut a straight length of timber, just long enough to cover the width or depth of each tread. Use it to compact the concrete with a chopping movement to get rid of any air bubbles, and then level it to the upper surface of the formwork using a sawing motion.

21 Allow the concrete to set thoroughly for about 24 hours before removing the shuttering. First, carefully prise the planks away from the front of each riser, using a screwdriver. Then pull the two side sections out of the ground.

22 If you wish, lay pavers over the top of the treads. First position them loosely over the concrete to see how they fit, and then mix mortar in a cement:sand ratio of 1:5. Lay them as described on page 39, using a trowel to fill the joints with mortar.

23 Once the steps are complete, you can lay the path. You will need pegs and string or a builder's line to mark out its position. Use additional pegs where it curves and measure the width at various points to ensure that the edges are parallel to each other.

24 Use flour or chalk to make more distinct lines on the grass, then carefully remove the turfs between them. Excavate the pathway to a depth of 100-150 mm to accommodate a 50 mm layer of gravel or crushed stone (hardcore) and 50-100 mm of concrete.

25 Compact the ground well with a punner or heavy pole and then pour in the hardcore. Distribute it evenly with a spade or rake, then compact it well. This will form the sub-base for the path, so it is vital that it is stable and there are no voids.

26 Cut hardboard or any other suitable flexible material to the depth of the concrete, and nail to pegs to form shuttering. You can re-use the upright sections of the step formwork if you wish. Position the formwork and hammer it in place.

27 Make sure that the tops of both sides of the shuttering are on an even plane, allowing for a very slight drainage slope across the path. A gradient of 1:40 is ample in this context. Do not forget to use a spirit level to check the alignment.

28 Instead of mixing the concrete on a flat surface and then transporting it to the site, you could mix it in a builder's wheelbarrow for convenience. Follow steps 14-18, adding a little more water if you find that the mixture is too dry.

29 Spray the compacted hardcore base lightly with water before you tip the contents of the wheelbarrow between the shuttering. Shovel it evenly, so that it completely fills the formwork next to the bottom step. Mix another batch and repeat.

30 Use a straight-edged piece of wood to compact and level the concrete. As you chop into it, water will rise to the surface. When the concrete has set, remove the formwork. Keep the concrete moist for several days to allow it to cure properly.

Whenever a patio and path are built at different levels, you will need to link them with steps. If you have used brick paving as the surface material, it usually looks best if you build the steps from the same brick.

Three steps, built into the slope, link this path and patio. Each step is built on a concrete foundation, while the paving is laid on compacted sand. On some sites, it may be necessary to excavate and lay hardcore or gravel to stabilise the sub-base.

For continuity, the risers of the steps are built in stretcher bond and the paving in the equivalent running bond. The paving is laid at a slight gradient (a run-off of 1:40 or 1:50 is recommended) to allow rainwater to drain away.

MATERIALS

A combination of ordinary facebricks and clay pavers has been used for this garden layout. Obtained from the same supplier, they match in both colour and texture.

The paving for both the path and the patio is laid on polythene. This is an optional step, which stops vegetation from growing up through the paving, although it does not prevent seeds from sowing themselves between the bricks. There is also a school of thought which strongly opposes the use of plastic under flexible paving (where the bricks are jointed with sand) on the grounds that it prevents water from draining away and may cause moisture movement.

1 Start off by establishing where the top and bottom step should be built. Measure both the horizontal and vertical lengths and make a simple profile (see page 40). Then cut away the general shape of the number of steps required from the soil.

2 Each tread is about 340 mm deep and 1 m wide. Mix concrete in the required ratio (see page 30) and lay a concrete foundation 50 mm thick and a little larger than the first tread. When it has set, lay one course of the thinner paving bricks on mortar.

3 Mix another batch of concrete and fill in behind the first tread up to the level of the first step. This will form the foundation for the second step. Use a plank to compact the concrete, expel all air bubbles and level the surface, then allow it to set thoroughly.

4 Each 225 mm high riser is built up with two facebrick courses and a single course of pavers, which also forms the surface of the tread. Use a corner block and builder's line to keep each course straight and lay the bricks using stretcher bond.

5 The top of the third step will be level with the surface of the patio. Build a one-brick wall and lay a single row of pavers on top as a header course. Fill the gap behind the step with concrete, level the concrete and leave it to set.

6 Peg out the area to be paved, then remove all vegetation and level the site, using the top step as a guide. You may need to excavate to allow for a 25-50 mm bed of sand. If the soil is unstable, you will need to allow for a sub-base of hardcore as well.

7 If necessary, spread hardcore and compact it well. Ensure that the surface slopes slightly away from the building (see page 36). If you are using polythene under the paving, lay it down now, overlapping the edges by 200 mm. Secure them with bricks.

8 Lay two adjacent sides of the edging, setting the paving bricks in a bed of mortar. Use a spirit level to check that they are level and a steel builder's square to ensure that all corners are at right-angles. A line will help to keep the edging straight.

9 You will need to bed the paving bricks on fairly coarse, clean building sand which is free from stones and vegetable matter. Spread it over the plastic so that it is more or less level with the mortar that holds the edging in place.

10 Use a straight-edged length of timber to smooth and level the sand. If the patio is large, you will not be able to smooth out the entire area at once. Work in manageable sections and use a spirit level regularly to check the gradient.

11 Start laying the pavers, working systematically from the edging to the other side. Decide which paving pattern to use and then push each paving brick firmly into the sand. Make sure they are level, and use a rubber mallet to tap down any that protrude.

12 Now you can excavate the path. First mark the line it will follow with pegs and string, making sure that the sides run parallel to each other. The steps are 1 m wide, so a good width for the path is 900 mm. Loose-lay a few bricks to check the width.

13 Level and compact the area then lay polythene sheeting down. Lay the edgings on mortar first, making sure they are the same distance apart along their whole length – in this case about 450 mm, to accommodate four bricks laid side by side.

14 Fill in between the edgings with about 25 mm of sand as before and use a straightedge to flatten and smooth it. Then lay bricks in running bond. When all the bricks are in place, trim the polythene with a sharp utility knife and remove the scrap pieces.

15 Lastly, brush fine sand into the joints. Alternatively, brush in a 1:6 cement:sand mix instead, spray the surface lightly with water, and make sure that all traces of mortar are removed (see page 53 for how to remove hardened mortar if it does dry).

Built alongside a house, this patio is raised above the ground, and incorporates a low retaining wall along the front and a short flight of brick steps leading up to the front door. Although the construction of the retaining wall and basic patio structure is not shown in the step-by-step photographs, the entire area was filled with several cubic metres of hardcore consisting of broken bricks, stones and gravel. This was well compacted before the paving was laid. If the garden is level, preparation will be the same as for the patio illustrated on pages 50 and 51. If a retaining wall is to be built, use 'brickforce' (a wire reinforcing mesh sold in rolls) on every third or fourth course, and make sure that there is adequate sub-surface drainage (see pages 35-36). If the wall is any higher than 1.2 m, consult an architect or engineer for specifications.

It is essential that the surface of any patio built adjacent to a house be located at least 150 mm below the underside of the interior floor slab, floorboards or the top of the plastic damp-proof membrane (if there is one).

The steps, which lead to the house, are built up from a flat surface, so a single slab is thrown and the steps are built on top of this. The gap behind each riser wall is filled with hardcore.

Since in this case the patio was bounded on three sides by existing walls, no edging was necessary. However, it was essential to insert a drainage pipe in the wall to cope with excess rainwater. If your patio is freestanding, you will need to lay an edging of some sort (for instance bricks set in mortar as illustrated on page 51), and the drainage outlet will not be necessary.

MATERIALS

The steps are built with facebricks and matching pavers laid in a stack bond, although to save costs, ordinary stock (plaster) bricks may be used on the inside of the steps where they will not be visible (see pages 28-29 for quantifying bricks and pavers). The same paving bricks, laid in a neat basketweave pattern, are used to pave the surface of the patio. Coarse building sand is used to bed the bricks, and a fine sand to joint them.

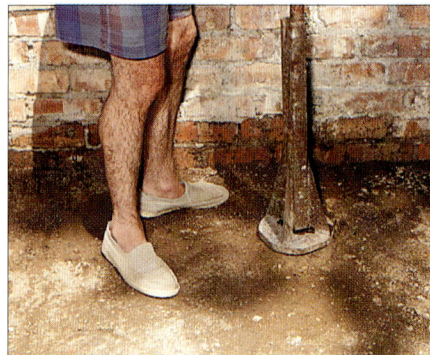

1 If the patio is to be built above the level of the ground, build retaining walls and fill the area with hardcore and gravel. Use a punner or ramming tool to compact the entire surface, or use a compacting machine to speed up the operation.

2 The sub-base must be level before you can pave over it. Aim for a gentle gradient of about 1:40 to allow water to run off the finished surface. Use a spirit level to check the slope at several points along the width and length of the patio.

3 Peg out an area of about 1.5 m x 1.2 m for the steps' foundation slab and excavate to a depth of 50 mm. Mix concrete and place it as described on pages 37-38. When it has set, mark out the steps with chalk, checking with a square that the corners are at 90°.

4 Lay a stepped one-brick wall on one side, using facebricks for the outside skin and plaster bricks for the inside. Lay the first course on mortar, pressing the bricks down firmly. Spread more mortar on top, make a furrow with a trowel, then lay the next course.

5 Mark the position of the top tread, and then lay a half-brick wall, in stretcher bond, along the full width of the step. Scrape off excess mortar as you work. You do not need to use facebricks for the first four courses as they will not show.

6 Repeat the process, building three half-brick walls to form the risers. String a line along the front of each one as you work; this will help you to ensure that the brickwork is straight. Use a spirit level regularly to make sure that each wall is level.

7 Although the top course or two of each wall should be built with facebricks (the number of courses depending on the height of the riser), any bricks can be used for the lower courses. Complete these walls and both side walls and allow the mortar to set.

8 Fill the spaces behind the risers with broken bricks, crushed stone, gravel and soil. Compact this hardcore well, making sure that there are no voids. Water lightly before topping with a thin layer of weak mortar, mixed in a 1:6 cement:sand ratio.

9 Mix a new batch of mortar in a 1:4 cement:sand ratio and lay paving bricks on the wet mortar already on the tread. Butter one end of each paver as you work, and use a trowel to fill any gaps which may be left. Scrape off the excess mortar.

10 Before the mortar dries, sprinkle dry building sand over the treads and use a sponge to wipe the cement off the surface; mortar stains, and once dry it has to be removed with spirits of salts (mainly hydrochloric acid) or a weak solution of muriatic acid.

11 You can now pave the patio. Spread a 25-50 mm bed of sand over the entire area. Flatten and level it with a straightedge (see page 51), or make a punner from a block of wood and a batten, and tamp the sand down firmly to compact it.

12 Decide on a pattern before you start laying the pavers. Begin at a wall (or edging) and lay the bricks very slightly apart. Tap them firmly into place with a rubber mallet and check regularly with a spirit level that you are sloping the surface correctly.

13 It is essential to lay a drainage pipe to prevent rainwater from collecting on the surface. Knock a hole in the retaining wall and insert a length of 100 mm PVC pipe right through it. Use a little mortar to secure it and to patch the hole.

14 When all the paving bricks are in place, spread fine sand over the entire surface and sweep it into the joints. Hose the surface down lightly and then repeat, to make sure that there are no gaps. If the sand settles over time, add more later on.

A very ordinary cast concrete stairway is transformed by affixing timber at the front of the treads and pushing round river stones into wet mortar at the back of the treads and on the risers. The steps are constructed using formwork as shown on pages 46-49, but the use of hollow retaining blocks simplifies construction and helps to stabilise the embankment before the concrete is placed. If you are building on a steeper or longer slope, you will need to extend the stairway; here the path slopes gradually from the top of the fifth tread, and materials specified will enable you to lay five steps and 2 m of pathway.

MATERIALS

15 x 425 mm x 340 mm x 225 mm hollow retaining blocks
335 kg cement (about 310 kg for concrete and 25 kg for mortar)
1 350 kg or 1 m³ sand

1 250 kg or 0.95 m³ stone
12 x 1.5 m x 250 mm x 50 mm hardwood planks
72 x 8 mm x 75 mm coach screws
river stones
scrap timber and nails for formwork

1 Measure and peg out a line 1.5 m wide across the base of the slope where the bottom step is to be.
2 Excavate five rough steps in the embankment, ensuring that the upper surface extends backwards about 400 mm to accommodate the tread, and that the steps are each about 150 mm high.
3 Compact and level the soil for the bottom step. Position three blocks across the width of the excavated tread with the 425 mm rounded section in front.
4 Compact and level the soil and position the blocks for the rest of the steps, then compact and level the path area.
5 Erect a 250 mm deep formwork to contain the concrete for the stairway, and a 100 mm deep one for the path.
6 Drill six holes in each piece of timber and screw in the coach screws so that at least 25 mm of the head and shaft protrudes.
7 Mix concrete in a cement:sand:stone ratio of 1:4:4 and place it along the path. Then cast the concrete for the stairs, starting from the top step and placing it around and in the hollows of the concrete blocks.
8 Before the concrete sets, position planks along the path and at the front of the treads, pushing the coach screws firmly into the concrete. Leave overnight.

9 Mix mortar in a 1:4 cement:sand ratio and fill in the gap between the timber and the riser of each step. Then spread mortar to cover the surface of each riser. Press river stones into the wet mortar.
10 Allow to set thoroughly before removing the formwork.

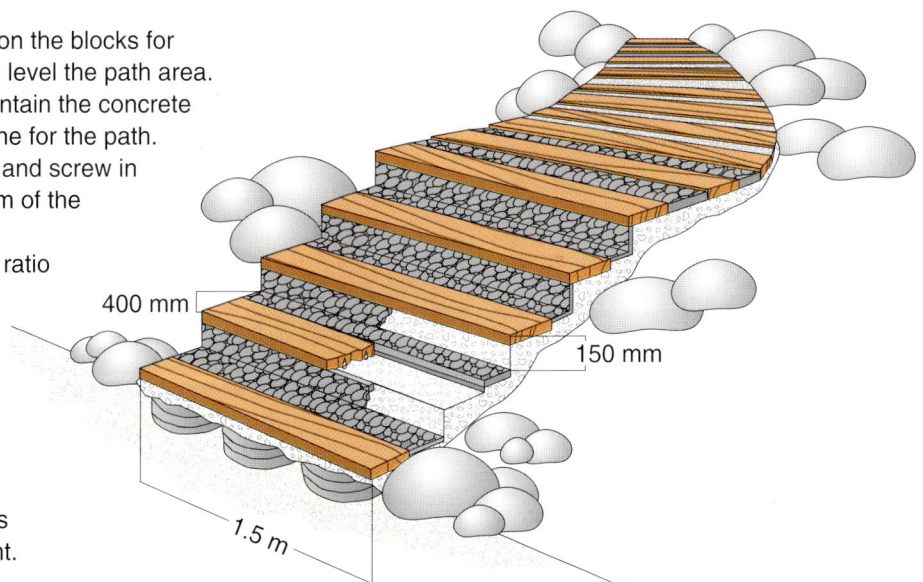

Expansive brick steps invite one to walk at a leisurely pace from one level to another in the garden. Two 1.5 m x 800 mm planters at the top of the steps, one on either side, are rendered and painted to add contrast and interest to the structure, and also incorporate light fittings. These planters, like the steps themselves, are topped with flat-faced bricks, although pavers could be used instead. The materials specified are sufficient for six steps, rising up a 5.5 m wide slope, but if you wish, the stairway could be extended at either end if the site is suitable.

MATERIALS
Steps
519 bricks
210 kg cement (about 70 kg for foundations)
850 kg or 0.5 m³ sand
70 kg lime
360 kg or 0.25 m³ stone
400 kg or 0.3 m³ fill, soil or sand

Planters
790 bricks
400 kg cement (about 140 kg for foundations)
130 kg lime
1 625 kg or 1.2 m³ sand
560 kg or 0.4 m³ stone
2 x weatherproof light fittings with conduit (optional)

1 Measure out and peg a sloping area about 5.5 m wide and 2.2 m long from top to bottom.
2 At the lowest point, excavate a 5.5 m x 400 mm trench to a depth of about 50 mm.
3 Dig away the bank immediately behind the trench to form a rough step. Then fill the trench with concrete mixed in a 1:4:4 cement:sand:stone ratio and allow to set.
4 Lay a row of bricks 50 mm in from the front of the foundation slab to form a stretcher course.
5 Fill in behind the bricks with soil or sand, leaving space for a 25 mm layer of concrete, measuring 350 mm from front to back, on top. Compact the soil before laying the concrete to form a foundation for the front of the second tread.

6 When the concrete has set, lay bricks to form the tread as illustrated.
7 Build a two-course wall in stretcher bond to form the next riser so that the top of the first course of bricks is at the same height as the top of the first tread.
8 Repeat steps 3, 5, 6 and 7.
9 Build the third step the same way. Then build the next two steps 3 m wide, centring them on the lower steps.
10 Dig away the slope on either side of the two 3 m wide steps and excavate an area of about 1.4 m x 900 mm to a depth of 50 mm below the top of the third step.
11 Erect formwork to prevent the bank from collapsing.
12 Place a few bricks in the centre of the planter to create drainage holes. Then mix concrete in a cement:sand:stone ratio of 1:4:4 and spread evenly over the entire area to a depth of 50 mm.
13 Allow the concrete to set overnight, but remove the bricks before it hardens too much.
14 To construct the planters, build up one-brick walls five courses high to form two rectangular 'boxes'.
15 Leave a gap in the front of the outer course to accommodate the light fitting if required. Get an electrician to complete the installation before you go any further.
16 Now build the riser of the top step as for the previous steps.
17 Render the exposed, outer surface of the planters using a 2:1:8 cement:lime:sand mix.
18 When the mortar has set, lay bricks around the top of the planters and along the top tread.
19 Fill the base of both planters with broken bricks and stones, then fill with soil and plant.

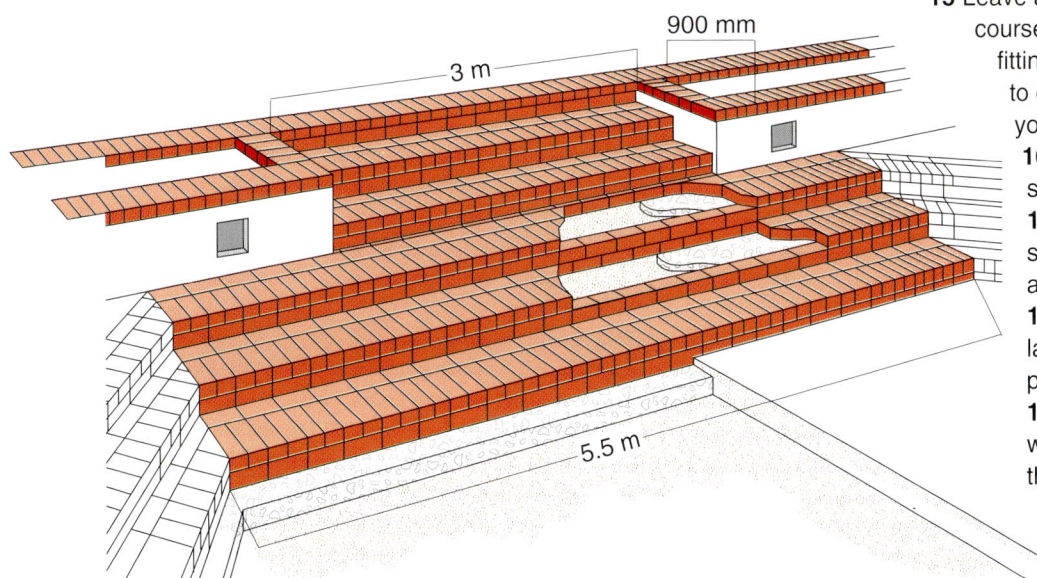

This lovely, random stepping-stone path, leading to beautifully overgrown brick steps, beckons one to explore more of the garden. Created with ordinary precast concrete slabs, the path is well planted with ground covers which soften the effect and give it life and colour. The path widens as it nears a brick patio (not included in this plan). Materials specify sufficient bricks, cement, sand and aggregate for the steps, the retaining wall on both sides of the steps, and an additional 2 m of wall along the front. You will also be able to build a pathway which is about 3.5 m long and covers a total of 6 m^2. The design can easily be expanded so that the stepping stones create an informal patio area.

MATERIALS
Steps
144 bricks
60 kg cement
250 kg or 0.18 m^3 sand
18 kg lime
100 kg stone

Walls
288 bricks
225 kg cement

35 kg lime
890 kg or 0.7 m^3 sand
hardcore for drainage

Walkway
810 kg or 0.6 m^3 crushed
 stone or hardcore
 (optional)
405 kg or 0.3 m^3 sand
33 x 420 mm x 40 mm
 round slabs

1 Mark out and excavate the steps, roughly cutting out the general shape required (see pages 46-49).
2 Lay a concrete foundation, 1.4 m x 240 mm in area and 50 mm deep, for the bottom step. (A 1:4:4 mix will use 25 kg of the cement.) Leave to set.

3 Lay the first course of bricks, with a stretcher course in front and header course behind.
4 Then lay the second course with the header course in front and stretcher course behind.
5 Fill in behind the first tread with concrete to create a second 1.4 m x 240 mm foundation, 50 mm deep and level with the top of the first tread. Allow to set.
6 Build up all four treads in the same way. Allow the mortar to set thoroughly.
7 Dig away the soil along the sides of the steps. If necessary, erect formwork to prevent the soil from collapsing.
8 Dig foundation trenches 250 mm wide and 100 mm deep. Mix concrete in a 1:4:4 mix using 150 kg of the cement specified, and fill the trenches. Allow to set.
9 Lay a one-brick wall in stretcher bond along the sides of the steps and extend the walls, if necessary, along the front.
10 Once the mortar has set, fill behind the wall with hardcore to aid drainage.
11 Level the area where the pathway is to be laid and compact the earth well.
12 Spread a 100 mm layer of hardcore and compact it again.
13 Cover the hardcore with a 25-50 mm layer of sand.
14 Lay the slabs, ensuring that they are flat and level.
15 Fill the gaps between them with good quality soil and plant with a suitable ground cover.

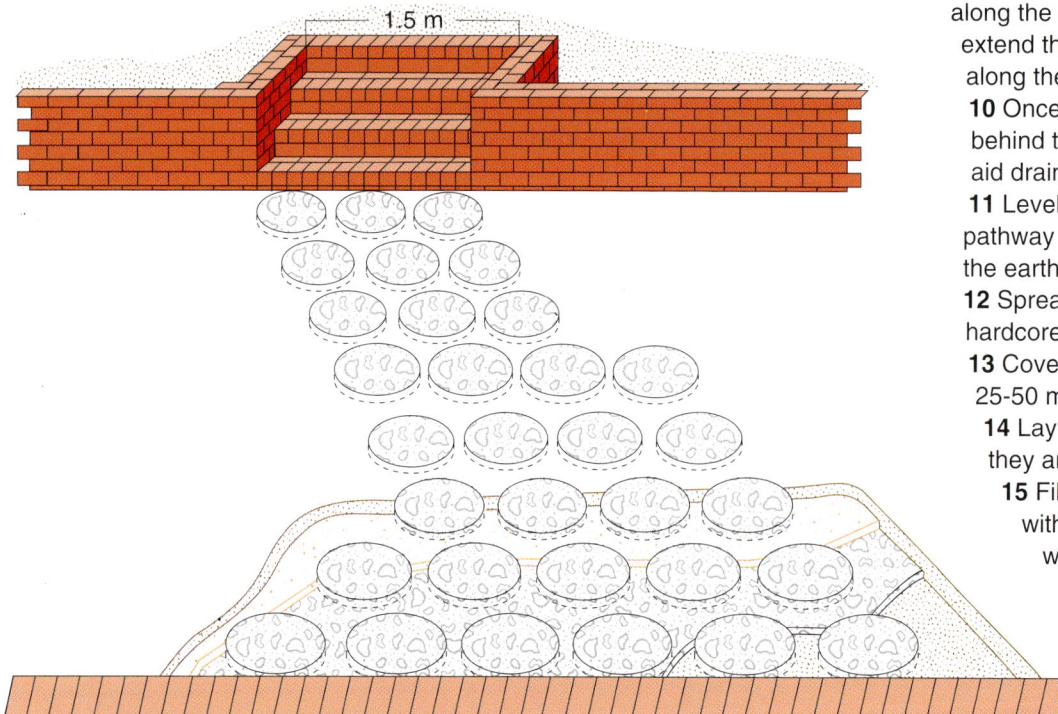

1.5 m

These charming rustic steps are set at the base of a grassy bank and link a stone patio/walkway with a slightly raised garden. Made from timber sleepers and split poles, which have been sunk well into the ground, they are built along the same lines as the adjacent split-pole retaining wall and rustic planters. Materials specified will enable you to build four steps set into a similar slope, and a simulated stone slab patio or walkway of 12 m². If you cannot find poles that are long enough to span the treads, simply abut two shorter ones to fit, and adjust any of the dimensions to suit your site.

MATERIALS
Steps
4 x 1 m x 250 mm x 150 mm timber or precast sleepers
1 x 2.7 m split pole, 90 mm in diameter
1 x 2.07 m split pole, 90 mm in diameter
2 x 1.8 m split poles, 90 mm in diameter, for the sides
1 x 1.44 m split pole, 90 mm in diameter
1 x 900 mm split pole, 90 mm in diameter

36 x 400 mm split poles, 90 mm in diameter
78 x 300 mm split poles, 90 mm in diameter
78 x 75 mm anodised nails

Patio/walkway
0.6 m³ sand
23 x 500 mm x 500 mm reconstituted stone slabs
23 x 500 mm x 250 mm reconstituted stone slabs
23 x 250 mm x 250 mm reconstituted stone slabs

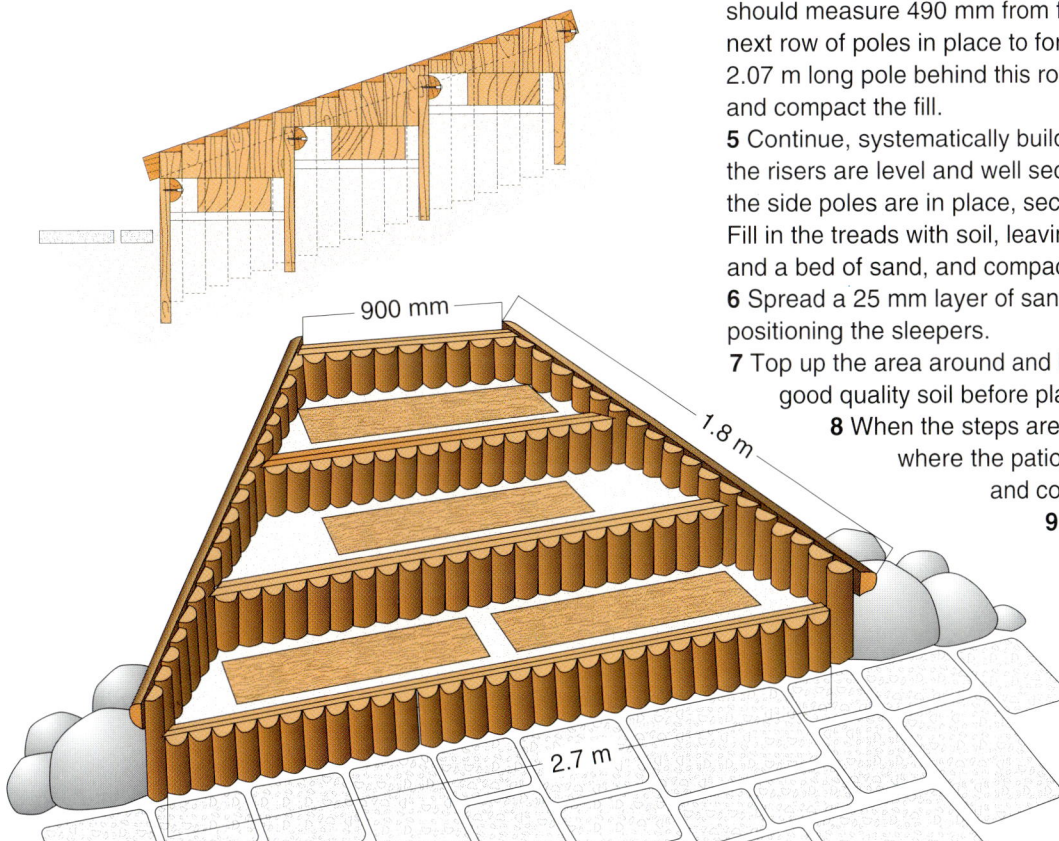

1 Excavate the area of the steps, cutting away roughly to the shape required.

2 Dig a 200 mm deep trench along the front and set thirty 300 mm long split poles in place. Nail the 2.7 m long pole (or two 1.35 m poles) to the back of these, so that the upper surface of all the timber is straight and level. Fill in the excavated soil in front of the step and compact it well.

3 Dig a 200 mm deep trench on either side of the steps, following the slope of the ground. Position the first six or seven 400 mm long poles on either side.

4 Dig another trench at the back of the first tread (which should measure 490 mm from front to back), then set the next row of poles in place to form a second riser. Nail the 2.07 m long pole behind this row as before, fill the trench and compact the fill.

5 Continue, systematically building each tread, making sure the risers are level and well secured from behind. When all the side poles are in place, secure these in the same way. Fill in the treads with soil, leaving 175 mm for the sleepers and a bed of sand, and compact.

6 Spread a 25 mm layer of sand on top of the soil before positioning the sleepers.

7 Top up the area around and between the sleepers with good quality soil before planting.

8 When the steps are complete, level the ground where the patio or walkway is to be sited and compact it well.

9 Spread 25-50 mm sand over the surface and water it lightly with a hose to aid compaction.

10 Lay the slabs in a random fashion, ensuring that they are level.

11 Fill the gaps with good soil before planting.

900 mm

1.8 m

2.7 m

Railway sleepers and bricks are cleverly combined to create a slightly winding, gradually stepped path leading to an informal garden. These materials are laid on a concrete slab which is stepped up the slope. Materials listed will enable you to construct a walkway about 5 m long; the number of steps you decide to build will depend largely on the gradient of your site. If timber sleepers are not available, hardwood planks or precast concrete imitation sleepers could be used instead. Although most of the sleepers will stay in place without bolts or screws, it is a good idea to secure those on the treads firmly in the concrete with coach screws.

MATERIALS
230 bricks
225 kg cement (135 kg for foundation)
1 180 kg or 0.9 m³ sand (270 kg for bedding bricks)

535 kg or 0.4 m³ stone
11 x 2.3 m x 250 mm x 150 mm railway sleepers
33 x 100 mm coach screws (optional)
scrap timber for formwork

1 Mark the line of the walkway and excavate an area 50-100 mm wider than the path on either side and 200 mm deep. Use formwork where the foundation is stepped and overlap the levels of concrete by at least 50 mm.

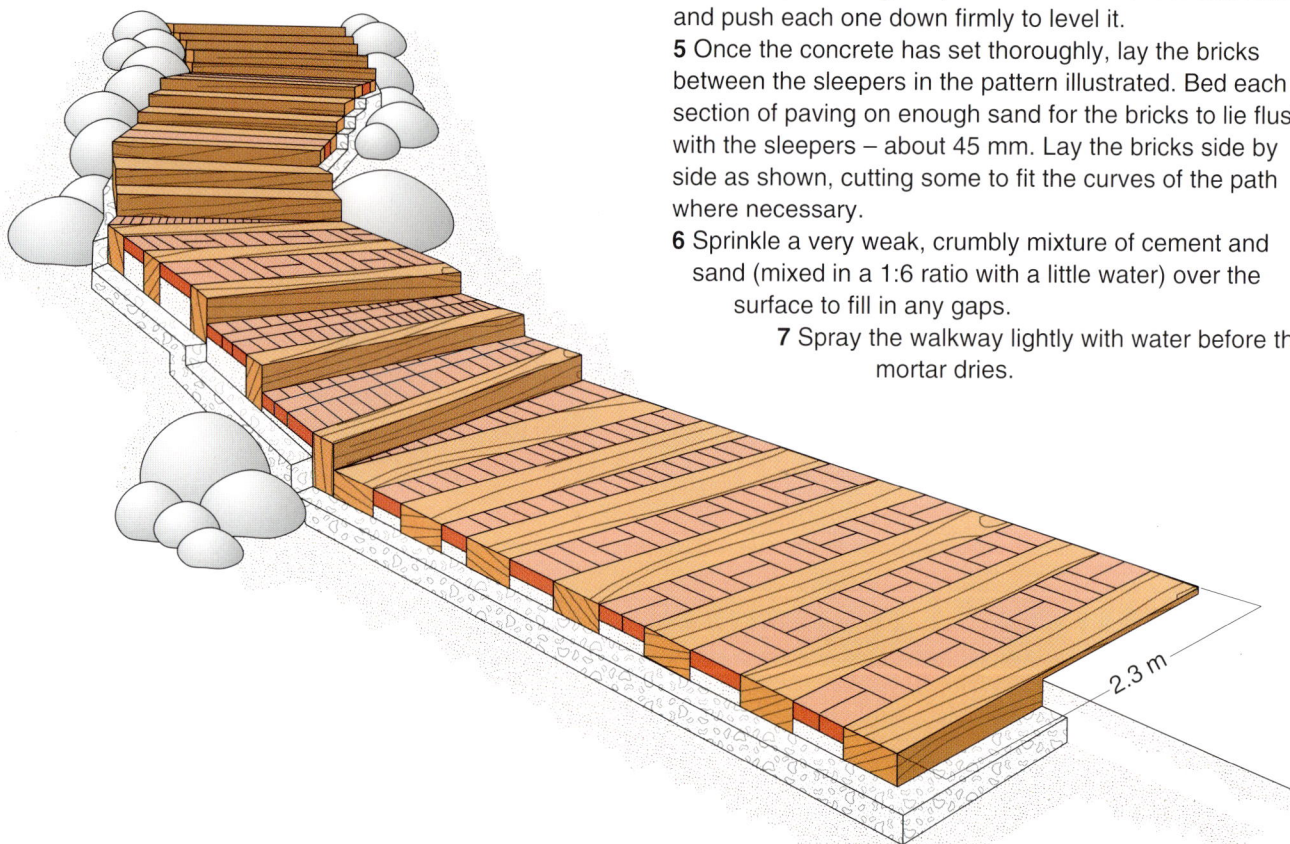

2 Mix the concrete (materials listed are for a 1:4:4 ratio of cement, sand and stone) and place it over the entire excavated area to a thickness of about 50 mm.
3 If you wish, insert about three coach screws part way into the underside of each sleeper, ensuring that the head and at least half of the screw protrudes from the timber.
4 Before the concrete sets, position the sleepers about 230 mm apart along the path and at the front of each tread and push each one down firmly to level it.
5 Once the concrete has set thoroughly, lay the bricks between the sleepers in the pattern illustrated. Bed each section of paving on enough sand for the bricks to lie flush with the sleepers – about 45 mm. Lay the bricks side by side as shown, cutting some to fit the curves of the path where necessary.
6 Sprinkle a very weak, crumbly mixture of cement and sand (mixed in a 1:6 ratio with a little water) over the surface to fill in any gaps.
7 Spray the walkway lightly with water before this mortar dries.

2.3 m

This small, simple, and very practical patio area alongside a boundary wall is linked to the house by a small, gradual flight of steps. Similar to the steps and patio featured on pages 52-53, the project requires only basic skills. Although facebricks and pavers are specified throughout, ordinary stock bricks could be used where brickwork is not visible, just as they are in the step-by-step project. If you need to build more than three step, or if you want a patio bigger than 12 m², you will need to adjust the relevant quantities.

MATERIALS
Steps
123 facebricks
198 paving bricks
140 kg cement (60 kg for concrete and 80 kg for mortar)
560 kg or 0.4 m³ sand

240 kg or 0.18 m³ stone
40 kg lime (optional)

Patio
540 paving bricks
810 kg or 0.6 m³ bedding sand
fine sand for jointing

1 Peg out an area of 2.5 m x 1.5 m for the steps.
2 Excavate to a depth of 50 mm and compact the soil to create a firm sub-base.
3 Mix concrete in a cement:sand:stone ratio of 1:4:4 and throw the foundation slab. Compact, level and leave it to set.
4 Chalk out the area of each step before laying stepped side walls. Build up two courses for the first two steps and five for the top one using a 2:1:8 cement:lime:sand mix for the mortar.
5 Now build the back and front risers by laying two walls between the side walls, five and two courses high respectively.
6 Allow the mortar to set, then fill the two cavities with broken bricks,

stones and soil or sand. Compact so that the material is about 10 mm below the top of the bricks.
7 Top the fill with about 10 mm concrete.
8 Lay pavers over the lower surface.
9 Lay a stretcher course of bricks on the paving to form the middle riser. Fill in with bricks and a 10 mm layer of concrete, then top with pavers as before.
10 Finally lay pavers to cover the top tread.
11 When the steps are complete, level the ground in front of the steps and compact it well.
12 Spread a 25-50 mm layer of sand over the compacted area, then compact and level it.
13 Lay pavers in a running-bond pattern, working away from the wall.
14 Set edgings in mortar.
15 Spread fine sand over the surface and sweep it in to fill all gaps between the bricks.

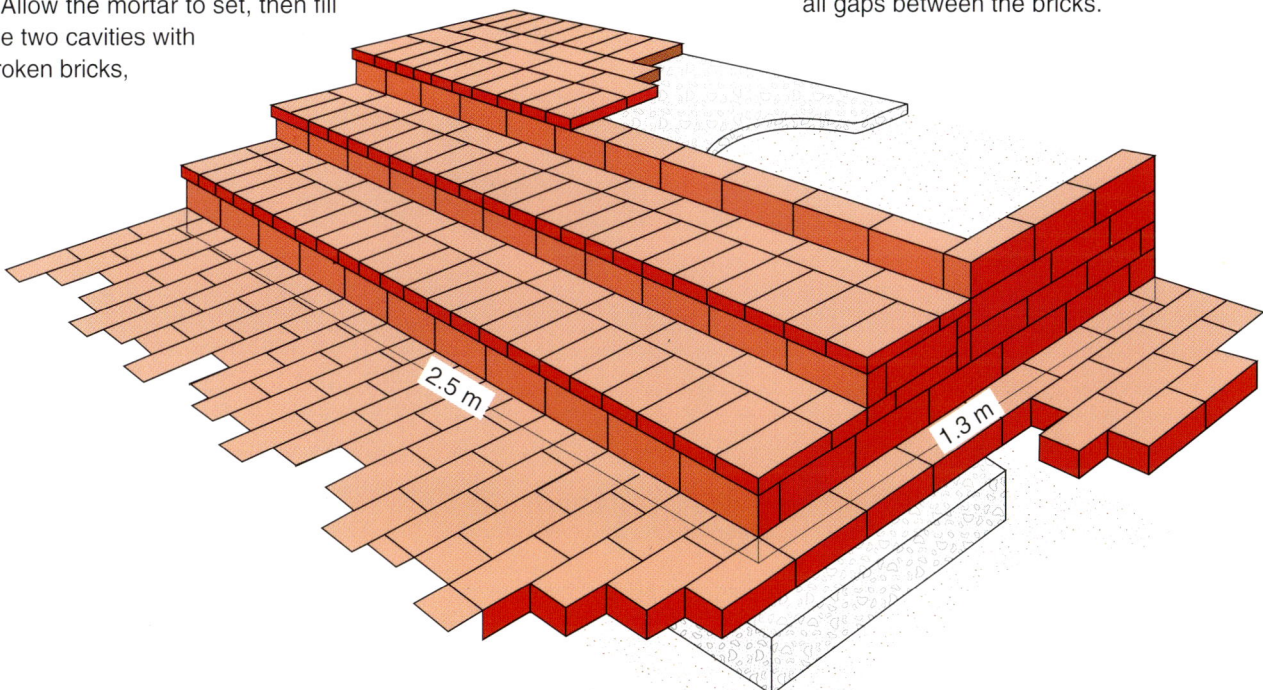

2.5 m

1.3 m

Well-coordinated brickwork is the key to this attractive entrance area which features low walls, a paved walkway, a planter and two flights of steps, one of brick and the other cast concrete with a tile finish. The site slopes slightly, and the elements can easily be adapted to many sites. Although this is a relatively complicated project, it does not require any special building skills. The secret is to tackle it systematically – each element should be marked out exactly before construction begins, and brickwork should be completed before the surfaces are paved and tiled. The materials listed will enable you to build the planter, both sets of steps, as well as an 800 mm x 2.2 m landing at the top of the steps and a 3.2 m long pathway. Bricks for the patio are laid in the same way as the path; quantities specified will cover about 20 m².

MATERIALS

Foundations
255 kg cement
1 030 kg or 0.8 m³ sand
1 030 kg or 0.8 m³ stone

Tiled steps
245 kg cement
990 kg or 0.7 m³ sand
990 kg or 0.7 m³ stone
187 x 200 mm x 200 mm
  ceramic floor tiles
15 kg cement-based tile
  adhesive
4 kg grout

Brick steps
384 facebricks
130 kg cement
525 kg or 0.4 m³ sand
525 kg or 0.4 m³ stone

Planter
720 facebricks
180 kg cement
90 kg lime
725 kg or 0.5 m³ sand

Walls
260 facebricks
90 kg cement
45 kg lime
365 kg or 0.3 m³ sand

Path & patio
1 125 paving bricks
1 080 kg or 0.8 m³ bedding
  sand
15 kg cement
60 kg sand for edging
fine sand for jointing

1 Peg out the entire area marking steps, planter and walls as shown on the illustration.
2 Excavate foundation trenches, allowing for slabs of at least 100 mm under the steps and planter, and 150 mm for walls.
3 Mix cement, sand and stone in a ratio of 1:4:4 and place concrete in all the trenches. Put a few bricks in the base of the planter to create drainage holes. Allow concrete to set, but remove bricks before it firms thoroughly.
4 Build tiled steps first. Dig away a rough stairway and set formwork in place.
5 Mix concrete and place in the formwork, then allow it to set.
6 Mix mortar in a 2:1:8 ratio and build up the planter in stretcher bond.

7 Now build the brick steps. Start in front, ensuring that the back row of bricks lines up with the planter and proposed position of the front wall. Lay all on edge as illustrated, starting with a stretcher course in front.
8 Lay a second course over the first, this time starting with a header course; the two courses will form the first tread.
9 Lay the second and third steps in the same way.
10 Build one-brick side walls for the path in stretcher bond. Finish the tops with a header course of bricks laid on edge.
11 Clear the area to be paved and compact the ground.
12 Spread a 25-30 mm layer of sand over the entire area; compact and level it.
13 Lay edgings against steps and walls. If the patio does not abut a wall, lay an edging in mortar along one side.
14 Lay bricks in a herringbone pattern; leave cutting till last.
15 Lay the rest of the edgings in mortar.
16 Spread fine sand over the surface; brush into the joints.
17 Finally, spread tile adhesive over the concrete steps, lay the tiles and grout.

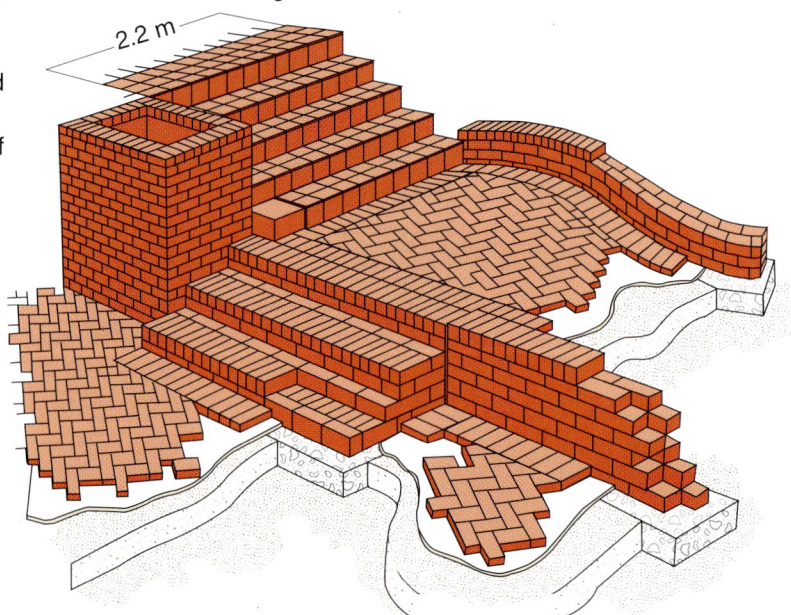

2.2 m

This well-proportioned stairway steps up gradually at right angles. Bricks are laid on edge in a basketweave pattern and the steps are held in place by a header course of bricks placed on edge at the front of each tread. Risers are constructed by building up two stretcher courses in the usual way. The amount of paving laid at the top of the steps may vary between sites; the quantities given here will allow you to pave about 8 m². An attractive 2 m x 1.2 m planter edges one side of the stairway, and matches an existing 1.3 m high facebrick wall. If you wish to build a wall as well as the steps and planter, you will need extra bricks, cement and sand, as well as stone for the foundations.

MATERIALS
Steps
900 paving bricks
455 kg cement (155 kg for
  foundations)
1 838 kg or 1.4 m³ sand
625 kg or 0.5 m³ stone

Planter
670 facebricks
250 kg cement (25 kg
  for foundations)
115 kg lime
1 010 kg or 0.7 m³ sand
200 kg or 0.15 m³ stone

1 Peg out the edges of the area where you plan to build the steps. Then measure and mark an area of approximately 1.8 m x 700 mm where the lowest step will be built.
2 Excavate about 50 mm from the bottom step, then fill with concrete mixed in a cement:sand:stone ratio of 1:4:4. Level and compact it and allow to set.
3 Lay a header course of bricks about 50 mm from the front of the slab, and a stretcher course along the right-hand side.
4 Now dig away the bank immediately behind this first tread, at the back and on one side, roughly forming the second tread. Excavate to the height of the header course.
5 Mix more concrete and place behind the header course and in the excavated section to create a foundation for the second step.

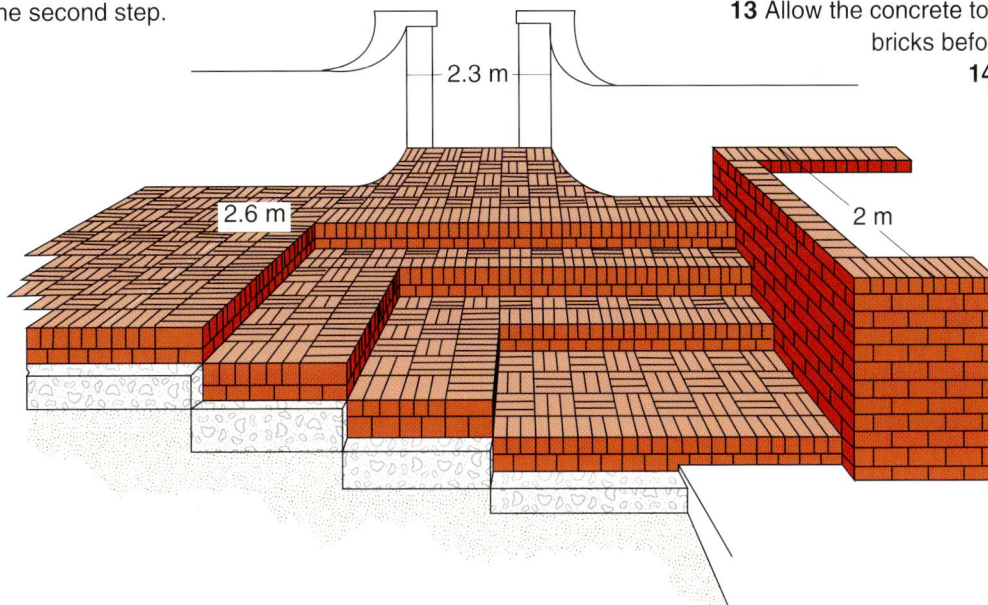

6 When the concrete has set, lay two header courses along the front of the second step to form the required right angle. Lay two stretcher courses on the right-hand side.
7 Lay the paving over the first tread, setting bricks on edge to form a basketweave pattern. End with a brick-on-edge header course at the front.
8 Repeat steps 4 to 7.
9 Repeat these steps a second time, but this time throwing a concrete slab for the upper section of paving rather than another tread. Pave the upper area using the same pattern.
10 Dig away the slope to the right of the steps, excavating a foundation trench for the planter about 50 mm below the bottom step.
11 If the earth is soft, erect formwork to prevent the bank from collapsing.
12 Place a few bricks on end in the centre of the planter to create drainage holes. Then mix the concrete in a 1:4:4 ratio and place to form a foundation slab.
13 Allow the concrete to set overnight, but remove the bricks before it hardens too much.
14 Construct the planter by building up one-brick walls to form a rectangular box 11 courses high.
15 Lay a header course of bricks on edge around the top of the planter.
16 Place broken bricks and stones in the base of the planter, then fill with soil and plant.

2.3 m

2.6 m

2 m

An attractive flight of steps built from dressed stone slabs allows a gradual descent from one level of the garden to another. The lower section of the steps spreads out from a central landing topped with crazy paving. A water feature (not included in the project) adds charm and character. You could continue the stairs across the full width of the area, or you could construct a stepped planter in place of the water feature. A precast pond could also be positioned in between the two lower flights. The stone you use to build the steps will depend on what is available in your area.

MATERIALS
94 slabs of cut stone, average size 300 mm x 200 mm x 100 mm, or stone slabs to cover 8 m^2
crazy paving to cover about 2 m^2
90 bricks
260 kg cement (175 kg for concrete and 30 kg for brickwork)
1 050 kg or 0.8 m^3 sand
700 kg or 0.5 m^3 crushed stone
plywood and scrap wood for formwork
2 x precast concrete lamps (optional)

1 Use a profile to establish where the steps will be located. Peg out the area.
2 Roughly excavate the stairway.
3 Construct the formwork in three sections, with treads about 200 mm deep and risers about 100 mm high. Use plywood wherever curves are required. Hammer into place, leaving the central landing untouched.

4 Compact the earth within the formwork. Mix concrete in a ratio of 1:4:4 (cement:sand:stone) and place it to form the foundation slabs for the steps. Level and compact the concrete and allow it to set thoroughly.
5 Excavate the earth between the two bottom flights of steps, using formwork to prevent the bank from collapsing.
6 Dig a trench between the two bottom stairways, 300 mm wide and 100 mm deep, for the foundation of the front wall of the landing.
7 Mix concrete in a 1:4:4 ratio using about 10 kg cement. Place in the trench and allow to set.
8 Build a one-brick wall six courses high in stretcher bond at the front of the landing, leaving drainage holes at the base. Allow the mortar to set thoroughly, then render the front of the brickwork. If you are building a water feature, construction may also take place at this stage.
9 Remove the formwork and backfill the gap behind the wall with crushed stone and soil.
10 Excavate and flatten the earth on the landing. The surface should be level with the base of the concrete which forms the bottom step of the top flight, and the top of the concrete which forms the top step of each lower flight.
11 Mix another batch of concrete and place on the landing. Level and compact it and leave to set.
12 Lay the stone slabs to form the steps, working from the bottom step. If they do not fit exactly, fill in the gaps with mortar or smaller pieces of stone.
13 Lay the crazy paving in mortar on the landing.
14 If you are installing lamps, get an electrician to do the wiring, and then concrete them in place at the top of the steps.

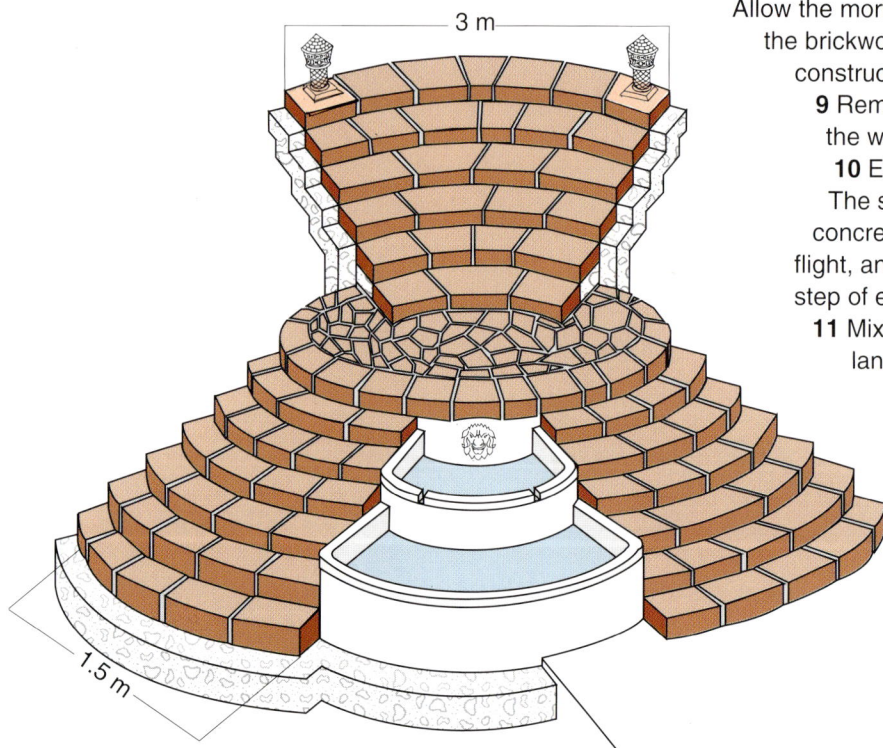

3 m

1.5 m

A formal garden staircase, which is a feature in itself, has been rendered and painted and the treads topped with attractive slate tiles to blend with the architecture of a large house. Relatively deep 600 mm treads combine with minimal risers up the slight slope. Although the project specifies 290 mm x 90 mm x 90 mm concrete blocks, the steps may be built with bricks or blocks of a different size. If you do need to adapt the materials, some of the other materials and the proportions may vary. You may also prefer to tile the treads with ceramic, terracotta or quarry tiles. All are suitable provided they have a matt, non-slip finish. If lighting is to be incorporated, you will need to employ the services of a professional electrician.

MATERIALS

190 x 290 mm x 90 mm x 90 mm blocks (some broken)
175 kg cement (about 75 kg for foundations and 70 kg for render)
50 kg lime
700 kg or 0.5 m³ sand
300 kg or 0.2 m³ stone
100 x 300 mm x 300 mm slate tiles
4 x 500 mm x 500 mm slate tiles
20 kg cement-based tile adhesive
2 x sealed light fittings with conduit (optional)

1 Peg out the 4 m wide staircase, marking the position of the two front pillars.

2 Dig two 490 mm x 490 mm foundation trenches, 50 mm deep, for the pillars, and a 3 m x 190 mm trench of the same depth for the wall which will form the first riser.

3 Mix concrete using a cement:sand:stone ratio of 1:4:4 and place in the holes. Allow to set. If lighting is to be installed, set conduiting in place before placing the concrete.

4 Build the two lower pillars five courses high and lay the two courses of the bottom step in stretcher bond, about 50 mm in from the edge of the concrete.

5 When the mortar has set, cut away the earth behind to form a rough second step.

6 Dig a second foundation trench for the next riser wall and fill it with concrete.

7 Once the concrete has set, fill the gap between this and the front wall and compact the fill so that the surface is about 25 mm below the top of the front bricks. Top with concrete.

8 Repeat this procedure for each riser, building up the side walls at the same time.

9 Build two more pillars at the top of the steps.

10 Use broken blocks to fill in the slope of the walls between the top and bottom pillars. Allow the mortar to set.

11 If light fittings are required, install them or have them fitted now.

12 Render the side walls and risers with a 2:1:8 mixture of cement, lime and sand.

13 When the rendering has set, tile the treads and the top of the pillars. Grout the tiles with a little mortar.

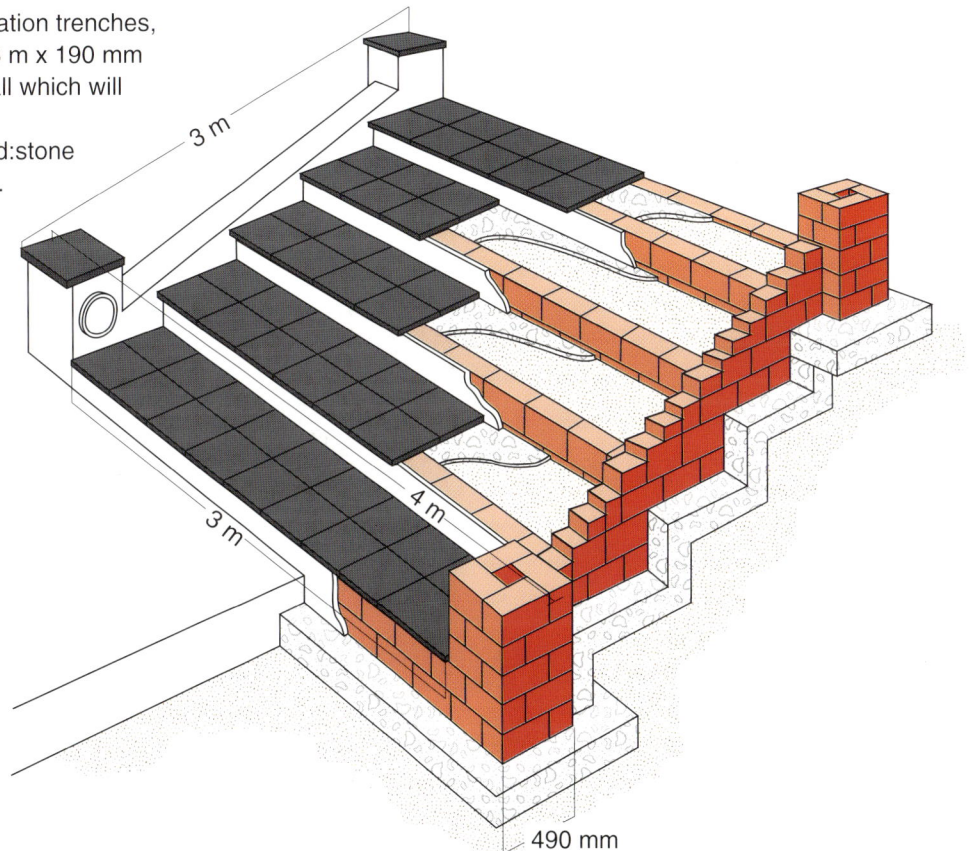

3 m

3 m

4 m

490 mm

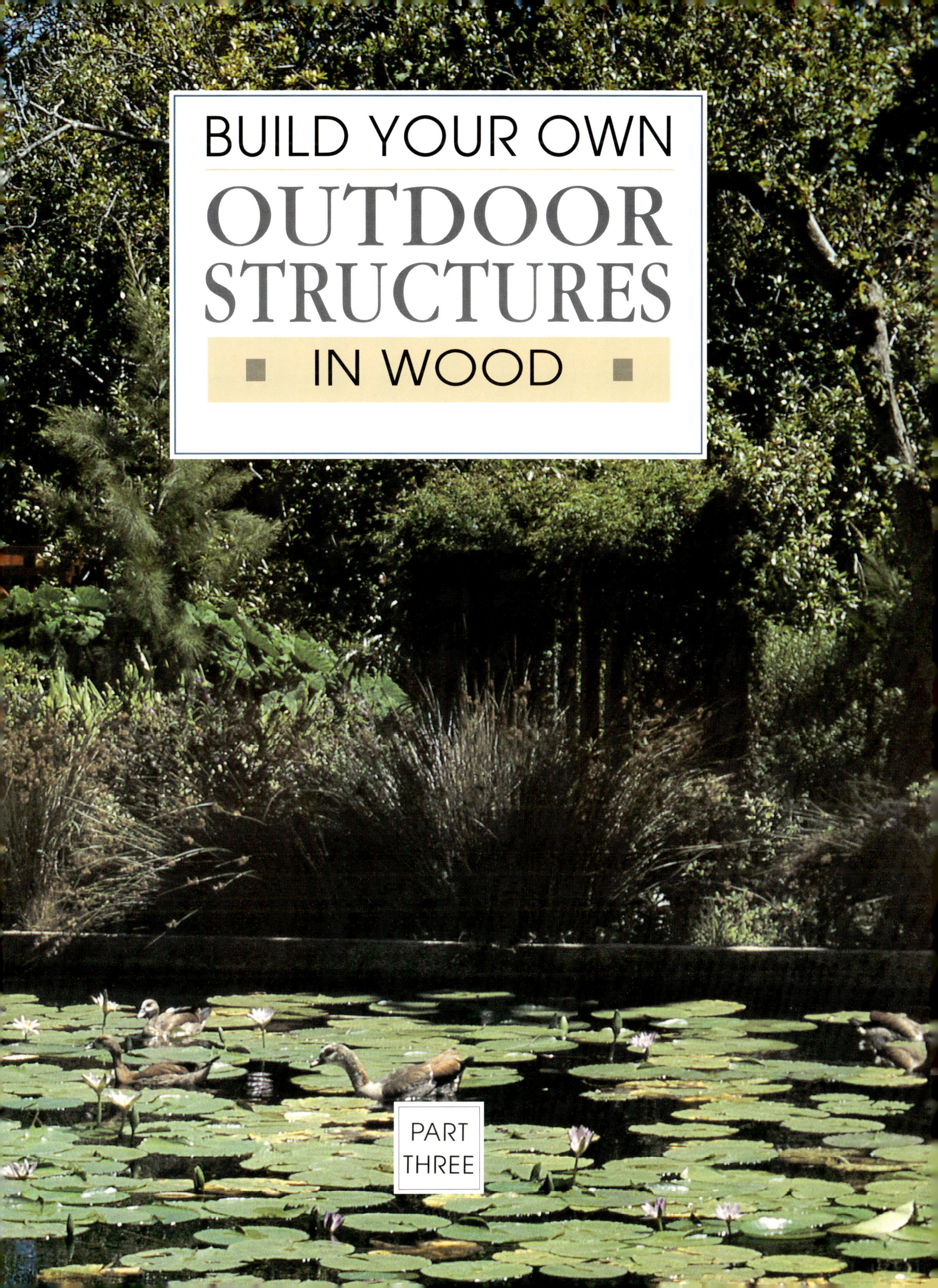

BUILD YOUR OWN OUTDOOR STRUCTURES IN WOOD

PART THREE

INTRODUCTION

Timber is one of the most popular and versatile materials available for garden constructions. It is relatively light-weight, strong and rigid, and has a pleasing appearance. Furthermore, with the most basic carpentry skills, it is possible to build shelters and simple buildings, decks, steps, fences and a myriad decorative features.

There are many reasons for choosing to use wood rather than other building materials, not least of these being the ease of construction and reasonable cost. It is usually quicker to erect a wooden structure and the process is less messy than working with bricks, blocks or stone and mortar. Some wooden buildings are available in kit form, and small utility structures are often supplied prefabricated. There are countless design possibilities, ranging from traditional types to rustic units which blend harmoniously with the garden environment.

While the most common structures found in any garden are limited to fences, walls and steps, there are many more possibilities suitable for 'do-it-yourself' (DIY) construction, and a large percentage of these are built from wood.

Partial shade is created by a slatted roof.

The most obvious examples are pergolas (sometimes referred to as arbours) and walkways, many of which consist of a basic framework made from wood. Either attached to a house or freestanding, these structures may have a solid roof for shelter or be left partially open to the sky.

A deck is another popular type of timber structure, with more complex variations featuring built-in seating, attractive handrails and sometimes screen walls. Imaginative designs may also incorporate planters, hot-water spas and outdoor storage facilities.

Particularly useful in sloping gardens or hillside locations, decking eliminates the need for traditional terracing which can be expensive and may not suit your lifestyle. It also overcomes the problem of cumbersome earthmoving and extensive landscaping.

Of course, wood may be used to build a conservatory or sunroom, which will provide you with a welcome transition from house to garden. Similar extensions, using a large percentage of glass, are also popular for hot spas (or whirlpools), which many people prefer to site under cover in the garden.

A 'glasshouse' does not have to be attached to the house; sited beside a swimming pool or tennis court, it can become a haven for relaxation and casual entertaining. This particular method of construction may be used for a utilitarian but traditional-style greenhouse, designed to trap the sunlight and protect the plants inside.

A simpler alternative for plant enthusiasts is a straightforward wooden lean-to where pot plants are sheltered and adequately shaded from sun, wind, hail or snow. Even a freestanding structure can easily be constructed around a very basic framework of wood, using either fibreglass or an awning material like shadecloth or canvas for protection.

If you are a bird-lover, a garden aviary or even a raised bird house or covered bird-feeding table for wild garden birds may appeal. Dog kennels, too, may be constructed from wood, and if you live in the country and keep ducks and chickens, it is the most obvious material to use for a simple A-frame shelter. You may want to tackle a more elaborate gazebo with latticework, or a traditional pavilion similar to the bandstands sometimes found in public parks.

For those who are lucky enough to live alongside a lake or waterway, a timber boathouse is a useful project. Another option is a dual-purpose shelter which can be used as a summerhouse as well as for storing movable garden furniture and other items not required indoors. Bridges, too, may be constructed from wood, whether designed for the practical purpose of crossing water, or purely as a decorative feature in a water garden.

For families with children, a wooden play structure can be a most rewarding project. Tree-houses are an all-time favourite, but they must be securely fixed in the branches to prevent accidents. A simple platform built in a sturdy tree will provide hours of fun, and you can erect a small deck around the trunk so that the timber floor doubles as a roof for a makeshift shelter below. It may be necessary to build a step-ladder for easy access.

The simple wooden structures described in this book cover most of the above options, as well as timber extensions and additions. You will find various options for a range of utility buildings including garden sheds and outdoor workrooms or studios, although we have avoided buildings larger than 50 m² in size. Also included is a section on building methods to help you adapt these projects to suit your own needs.

The focus of the book is on timber structures which are practical rather than simply decorative, but there is advice on improving the appearance of an existing structure or one that you plan to build. You will find that a coat of paint or the addition of latticework, wooden cut-outs and carpenter's work, or potted and hanging plants, will give ordinary structures a special charm. Photographs throughout the book aim to inspire, while the accompanying text gives sound, practical advice and a host of good ideas.

The first section will help you to plan your project systematically and sensibly; it will enable you to identify your own needs and determine exactly what and where you should build. It will also help you to estimate the cost of the project and decide whether or not professionals should be employed.

Various design options are discussed and illustrated, ensuring that your structure will look attractive and will be compatible with the garden plan as a whole, whether it is a gazebo, a children's playhouse (Wendy house) or a functional tool shed. In addition, a wide range of flooring and roofing possibilities are considered.

For those wanting to build a traditional timber structure, there is some interesting information relating to small pavilions, gazebos, arbours and pergolas. The history of more substantial garden houses, rustic country huts and other small, open shelters which were usually built of wood, is also examined.

Materials are discussed and the relevant tools detailed, along with various construction methods which are clearly explained (also included is a box on plumbing and electrics).

There is a section with step-by-step photographs, showing you how to build a range of structures. Although it follows the construction of only two structures – a pole structure and a stud-frame structure – the instructions and illustrations also guide you through a simple method of deck-building, explaining how railings are built, decking slats installed, and how to assemble tongue-and-groove flooring.

The sliding doors of this 'glasshouse' may be opened wide on hot, sunny days.

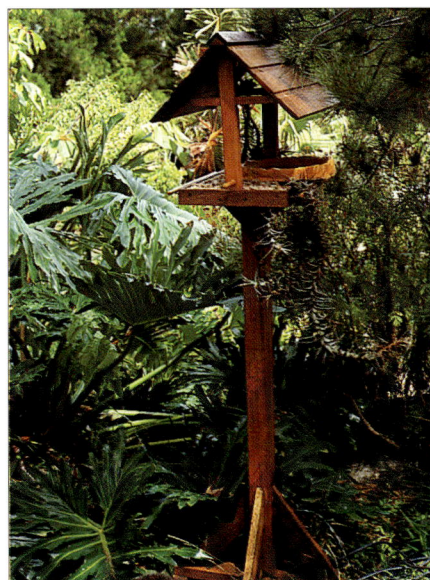

A simple, wooden bird-feeding table.

Reeds clad this delightful hide-out.

Two possible construction procedures for walls are described: one uses pre-assembled panels, and the other, the pole-building (or stick-frame) method. You can also see how windows and doors are fitted, and how a simple roof is erected.

In the latter part of the book, there is a series of ten different plans, together with detailed check-lists of materials.

Although formal building plans may be required for these designs (see page136),these may certainly be used as presented, or adapted and changed to suit your own needs and site.

Whether you aim to do all the work yourself or plan to employ others to help, *Build Your Own Outdoor Structures in Wood* is an invaluable guide to have at hand at all times.

Proper planning is essential, even for the simplest of timber structures. It really does pay to evaluate your needs carefully and establish exactly what purpose you want the structure to serve. Decide from the outset where you want to site it and make sure there are no obstacles or major disadvantages in that position.

Unless you are fortunate enough to have an unlimited budget, costing the project in the planning phase is also imperative. Rather make the changes in the initial stages than wait until you have a half-built structure.

Even if you are determined to do-it-yourself, you may have obvious difficulties at this early stage, and it is often best to call in professional assistance (see pages 135–138) before you begin. You can always minimise costs by doing a lot of the hard, physical work yourself at a later stage.

YOUR NEEDS

Your own preferences and the needs of your family should help you to determine exactly what to build. Most of these considerations are practical and you can be guided by common sense. Still, a little extra thought and preparation will ensure that you make the most of your building efforts.

For instance, if you are a keen gardener you may want a shed to store tools, a wheelbarrow and compost; but why not construct a shelter which will enable you to use it as a mini-greenhouse as well? Alternatively, a greenhouse may be built to house outdoor furniture. By locating it alongside your house or beside a pool, you can create the character of a traditional conservatory, with seating and pot plants, rather than just erecting a functional place to pot and tend seedlings.

Even a simple deck can have many uses, and it pays to consider these from the start. By incorporating a pergola and timber screen, it will immediately become more of an outdoor room. And by building in benches and perhaps a table, its function can be further extended.

A lot is dependent on your lifestyle. If you want an area for entertaining, consider whether children will make use of it. You may have your heart set on a traditional gazebo, but if it is likely to double as a play area, it may not be a realistic choice. A more expansive summerhouse, on the other hand, could be a far more practical option which would meet both needs.

Where space is at a premium, you may be able to create a multifunctional structure with an open area for seating and storage for tools and other garden items.

SITING THE STRUCTURE

Some wooden structures (including those which are assembled in factories) can be moved if necessary, but most are permanent additions designed to stay where they have been erected. Having established that you want a garden structure of some sort and planned its use, you must carefully consider where to site it.

You may be limited by space, but there will often be several possible locations in your garden. The best advice is to contemplate and explore them all, and to weigh up all the pros and cons before making a decision.

One of the most important factors is the accessibility of the structure, and this should relate to function.

You may want to use a deck for alfresco meals; if so, it should be close to the house (or, preferably, attached to it) and large enough to accommodate a table and chairs. If you aim to use it as a sunbathing deck, it should quite obviously be

A clever solution for a hillside property with limited space.

adjacent to the pool (if there is one) or in a spot which remains sunny for most of the day. A garden shed is better sited out of view, but in a location which enables you to retrieve the lawnmower, wheelbarrow and so on without any difficulty or inconvenience.

A cottage or studio in the garden may be tucked away for privacy; but if you plan to work there and invite clients or customers to visit, it should be accessible from the road or from an area on the property where visitors' cars can be parked safely.

If you have lived in your house for some time, you will know which parts of the garden tend to be windy, cold and damp, or otherwise unpleasant. If not, make a point of spending time outside and note the direction of prevailing winds, and areas which are constantly shaded from the sun. You may have pinpointed a site with a lovely view, but if it is too exposed, it may be unpleasant most of the time.

Wood is a sensible material for a difficult site, and obstacles like large rocks, trees and even sloping ground can be turned to your advantage.

An attractive, Oriental-style lattice structure designed to shelter bonsai.

Latticework and clever cut-outs transform a reasonably simple wooden structure.

For instance, most wooden structures can be built on stilts (or posts) where the ground is not flat, and trees can be incorporated into your design. This will enable you to use areas of the garden which would otherwise be useless, but consider whether this approach will increase your costs.

EMPLOYING PROFESSIONALS

The size of your structure and the complexity of its design will influence any decision to seek professional help. Even if you are confident that you can do the building work yourself, you might prefer to ask an architect or designer to help with plans and specifications. If you have difficulty visualising a final effect, the solution may be to consult a landscaper or another specialist for ideas. You may know exactly what you want to build, but do not have the time or expertise to erect the structure yourself; in this case you may require the services of a building contractor.

Before you start erecting even the simplest wooden structure, it is always advisable to contact your local authority to check on building codes and regulations, as well as any possible legal restrictions which may be applicable. Ascertain whether plans must be submitted and if a building permit of any kind is required. Remember that you could find yourself demolishing or dismantling the results of many hours of hard labour if you do not have the necessary permission to build.

While some structures will not be regulated, it is universal practice to have specific rules which set minimum standards in the building industry. You will find that many of these relate to safety (to ensure structures do not collapse and people are not injured), and common sense indicates that they should never be ignored. Even if formal plans do not have to be submitted to your local council or building department, it is sensible to examine local regulations for guidelines relating to foundations and footings, timber dimensions, the recommended height of structures and so on, especially if you decide to build your structure without professional assistance.

In certain instances, structural timbers will be governed by regulations, and specified grades may have to be used. Where strong winds and snow are a factor, it is particularly important to use adequately sized uprights (posts and poles). The framework of any structure must be constructed in such a way that it copes with the weight of the timber and roofing materials if it is to be covered, and also with possible maximum wind speeds and snow loads. Various codes specify minimum spacings for upright timber as well as the depth to which they should be sunk into the ground, and the dimensions of foundations, footings and other structural elements.

Suitable preservatives may also be stipulated (see page 29), particularly if a structure is to be used to house animals.

You may discover that there are limitations governing the location of wooden structures. You will need to work within building lines, and usually a specified minimum distance from the boundaries. In some developments there may be a height restriction to protect the view of neighbouring properties, and an architectural style may be specified.

Where formal plans are required, you will probably have to produce a site drawing indicating the position of the structure, as well as elevations, sections and drainage arrangements. If you are not using professional assistance, your local authority will provide a check-list of what is required. Note that plans based on the diagrams and illustrations featured on pages 52-63 will not usually be sufficient for submission to the authorities.

An A-frame garage made of wood.

A timber cottage owner-built from a kit.

An attractive pergola, designed by a landscape architect, is sited over a walkway.

Architect or designer

These trained professionals are well equipped to design garden structures which will blend with the existing architecture of your home. They should have a sound knowledge of construction materials and suppliers, as well as contractors and other experts. Most charge an hourly fee for consultations or agree on a specified amount to draw up plans and possibly even oversee the job. An architect (or landscape architect, see at right) will usually be registered or licensed with an official institute or body, while a designer often has unauthenticated training or a qualification which is not officially recognised.

Draughtsman

If regulations call for formal plans, these should be drawn by a specialist. An architect or designer will certainly do this for you, but a draughtsman will provide a less expensive service. In fact many architects and designers employ them to prepare their own working drawings. Although some draughtsmen have good ideas and a knowledge of specifications and materials, it is generally best to approach these professionals with a clear vision of what you want.

Landscaper

Landscape architects and garden specialists (who may or may not have formal qualifications), will sometimes undertake design and/or construction of garden structures, particularly if these form part of a greater landscaping plan. Some professional landscapers prefer to subcontract structural work and concentrate on planting.

Contractor

The majority of small-scale builders will undertake garden projects and some will even suggest designs and submit plans. If you decide to employ a contractor to build your structure, ensure that he has the necessary experience and has completed similar projects. Ask for a portfolio of work completed to date or visit the sites of projects that he has already finished building. The best option may be to approach specialist contractors in your area, such as timber merchants who sell prefabricated or kit-form wooden structures, and who may also build personalised, custom-designed units.

Subcontractor

A good compromise between doing all the work yourself and employing a contractor to do it for you is to enlist the services of subcontractors, provided that you have the time and energy to oversee the building operation.

An experienced carpenter will be particularly valuable if the design incorporates complex joinery or intricate decorative work. If there is glazing to be done, you may prefer to subcontract this part of the project. Suppliers of glass will usually install the panes for an additional labour fee.

A lean-to alongside a timber cabin is used for storing cut firewood.

Where electric wiring is required (in a shed, studio or garden cottage, for instance), it is usually advisable to subcontract a qualified electrician; in fact your local authority may insist on it (see page 139).

Specialist consultants

Various consultants, including engineers, can provide valuable services, particularly if your site is an unusual or difficult one. If you are building on a steep or unstable slope, a structural engineer will be able to specify foundation dimensions, as well as wind- and load-stress calculations, and will advise on design.

A geotechnical or structural engineer will analyse soil (if it appears to be problematic) and evaluate what steps should be taken to ensure that the structure is safe.

COSTING THE PROJECT

It is important to finalise your design in the planning stage (see pages 140–153) prior to quantifying and costing the materials required. This will help to ensure that you have the necessary funds and can budget carefully for each phase of the project.

First make a detailed list of all the materials you need, from cement, sand and stone for foundations and footings, to nails and screws. Price the timber carefully and try to avoid unnecessary waste. Standard dimensions and lengths are invariably cheaper than wood that has to be planed (or dressed) and cut specially for the job; if necessary, alter the design to suit what is readily available. It pays to shop around and to be absolutely meticulous in your calculations.

You will now need to cost labour. Find out what professionals, labourers and subcontractors charge in your area. If any helpers are to be paid by the hour, always be generous with estimates. It is better to have a little cash left over at the end of the project than to be caught short.

Finishes and decorative features should also be included in the costing – even if you leave some of them until a later date (see pages 151–153).

An imaginative timber arbour designed by a landscape architect for a park-like garden.

A hot-water spa is set in an attractive deck constructed by a contractor.

Although a multitude of wooden garden structures are built without electricity or plumbing facilities, there are times when these conveniences make life much easier, or even when they are essential for the structure to be functional.

If you are planning on using your outdoor structure for entertaining guests or as a workroom, you may want running water, lighting and a couple of power points for small appliances. Larger structures usually require more sophisticated facilities, but even a rudimentary tool shed will become a much more useful place with the addition of plug points if you plan to use it as a workshop, and an outdoor cooking area will be more convenient if you have a plumbed-in sink, or at least a nearby tap. If you are ambitious, and plan to build a habitable structure, you may even want to incorporate a bathroom or kitchen of some sort.

You will usually need to hire professionals to undertake the work for you, but it is essential to plan for these services from the very start and to incorporate pipework, conduits and so on when you build.

Plumbing Local authorities almost always insist that a registered plumber undertakes or at least oversees basic plumbing and the laying of drains in any building, and a wooden garden structure will be no exception. Building and health inspectors will be even more stringent if sewerage, rather than simply a water supply, is involved.

Piping and related materials required for plumbing should conform to local

With imagination even a small structure can accommodate plumbing fixtures.

building regulations, but it may be possible to use cheaper items than you would choose for your house. Using plastic (or PVC) rather than copper piping for the water supply, for instance, will inevitably result in a cost saving.

Electricity Electricity supplied to homes by means of an underground or overhead mains cable is potentially extremely dangerous, and should be handled only by those who know what they are doing. For safety reasons, the best advice to DIYers is to leave all electical installations and major electrical extensions to a licensed professional.

If a pergola or enclosed patio is to be attached to the house, you will probably be able to utilise the existing wiring to provide additional lighting. Furthermore, you may even be able to install new fittings yourself.

If you have built at some distance from the house, you may need a separate circuit altogether. Alternatively, the electrics could be linked to an existing outdoor circuit which, for instance, services a garage, swimming pool or spa. Waterproof or armour cabling should be used underground where possible, and if light fittings are installed in an exposed position, sealed units must be used. If the regulations permit, you can lay cables and fix fittings yourself, but the wiring itself must be connected to the mains supply by an authorised electrician.

Wiring is fixed into wall panels before cladding.

Hot-water pipes are fitted before the floor is screeded.

DESIGN DETAILS

Whether you are building an elaborate gazebo, a garden shed or a child's playhouse, it is essential to consider all aspects of design. Ensure that your structure is compatible with the rest of your garden design, so that it is an architectural and landscaping asset. There is little point in spending time, effort and money on something that looks out of place or inferior.

existing trees and bushes you want to retain, rocks and natural water. Indicate the direction of prevailing winds, as well as views which can be exploited, and note areas which get more than average sun or shade. To avoid any confusion and the need to redraw the site on paper several times, use an overlay of tracing paper for the new plan.

This does not mean you have to match materials exactly, or slavishly copy existing architectural styles. While these elements will be more important if the structure is attached to or is constantly visible from the house, a sensitive juxtaposition of contrasting materials will often add unusual character and interest, especially in the outdoor area or garden itself.

A simple gazebo provides shelter.

Another charming gazebo, made from poles and sawn timber.

DESIGN BASICS
Successful garden design relies on a clearly defined plan which is carried out in an orderly fashion. If you are starting from scratch, decide on a basic layout for the whole area and determine where paths, walls, patios, service areas and so on are to be located. Identify sections which will best accommodate a children's play area, kitchen or herb garden, pond or pool, and then decide where additional structures will go. Make sure from the start that all the elements you plan to introduce create a harmonious whole.

Whether you can visualise the final effect or not, it helps to work on a site plan drawn to a scale of at least 1:100. Draw in all existing buildings and features – the house, outbuildings,

Once you have a basic layout, you can decide which materials will be used for the structure itself and for hard landscaping (walls, paths, fences and so on) and work on planting.

If yours is an established garden, the layout will already be determined and you will, in all likelihood, have a host of well-developed plants. There may even be existing structures and features which have been developed over the years.

Anything you decide to build in the garden must be part of the design as a whole, so it is essential that the style of a pergola, a gazebo or even a simple tool shed fits the general plan. The structure should also blend with the architecture of the house and any existing outbuildings.

A lot can be learned from traditional structures (see page 143), many of which have been designed and placed to create a feeling of surprise and secrecy, for example, pathways that lead to sheltered arbours and shaded retreats, or plant-smothered pergolas and walkways that invite one to venture towards a rose or herb garden. Frequently, they are not seen in relation to the house at all, and so the suitability of materials is largely dependent on the structure itself.

Gazebos, on the other hand, are generally built to capture a view and they are seldom tucked away out of sight. Although the range of whimsical styles recorded over the years relates directly to architectural preferences of the past, these often mirror the dwelling. So a steeply-pitched hexagonal roof could, if you wish, be tiled to match the roof of your house, or you could use inexpensive latticework without threatening the authenticity of the appearance.

Remember that pergolas and so on may be used to identify and divide the garden space. Furthermore, if they are used as supports for colourful and scented climbing plants, they will immediately add visual interest and welcome shade. Other structures, like a gazebo or small pavilion, may be placed at a focal point in a formal rose garden, or designed as a feature of an outdoor entertaining area; and a wooden bridge can expand the idea of an established water garden, however small it may be.

It is a little more difficult when designing a utilitarian building like a tool shed or animal shelter, but imaginative finishing touches can make all the difference. Consider painting a shed so that it blends with the surrounding environment, or mount a container below the window and plant it with colourful annuals or perennials (see pages 152 and 153).

FLOOR SURFACES
In addition to aesthetic considerations, the type of structure and its function will help you to determine the most suitable floor surface. While wood is often the obvious choice for a timber structure, you may prefer to use a concrete slab, brick paving or a

USEFUL TERMS

Bargeboard Lengths of timber used to neaten the edge of the roof at the gable ends of a building.

Batten Long, narrow, piece of timber, often square in section; commonly used as part of the roof structure, particularly when tiles or slates are used.

Beading Narrow moulding or strip used to neaten various elements in building.

Beam Squared timber used horizontally at base of roof structure and supported at both ends.

Bearer Larger supporting beam or girder used at base of floor structure.

Capping Covering manufactured to protect apex of pitched roofs.

Carpenter's work Term given to various types of period-style decorative trim fashioned from wood.

Cladding The material used to cover and finish the timber framework of dry walling. There are types suitable for use both inside and out.

DPC The damp-proof course of impervious material (usually polythene plastic) laid under concrete floors and in walls to minimise damp in buildings. A damp-proof membrane may also be laid under the roof structure.

Dry wall A timber-framed wall which, unlike conventional brick and block walls, does not involve any 'wet' work (bricklaying, rendering, and so forth) during its construction.

Fascia Timber used to neaten the back and front of buildings at the ends of the rafters; this is the surface to which gutters are usually affixed.

Flashing Waterproofing which is used to seal the joins between the roof and various protrusions (chimneys, dormer windows, skylights and so on).

Footing Term used for foundations, particularly of pillar, pier, commonly cast concrete, timber post or pole.

Foundation A solid concrete base (dug into the ground) on which a building or wall is anchored.

Gable The upper section of a wall at the side of a pitched roof, extending from the level of the eaves upwards. Gable may also refer to a gable-topped wall.

Girder Large beam which supports floor joists. See also Bearer.

Half-brick wall A brick wall that is equal in thickness to half the length of a standard brick. A one-brick wall is built with two rows of bricks which are laid end to end, so that the thickness equals one brick-length.

Joist Parallel timbers used to support flooring and decking slats.

Lath Thin, narrow strip of timber used for trellises and latticework; also useful as a cover strip, for instance where sheets of cladding or boarding meet.

Latticework Structure made with laths which cross each other diagonally or at right angles; used as a decorative feature or for screening.

Plank Long, wide, thickish piece of timber. May be used to form various parts of a structure including beams, joists and even decking slats.

Pole-building Term used for construction method using a basic framework of posts or poles set securely in the ground.

Post A stout length of cylindrical or square timber used as a vertical support in building.

Post anchor Metal base or bracket set in or on a concrete foundation to anchor posts and poles.

Purlin Slightly larger version of a batten, usually used to support roof sheeting.

Quadrant Quarter-round timber used to finish edges where two sides of a structure meet. Useful at external corners and in place of a cornice at ceiling height.

Rafter Sloping beam that forms part of the framework of the roof. Lean-to rafters are found in mono-pitch roofs or over verandahs and decks which are attached to a house.

Rail Horizontal timber used in building; sometimes referred to as noggin. The term may be used in relation to various elements, like a stud wall, a panelled door or the top of a verandah railing.

Railing Arrangement of posts and rails (sometimes with diagonal crosspieces) constructed around the edge of decking, stairways and so on.

Skirting Timber trim used to neaten the junction between internal walls and floors.

Stay Prop or support, usually of timber, used to brace a structure during the building process.

Stick frame The framework of a structure put together using the pole-building system.

Stud Vertical post of timber-frame houses and panelling.

Stud frame Framework for dry walling or partitions made with studs and rails. There are no vertical posts anchored into the ground, and the lowest rail, or floor plate, is nailed or screwed to the floor.

Trelliswork Criss-cross structure made of wood or some other material, used to support plants.

Truss Pre-manufactured or built on site, roof trusses consist of various rafters, beams, posts and struts which will brace the roofing timber.

ceramic tile surface instead. If the structure is an extension of your house, you might like to continue the flooring used inside. When linking a pergola-covered patio, conservatory or additional room, this can be a very effective way of achieving visual unity.

In most instances, you will want a smooth, level surface, with a low-maintenance finish which is both durable and attractive. If the structure is open-sided, or partly enclosed but with no roof, drainage will be an added factor. Water must be channelled away from adjacent buildings and it may be necessary to slope the surface slightly (a gradient of about 1:40 is normal) to allow for run-off. The finished patio floor should be at least 150 mm below any damp-proof course (DPC) or vapour barrier in the wall of the building.

Any structure which is to be used for storage or play, for entertaining or even for work, however temporary, should always be built on a damp-proof base. A timber floor should be suspended above the ground and a polythene DPC should be laid beneath

concrete and other hard surfaces. In addition to the more permanent hard materials considered here, you could use grass, stepping stones combined with ground-cover plants, gravel, pebbles and so on to form an acceptable surface beneath an arbour or informal walkway.

Timber
Timber is relatively lightweight and easy to work with, and is appropriate for a wide range of structures including sheds, Wendy houses, workrooms, gazebos, and of course decks. The type of timber used will depend on what is obtainable locally, but the basic choice is between softwoods and hardwoods (see page 154). You will usually find that hardwoods are more pricey, but they are often better suited to exposed decking than a lot of the softwoods which are readily available.

Both square-edged and tongue-and-groove floorboards are suitable for garden structures. Decking slats may be slightly thicker than internal boards where a very soft wood is used, or

where bearers and/or joists are widely spaced. It is best to choose timber that has been planed (or dressed) all round in the factory.

Man-made board
Manufactured in various forms from timber, most man-made boards are cheaper than solid wood.

Both ordinary plywood (made from several very thin layers of wood) and chipboard or particle board (made from bonded fragments of timber) are adequate choices for the internal floors of sheds, playhouses and similar buildings. Waterproof shutterboard (or shuttering plywood) is particularly strong and stable. All these materials should be laid over bituminous felt to prevent damage from rising damp and excessive moisture. Alternatively, the lower surfaces could be painted with a suitable rubberised bitumen sealer.

Unless particle board has a veneer finish of some kind, it is usually best to paint it, or to cover it with vinyl sheeting. Plywood is reasonably attractive and can be left as it is.

A low-level timber deck alongside a cabin in the garden is practical.

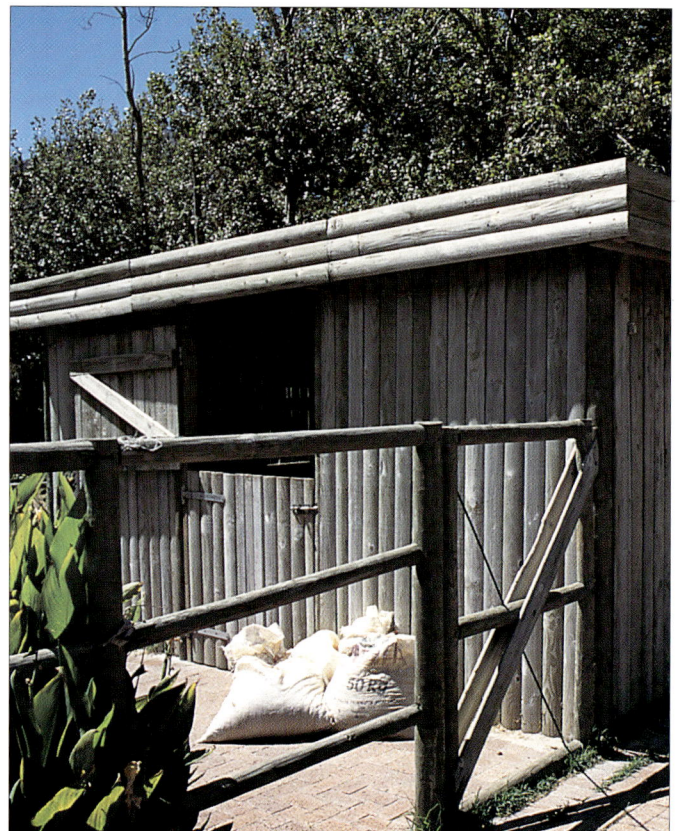

Split poles are often used to clad garden outbuildings.

Timber has been used to build a wide range of structures and garden buildings for centuries. In Ancient Egypt, grape arbours were grown to provide shelter from the harsh desert sun, while in China, covered walkways and small pavilions were often constructed from wood. In Japan it was a primary material used to build traditional tea houses, and in 19th-century England and Europe it was the obvious choice for rustic yet decorative utility buildings such as cow sheds, chicken runs and barns.

For many centuries, bird lovers have built garden aviaries from timber. While early Chinese aviaries were usually crafted from bamboo, the Egyptians seem to have preferred wood. Bird houses and bird feeders, popular from the 19th century, have traditionally been made from wood. These small garden structures were generally rustic in style and designed to blend with nature.

The origin of boathouses can be traced to Ancient China where lakes were a prominent feature in the royal gardens. Traditional Chinese bridges, which had decorative latticework along the sides, were often built from timber.

Galleries, pergolas, arbours and open-sided walkways have been extremely popular in various forms for many centuries. Found all over the world, these range from colonnaded pergolas, so typical of both ancient and Renaissance Italy, to arched lath tunnels favoured in 16th-century France, and elaborate galleries preferred by the English of the same period. In colonial America, more modest arbour walkways were established in the gardens of the wealthy.

Decks, viewing platforms and relatively elaborate gazebos have had an equally long history. While the modern timber deck is very often free-standing in a garden, or is used as a landscaping feature to terrace sloping ground, the traditional structure was more commonly attached to the house. Typical Japanese decks, for instance, led directly from the dwelling and served as a viewing platform to the garden beyond.

Some say that the gazebo, which is frequently constructed in timber, originated in the Netherlands, although the classic English gazebo is probably better known. Initially a feature of grand, formal gardens, it was invariably built in a location where there was a good view of the garden and landscape beyond. Unlike summerhouses, these structures were partially open-sided and usually square or octagonal in shape.

Although early pavilions were actually tented shelters, made with painted canvas and metal poles, by the 19th century many were being constructed with wood. Gazebo-like bandstands or music pavilions, which were mostly found in public parks and gardens, were also made of wood; so too were smaller sheltered seats, built in a range of exotic styles similar to those favoured for a variety of garden buildings.

Small, open shelters, often built of wood, were also popular in both China and early Japan. Roofing materials included thatch and shingled bark, and built-in seating was another common feature.

Although a greenhouse was the obvious shelter for growing seedlings and exotic plants in a cold climate, in some countries decorative lath or latticework houses were constructed to shade plants from the sun.

More substantial garden houses go back a long way. In China, for instance, country huts built from wood and timber structures with screened doors and windows were popular many centuries ago. While brick and stone was more favoured in some countries, in the United States of America, Australia and New Zealand, garden houses and some main dwellings of yesteryear were frequently made of wood. In the southern part of the USA, for instance, early summerhouses often combined solid roofs with lattice walls for shade and fresh air.

In England, where summerhouses were fashionable for centuries, they were originally called 'shadow houses'. While 18th-century versions usually mirrored the style and materials of the house, during the Victorian era, the style changed to rustic wooden buildings which were built by handymen and country carpenters.

Even tree-houses have a history. Since their recorded popularity during the 16th and 17th centuries, they have been called by many names including bowers, crow's nests (usually without a roof) and tree rooms. Although generally thought of as play structures, pleached tree-houses (made by painstakingly clipping and training branches to form a room above ground), look-out or observation platforms built in tall trees, and elaborate structures similar to those built in Persia three or four centuries ago, were certainly not meant for children. Even the modern, well-built tree-house is sometimes used as a workroom or sanctuary for adults.

An attractive gazebo with decorative detail, built in traditional style.

Concrete

Basic but versatile, concrete is frequently used both structurally (for foundations and footings) and as a smooth base for flooring. For instance, a stud-frame garden building, built with factory-manufactured panels, can be erected on a concrete slab (see pages 164 and 173–176). The prepared surface is then screeded, and tiled, carpeted or finished in any way desired.

Tiles

A wide range, including terracotta, terrazzo, slate and clay quarry tiles, is well suited for use in the garden, both on patios and on floors within most outdoor shelters. These tiles should be laid on a solid concrete base, which is usually screeded to give a smooth surface prior to tiling.

Tiles which are exposed to the weather should always have a non-slip, matt finish, and if your area experiences frost and snow in winter, they should be resistant to freezing.

Bricks and blocks

Clay brick pavers, concrete blocks and a range of simulated flagstones and pre-cast slabs are all possibilities for patio floors in a range of wooden structures. They can be used as

A colourful pitched pergola.

A fort made with poles and rustic timber incorporates a swing and an upper deck.

flooring for some gazebo designs, and even for workrooms and shelters used for casual entertaining. If the area does not have to be watertight and rising damp is not a factor, bricks, paving blocks and slabs may be laid on a well-compacted base of sand. Otherwise it is best to throw a concrete slab (see page 164), if necessary over a layer of compressed hardcore, and to bed the chosen units in mortar.

CLADDING

The majority of garden buildings made from wood require some form of external cladding or siding and, if you wish, internal finishing as well. Although metal was a traditional material for cladding the exterior of some timber-frame buildings, it is not commonly used for ordinary garden structures. Instead, wood is a popular choice, and there are various options available, ranging from plywood sheeting to strips of weatherboard manufactured in different profiles. The choice of internal cladding is usually limited to either plasterboard or timber panelling of some sort.

While most types can be affixed to the structure on site, some buildings (including sheds, playhouses and even some quite substantial workrooms) are made from prefabricated panels. You may be able to buy ready-made panels, or you can make them by assembling the basic framework in your workshop and nailing the cladding to it before the structure is erected (see pages 172–176).

Plywood

An exterior-grade or weatherproof marine ply (ripped or used in sheets) is suitable for many garden structures. Ordinary plywood or the more decorative cladding board, which has false joins to make it look like vertical timber boarding, may be used to panel internal walls and partitions. The basic material is also useful for adding rigidity to pre-made wall panels.

If you wish, you can slice plywood into fairly narrow plank widths and nail them in place so that they overlap one another slightly. This will have a similar effect to weatherboard cladding, as the overlap creates its own angle.

Rounded loglap cladding on this shed creates a rustic, weather-resistant finish.

Shiplap cladding (top) and Waney boards.

Hardboard

Available in sheets, this man-made board (made of compressed and processed wood-pulp fibre) is favoured in some countries as a wall covering for sheds and barns. Seams may be hidden by nailing battens or cover strips of wood over them to create a more decorative effect.

Particle board

Only exterior-grade particle board is suitable for use as cladding. When properly treated, it has a high resistance to water; it does expand and it is necessary to use a suitable expansion joint filler between boards.

Sawn timber

Ordinary wooden planks may be used to clad a timber-frame structure, although it may be necessary to use battens or cover strip, either internally or externally, over the joins. This is a relatively labour-intensive option, but one which may be used when tongue-and-groove or other overlapping boards are not available. Alternatively, the planks may be affixed to plywood or another sort of panelling.

Trellises and lattice panels made from thin strips of sawn timber may be used for screen walls or to enclose structures which are left partially open to the elements.

Weatherboard

A popular and attractive option, weatherboard is designed so that horizontal boards overlap one another slightly. The profile you choose will affect the visual appearance of your structure. The most common types include traditional shiplap cladding board (see page 172), a rounded loglap, which gives the impression that the building has been made from logs, and slightly splayed lapboard.

Vertical boards

Both tongue-and-groove boards (if sufficiently thick) and V-jointed boards may be used vertically to clad garden buildings. As the widths and sizes of tongues and grooves may vary, it is best to buy all your timber from one supplier. Some weatherboard may be affixed vertically, although this not generally recommended.

Fibrecement

Made of a mixture of organic fibres and cement, high-density fibrecement cladding is relatively heavy and so better suited to the larger garden structure. It can be pressed during manufacture to give the impression of woodgrain once it is painted.

PVC

Although not available everywhere, PVC is a cladding option. It is fixed in the same way as wooden boards and can be used internally and externally.

Plasterboard

Suitable only for internal use, this dry-wall cladding is manufactured with a core of gypsum plaster. Joints should be taped and then skimmed with a mix of gypsum plaster prior to painting.

Climbing plants cover a simple, painted structure.

Striped awning material creates shade on a patio.

ROOFING OPTIONS

Even though some timber structures are open-roofed, many do provide at least partial shelter from the elements. Some arbours, pergolas, walkways and many other overhead structures may simply shade or define the area, while summerhouses and a variety of pavilions and gazebos will give added cover from rain, wind and snow. More substantial structures, including tool sheds, greenhouses, playhouses, cabins, barns and chalets, usually offer full protection from the elements.

Plant ceilings

Creepers and climbing plants trained over pergolas, arches and other garden structures will soon form a natural plant canopy which offers dappled shade. You may want to plant an evergreen climber, perhaps one of the jasmines, which will reward you with luxurious scent, or a species which bears colourful flowers. But choose your plants carefully.

A dense ceiling of creepers over a pergola constructed alongside a house will be a welcome retreat in summer, but may make the adjacent rooms gloomy and even cold in winter.

Here, it is safer to opt for deciduous plants which will lose their leaves in autumn. The many clematis species are great favourites, as is fragrant wisteria with its drooping racemes which precede thick leafy cover in early summer. Bougainvillea is a common choice in warm climates, but although fairly hardy, it may not survive very cold winters.

Although creepers and climbing plants enhance the appearance of most structures (especially the more utilitarian types), you must ensure that the timber is sturdy enough to support whatever you plant. Some mature plants can damage pergolas, arches and so on with their weight, while others (including some types of ivy) may become invasive, pushing shoots through cladding.

Awning material

Used when shade is the primary requirement, awning materials are not usually waterproof and few materials will last more than a decade; some have a lifespan of only about four years. Nevertheless, several fabrics are water-resistant and will add colour and interest to gazebos and patio roofs.

Various types of awning material are suitable, including treated canvas and shadecloth, a woven material popular with nurserymen for years. It may be fixed in place to form a permanent roof over the structure, or fitted so that it forms a retractable awning. Although there is nothing to stop you making a retractable device yourself, specialist suppliers in most areas will custom-make an awning to fit your structure.

Timber

Latticework and thin laths of wood affixed as open slats may be used as an open ceiling for a pergola or walkway, or as an attractive cladding for a pitched gazebo roof. Timber used for this purpose should be the best quality available, and should always be treated. Choose a reasonably rot-resistant type if possible (see pages 154–155).Once latticework and trellises start to deteriorate, they look shoddy and should be repaired immediately.

You may be able to incorporate ready-made lattice panels, but be sure these are of a quality consistent with the rest of the structure.

Reed and bamboo
Both reeds and bamboo make effective patio roofs. Although usually attached directly to a pergola or the purlins of a patio structure, unattached panels may be suspended overhead. This process is simpler if you can buy the material in woven rolls and all you have to do is trim it to size. Unfortunately though, rolls are not available everywhere. Alternatively, you can string or bind lengths together to create your own panels.

Used on their own, neither bamboo nor reeds will do more than shade an area. They may be used as a ceiling

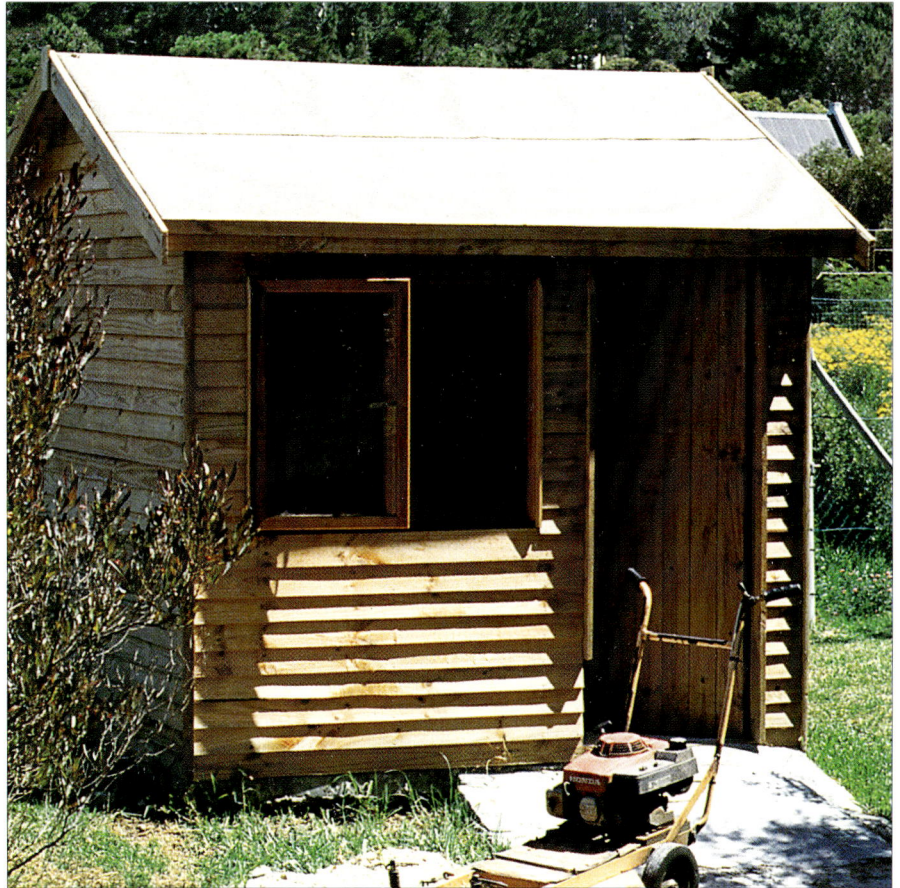

A small, outdoor tool shed with practical, weather-resistant roofing felt.

A larger-than-usual shed, used as a sewing room, has bituminous felt on the roof.

in conjunction with a roof sheeting of some sort – this is a particularly good idea for a cosy log cabin or to shelter a rustic patio at the side of a house.

If you are fortunate enough to find a supply of growing bamboo or reeds, make sure they are green when put in place. If they dry out before installation, individual lengths generally become brittle and difficult to work with.

Roofing felt
Nailed to tongue-and-groove timber, plywood or some other type of boarding, roofing felt is an acceptable option for sheds, garden workshops and greenhouses, and one that is usually chosen for prefabricated versions of these structures.

Sold from rolls of varying widths, it is well suited for flat roofs, those which have a very slight pitch, or for mono-pitch roofs which slope in only one direction. It may also be used as a base for some kinds of shingle. Alternative types of matting may be

An open lattice roof gives partial shade to plants.

Polycarbonate sheeting over a structure attached to a house.

used in conjunction with boarding. Like roofing felt, the material has to be coated with bitumen or some other waterproofing compound to make sure that the structure is watertight.

Remember to check your local building regulations for acceptability. For instance, you may find that two layers of ordinary roofing felt will be required to finish a roof.

Sheeting

Various materials are used to manufacture roof sheeting, some of which are better suited to simple wooden structures than others. Common types include corrugated iron, polycarbonate which may be transparent, opaque or tinted and either smooth or corrugated, and both translucent and coloured fibreglass, although you will get a disturbing colour cast from green and other shades. A tough, lightweight sheeting

made from organic fibres saturated in bitumen is ideal for cabins, cottages, garages and even playhouses and sheds (see page 170, steps 38–40). Although aluminium sheeting is popular for houses in coastal areas where rust can be a problem, it is an expensive option for the average garden structure. Fibrecement, although relatively inexpensive, is not generally suitable because of its weight. It may, however, be used for cabins and larger sheds.

While corrugated sheeting is available in a range of profiles, the simple S-rib is probably the most suitable for the type of structures featured here. Most roof sheeting may be used for flat and ridged roofs (with a minimum pitch of 5° to 10° depending on the material), but it is essential to make certain that the basic roof structure is compatible with whichever type you choose.

Check specifications for the maximum spacing of roof trusses, for purlin and batten sizes, and the standard purlin or batten centres which indicate how far apart they should be spaced.

When laying any type of sheeting, it is important to overlap consecutive lengths to avoid rain and moisture penetration. Holes should generally be pre-drilled and proper roofing screws used to affix the sheeting.

If the roof is pitched, you will need capping along the ridge, and if it abuts the wall of a house, flashing will have to be incorporated to prevent rain from seeping through.

Glass

The traditional material for greenhouses and conservatories, glass is relatively expensive and not usually the first choice of the DIY builder because of its fragility. It can also make interiors excessively warm and humid, especially when the walls and the roofing are both made of glass. While tinted and coated glass will help reduce some of the effects of direct sunlight (including glare and heat), it is also important to know what thickness and glass type (wire-reinforced, laminated and so on) to use. Building regulations usually offer some basic guidelines, but this is one time when professional assistance can be crucial.

Shingles

A common choice for period-style gazebos, shingles (and slightly thicker shakes) were originally made from wood in some countries. Nowadays they are also made from asphalt, which is easier to install and maintain, and from aluminium and fibreglass. If shingles are not easily obtainable in your area, a similar effect may be achieved with either flat slate or clay tiles (see below).

Tiles

A large number of traditional garden structures, including gazebos and summerhouses, are built with tiled roofs. If your house itself is tiled, this may be an excellent choice, as it will

A pole structure with a thatched roof offers sheltered seating.

enable you to match materials. The weight of most tiles is an important factor to be considered, and you will need a sturdy roof structure to support them. In addition, to reinforce the structure properly, battens or purlins will need to be spaced closer together

than those holding roof sheeting. As more timber will be required for this roofing method, your budget must be adjusted to reflect this cost.

A wide variety of tiles is available, although you will have to consider the pitch of the structure; smooth, flat slate tiles depend on a minimum gradient of 15°, while most cement and clay tiles require a pitch of at least 26°, unless a suitable waterproof underlay is used. Ridging tiles will have to be used unless the roof is mono-pitched and slopes in only one direction.

Thatch

A popular choice for open-sided summerhouses and detached pool rooms in some hot-climate countries, thatch is generally used in conjunction with wooden poles rather than sawn timber. An African-style thatched umbrella may also be constructed atop a single pole. Various grasses and reeds are used for this type of roof covering, which should be installed by a properly skilled craftsman.

As thatch is a fairly expensive item in some countries, even in those areas where the grasses grow wild, acrylic thatch has become reasonably popular in recent years.

A traditional-style gazebo, its roof covered with shingle-like tiles.

Wood is probably the most popular material used for children's play structures. Most playhouses are made of wood, and climbing frames are frequently built with debarked and planed poles. Sawn timber or poles may also be used for play frames and elevated decks, which often incorporate swings and step-ladders. Play forts with ramps and ropes are also easily constructed from timber. Simple sandpits may be made with planks of wood, while exterior-grade plywood can be used to make basic shelters, or to clad tree-houses. Smooth, exterior-grade plywood is also a possible material for slides, especially if it is coated with a plastic laminate of some sort. A metal or fibreglass slide could also be attached to the wooden structure.

Of course children will eventually outgrow most play structures. Properly planned and built on a reasonable scale, a playhouse may then be converted into a garden shed.

A well-built tree-house can be used as a den for older children and teenagers, or even as a secluded retreat for adults.

It is particularly important to ensure that the timber used for play structures is smooth and well sanded to avoid scrapes, splinters and snagged clothes. It should be well varnished or painted with a non-toxic and lead-free coating of some kind. Paint can hide defects, like split timber or broken knots, so use an alternative finish for climbing structures or little buildings and hide-outs erected above ground.

For safety's sake, round all hard edges, countersink screws and make absolutely certain no potentially dangerous nails are left even slightly protruding. It stands to reason that all play structures must be properly braced and built so that they are stable. Children weigh less than adults, but when several little people climb onto a structure together, it will have to be sturdy enough to hold their combined weight which can be fairly substantial.

Where space permits, play structures should be located in a separate part of the garden. However, a structure which is intended for toddlers or for very young children should be near to the house where you can keep a watchful eye without necessarily having to abandon household tasks.

Surface materials should be chosen with safety in mind. Where possible, falls must be cushioned. Grass is a universal favourite, even though it does tend to deteriorate under structures and in constant traffic areas. Sand is another possibility, and it is essential to use clean, coarse sand. Some building sands may be suitable, but make certain that lime has not been added as it can be harmful to the skin. Avoid ordinary garden soil as it will become muddy and stain clothes. Bark chips are very popular in some countries as they offer a safe and stain-free landing. Gravel is not a good idea as it tends to graze and can be very messy.

A playhouse on stilts promises hours of fun.

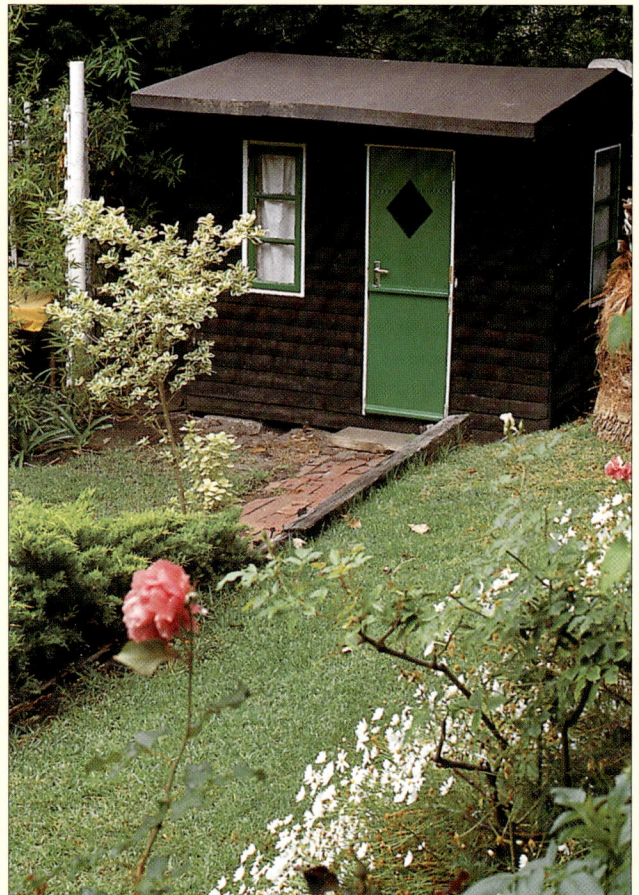

A pretty little playhouse at the bottom of the garden.

INTERIOR FITTINGS AND FIXTURES

A variety of fixtures and fittings, including built-in seating, shelves, cupboards, sanitaryware and various appliances, may be required inside your wooden structure.

A well-organised tool shed will need a workbench, as well as adequate storage facilities for hand tools, machinery and all those small items, like nails, screws and washers, which are inclined to get lost so easily.

A greenhouse will need shelves and working surfaces for potting and to accommodate seedlings and plants which are grown inside it; and a cabin used for sewing will benefit from shelving designed to store fabric and all the other items required.

There is no doubt that built-in storage is more practical than loose shelves and cupboards, especially when you are fitting out a small space. The type of structure you have built will determine the finish required, and in most cases, a handyman with basic carpentry skills will be able to do it himself. Quite basic arrangements are adequate for sheds and playhouses; for more complicated joinery, you may prefer to employ a carpenter.

Before installing cupboards, make certain that all the doors will open easily. In very small wooden structures it may be preferable to curtain the front of a cupboard or to install a sliding door to save space.

LIGHTING

Various aspects of lighting need to be considered, for both the inside and the outside of the structure. Decorative exterior lighting may be used to highlight planting around it, or to illuminate the structure itself. More important is lighting which has a practical value. You need to be able to approach your structure safely at night and to illuminate the seating area if you are using it for entertaining. You will not need many lights, and even one fitting may be adequate; it is best to avoid harsh spotlights and to aim for a reasonably subtle effect. By placing several fittings strategically, you can accentuate plant forms and particular features, and add a soft glow to the surrounding garden.

Of course, an open structure may also be lit from within, creating a dramatic effect which is functional and decorative at the same time. For instance, a pendant lamp hung in the centre of a period-style gazebo will cast interesting shadows and introduce a welcome element of charm and warmth to the structure at night. Workrooms, sheds and cabins may also be illuminated from within so that they can be used after dark.

Light fittings used in enclosed structures will be the same as any others used for dwellings. Those installed in the garden, on patios or in structures which are even partially exposed to rain and moisture must be sealed units. These are available in a selection of styles and it is sensible to choose fittings which will complement whatever you have built.

Connecting the electrics calls for specialised expertise (see page 139). You will need to use suitable water-proof cabling or conduit, preferably buried underground, and to ensure there is earth leakage.

FINISHES AND FINISHING TOUCHES

Having built your own wooden structure, it is important to finish it off properly and attractively. You will, of course, want a finish that protects the wood against weathering and decay, but appearance is equally important.

Steps combining a weatherproof finish with attractive fretwork.

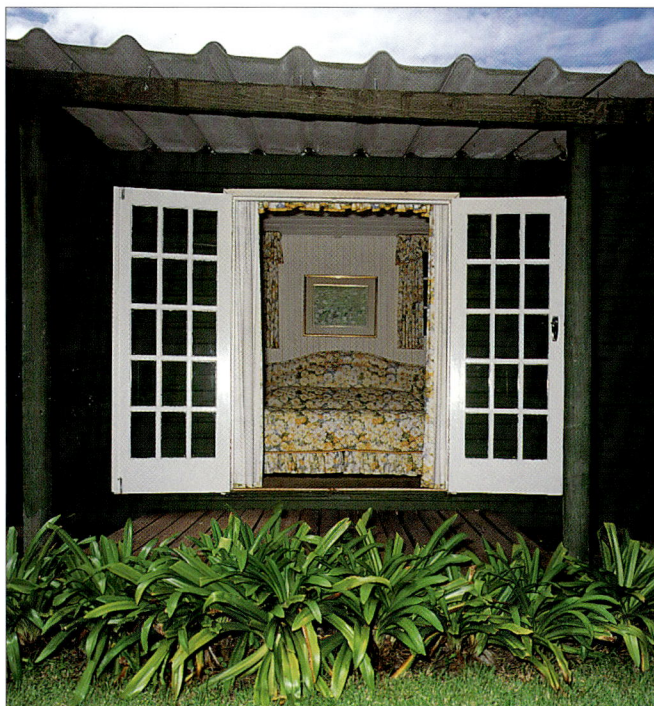

A tiny cabin for guests, charmingly fitted and finished.

Plants and ornaments add charm to an ordinary garden shed.

You should also seal resinous knots to prevent resin from seeping through the paint, and seal nail heads to stop them rusting and discolouring paint.

To retain the grain of the wood but change the colour, use a stain or a polyurethane wood coating. If you cannot find the colour you want, stain the timber before coating it; remember, though, that polyurethane varnishes tend to yellow and so alter the hue.

Decorative detail

Various types of decorative work and trim may be added to wooden structures. Ornamental railings not only finish off a deck and make it safe, but they can also be extremely attractive. Latticework transforms an ordinary pergola into something quite special, while simple wooden cut-outs and more intricate carpenter's work will enhance the plainest building.

If a structure has a verandah or adjacent deck which is covered, consider a decorative trim along the front just below roof height. Cut it out of wood or buy precast decorative cast-aluminium or wrought-iron edging and corner pieces. Another inexpensive idea is to cut a pattern in plywood and glue this to the fascia boards or even affix it directly to the

For instance, a playhouse will be a much more exciting venue if given a touch of colour, perhaps just on the door and window frames.
A plain garden shed can become a charming structure if a decorative wooden cut-out is affixed to the fascias; and if painted, it acquires a more cottage feel and looks less utilitarian and austere. Trelliswork, too, will add to the finish, especially if it supports climbing plants. Consider the area around the structure and decide where to plant or place containers and any other ornaments. You will find that these finishing touches make all the difference.

Finishes

Some finishes are intended primarily for the protection of materials, but it is important to consider their aesthetic value as well. Unless structures are built in a period style or designed to match an existing building, and need to be painted, wood is often simply sealed for protection. This is usually the cheapest option and it may be

the finish you desire, but it can look bland and unimaginative. If you decide to paint the structure, always use a suitable wood primer to give it the added protection required outdoors.

A rudimentary timber cabin, fitted and beautifully decorated for occasional guests.

The key to successful extensions and additions is to match materials and ensure that the old blends with the new. However, wood should be seriously considered even if the existing house is built with bricks and mortar. Although you may not save dramatically on materials, the erection of a timber addition takes less time and requires less labour. Whether you employ others to do the work or intend doing it yourself, this will save you money.

If your house is plastered and painted, a timber-clad extension may be painted the same colour so that it blends in, and the roof structure can be duplicated exactly. Alternatively, wire mesh reinforcing affixed to external boarding allows for a variety of rendered finishes. The mesh must be held about 9 mm from the surface of the board to accommodate the sand and cement render, which should be about 12.5 mm thick. This coating is scratched while it is still wet to provide a key for the finishing coat, which may be as rough or as smooth as you wish. This construction method, developed in the United States, increases the versatility of a timber-frame addition or extension.

For an existing facebrick house, the obvious solution is to clad the exterior walls with matching brickwork. The framework itself is timber, and internal walls the same as those in any other wooden structure. Instead of using timber cladding which is attached to the framework, a brick veneer is laid alongside or adjacent to the timber stud frame. This usually consists of a half-brick wall which does not support the roof structure or any other load, but which is securely braced to the frame.

A timber extension to a facebrick house provides work space for the owner.

Another common option is to use wood for a second storey. Weatherboards complement both facebrick and a plastered or rendered finish, and many timber-frame homes are designed with brick cladding or even solid brick walls beneath and wood above. Rooms created in existing roof spaces are usually constructed with a timber framework.

One of the simpler extensions to build is a glasshouse or conservatory attached to your house. To avoid leaks during wet weather, it is important that it is properly sealed, especially where the addition meets the existing building. Also ensure that it is well ventilated. While any conservatory should be light and bright, it can become excessively hot on sunny days, and shades, awnings and reflective film can help reduce the effect of the sun's glaring rays.

Although standardised modular conservatories are offered by various specialist companies, many of these structures are made with an aluminium framework rather than wood.

ends of battens or purlins (see page 170). It takes little effort with a jigsaw, yet will elevate most wooden buildings from the mundane in an instant.

Plants
Planting invariably improves the appearance of any structure. Many structures are planned with climbing plants and creepers in mind (see page 146). Flower beds should be considered as part of the garden plan as a whole, but also in relation to the structure.

Plant on either side of the door leading into a cabin, or on three sides of a pergola. Introduce pathways leading to the structure and plant a herbaceous border on both sides.

Tubs, pots and barrels will add character to a deck, while a window box will introduce colour and enliven the front of a shed or playhouse. Hanging baskets are a charming addition to a pergola; just be sure they are not in the direct line of prevailing winds or they could be damaged.

Ornaments
There is no need to be ostentatious, but some form of ornamentation can add an element of originality and individuality to a simple garden structure. A weathercock on top of a gazebo, a statue at the end of a patio or a plaque or decorative panel mounted on the structure itself are all possiblilities. Remember that any ornament chosen should be in keeping with the structure and the garden, in style as well as in scale.

The essential material for any wooden structure is, of course, timber; the type chosen will depend largely on what you are planning to build. While poles are suitable for pergolas and some rustic structures, most buildings will be constructed from sawn and often planed (dressed) hardwood or softwood. In addition to the timber, you will probably need concrete for foundations as well as the necessary nails, screws and bolts to fasten the various components. If there is glazing to be done, you will require glass; for roofing, you will need sheeting, tiles, slates or thatch (see pages 146–149).

If you plan to work or even stay overnight in the wooden structure, internal cladding and insulation materials are essential. See pages 144–145 for a range of cladding ideas.

TIMBER

The exact wood chosen for various garden projects will vary depending on what is available in your area as well as what is best for local weather conditions. In general, the choice is between softwoods and hardwoods, some of which are better suited to particular structures than others.

A typical example of softwood cladding.

You will also need to decide whether you want to use poles or sawn (and sometimes planed or dressed) timber.

Whatever your choice, it is essential to buy wood that is structurally sound and will be durable. Even if you are erecting the smallest shed or lean-to, it is good building practice to select timber treated with preservatives for structural use. Also consider the intended function of the structure and the method of construction to be undertaken. Remember that the workability and nail-holding capacity of different woods vary.

Once you have bought the timber for the project, store it under cover until you need it. It will deteriorate rapidly if left exposed outdoors or in damp conditions. If you have to leave it outside, stack it at least 300 mm above the ground with spacer blocks to aid the movement of air, and cover with plastic or a tarpaulin.

Softwood

Cut from coniferous trees, softwoods are easier to saw and plane than most hardwoods. Trees felled commercially for construction throughout the world include pine, red and white cedar, fir, larch, spruce, redwood and some cypresses. Since different species have different qualities, you will find that certain softwoods are more hardy than others. Redwood, for instance, is durable and renowned for its resistance to decay, while the wood from some quick-growing pines requires frequent maintenance if it is to last for any length of time.

Your choice should always be based on the best quality available at the most economical price.

Hardwood

Generally more costly than softwood, hardwood comes from various broadleafed tree species. Some of the more common types used in various parts of the world include mahogany, oak, several eucalypts, ash, elm, balau and meranti, a slightly softer hardwood.

Although many people limit their use of hardwood in the garden to outdoor furniture, several species are particularly well suited to deck building.

Even though the classification 'hardwood' is a botanical one and does not refer to the durability, strength or 'hard' qualities of the wood, hardwoods are often tough and very difficult to cut. This means that most need to be pre-drilled when nailing.

Poles

Ideal for pergolas and upright supports of decks and rustic shelters, poles have an intriguing rusticity which makes them suitable for arches, bridges and other structures. While this type of timber may be combined with sawn wood (see below), its versatility should not be underestimated. For instance, if you need flat sections, you can use split poles or even boards cut in a loglap profile. Furthermore, they are suitable supports for thatch or even for some kinds of roof sheeting.

There is usually a choice between poles that have been debarked (and branches removed), and those that have been machined to a smooth surface and reasonably regular size. Poles that have not been machined will taper, quite obviously, from top to bottom, and two poles will never be identical. Even those that have been milled are slightly irregular in diameter. This characteristic adds a rustic appeal, but will not suit all structures.

Sawn timber

Most timber sold commercially for construction purposes is sawn in the mill to form planks, beams, battens, posts and so on. Although rough-sawn timber is widely available, many people prefer to buy it planed all round (PAR) or dressed all round (DAR); this is a bit more expensive, but it has a smoother finish which makes it easier to work with. To finish a garden structure built with PAR (DAR) timber simply give it a light sanding and then oil, seal or paint it.

Waney board, which has an uneven edge with some of the bark remaining, is a less common choice, but one that will cut costs if suitable. If it is available, you may be able to use it to clad a rustic shed or workroom.

The lengths and sections of all timber components must be compatible with the scale of the structure itself. For instance, the garden shed featured on pages 178–179 uses 70 mm x 70 mm PAR (DAR) upright posts, but these will not be sturdy enough for much larger structures. Roof timbers must be chosen with the proposed covering in mind, as this will affect the design of the roof as well as the dimensions of purlins which support roof sheeting, and battens supporting tiles.

Standard sizes do vary, but this is seldom a major issue. In fact most suppliers will always quote nominal sizes, without taking the wastage lost during planing into account.

Timber sizes are given as a guide in the plans featured on pages 178–189; if the exact dimensions are not available, you can have timber planed to size, which can be expensive, or simply use the nearest size available and adapt accordingly.

If your structure requires long pieces of timber you may have a problem, as world supplies of long lengths have become increasingly scarce. An international solution, based on a German invention, is finger-jointed wood, accepted worldwide as a strong and reliable method of lengthening structural timbers in the factory. Alternatively, you can buy laminated timber, which is more expensive but considerably stronger and more stable than wood sawn from a single log. It is also reasonably simple to join two lengths by bolting, screwing, nailing or using timber connectors.

If the necessary thickness is not available, you can probably glue and clamp two lengths together. Just be

A timber umbrella (see plan on page 54) on a waterfront deck.

sure to use a suitable waterproof woodworking adhesive which will resist temperature changes and moisture.

Quality
While timber is graded throughout the world, specific gradings will vary. Certain universal standards do, however, apply.

For instance, all newly felled 'green' timber contains a large percentage of water and the wood must be dried to strengthen it. In factories this is done either in huge kilns or by air seasoning, where it is allowed to dry naturally. Both processes kill the spores of fungi and destroy pests including termites and beetles, as well as their larvae and eggs. Be guided by the grading; poor grades of wood may still contain a high degree of moisture.

Avoid twisted, bowed or split lengths of wood as these defects can affect the stability of any structure. Sawn wood with an excessively sloping grain should also be avoided as it is more likely to warp, while too many knots, especially hard, dead knots from old branches, are liable to fall out and create points of weakness.

Preservatives
Some wood, such as heart-grade redwood (where it is available), is naturally resistant to fungal decay and infestation, but the best advice to DIY builders is to use timber which has been pressure-treated in the mill.

If you do not treat wood adequately it will rot, and insects, termites and other parasites will eventually destroy it. On the other hand, if it is treated according to recognised specifications, it will be as durable as most other materials.

There are three basic types of preservative, coal tar creosote being the cheapest and probably the best known to DIYers. Although creosote is suitable for outdoor use and useful for coating the ends of poles and posts in the ground, it is highly toxic to plants and will cause some materials, such as shadecloth (see page 146), to rot. In addition, it has an unpleasant smell and cannot successfully be overcoated with paint or any other finish.

Certain types of organic solvent-based preservatives, including PCP (pentachlorophenol), which is banned in some countries, and TBTO (tributyl tin oxide), are also toxic.

Water-based preservatives are usually colourless and odourless, and can be easily overcoated with a finish. However some of these products, such as CCA (chromated copper arsenate), which is commonly used for pressure-treating poles and roof timbers, give the wood a slightly green tinge. Although CCA can be used outdoors, many of the water-based preservatives (including boron) are suitable only for interior wood. Toxicity levels vary, but any treated wood should never be burnt in an open fire or used for a barbecue (see page 163).

CONCRETE, MORTAR AND PLASTER

Concrete and mortar, as well as various plasters (renders) and floor toppings, are necessary for foundations, footings and any solid slab floor.

Mortar is used for bricklaying, rendering external walls and screeding concrete floors. Any building that has internal plasterboard cladding may be skimmed with gypsum plaster or with special skimming plaster.

The common components of concrete and mortar are cement and sand. Stone is added to concrete to add strength and give bulk to the mixture. Lime mixed into mortar will improve its plasticity and cohesiveness and aid water retention. This helps avoid cracking once it hardens.

Cement

Although there are various types of cement, Portland cement is most commonly used. Packaged in 50 kg or 40 kg (and sometimes smaller) sealed paper sacks, it hardens when mixed with water and gains its strength by curing, which necessitates being kept damp for a period of time. While it is in storage, cement must be kept dry. Never leave bags outside, and stack them above floor level.

Aggregate

Various aggregates are mixed with cement to form concrete and mortar. Generally, material that can pass

Screeding a floor with mortar.

through a 4.75 mm sieve, like sand, is referred to as fine aggregate, and coarser material (usually crushed stone) as coarse aggregate. Mortar contains only fine aggregate, while concrete includes both forms.

Suppliers of coarse aggregate usually supply what they refer to as single-sized stone. Crushed stone is sieved and natural pebbles screened to size. Gradings may differ slightly, but the most common size used by DIY builders is 19 or 20 mm, and all quantities given in the plans on pages 178-189 refer to this size. Although it is cheaper to buy stone in bulk, it is also available loosely bagged from most shops that stock builders' supplies.

Sand, available from the same sources as stone, is also graded and should contain particles of various sizes. It must be clean and should not contain any clay or vegetable matter. You need fairly coarse or 'sharp' sand for concrete, and softer sand for mixing mortar (used for render and screeds). Bedding sand beneath paving bricks should also be coarse, while that used between the joints should be fine.

Most natural sand is suitable for concrete and mortar. River sand is usually quite clean and free of clay, while pit sand, although well-graded, may have too much clay. Beach sand can only be used if it is thoroughly washed and processed.

Water

Water is a vital ingredient in concrete and mortar, and is not usually measured: just enough is added to the dry materials to make them workable. It is vital to use clean, pure water. Sea water may be used for unreinforced concrete (it will cause reinforcing to rust), but the salt will leave a white, powdery deposit on the surface. A good rule of thumb is that if you can drink the water, you can use it for building.

Lime

Hydrated builders' lime, sold in 25 kg bags, improves the cohesiveness and plasticity of mortar, especially when coarse sand is used in the mixture. Otherwise use a proprietary plasticiser.

Agricultural lime, road lime and quicklime (calcium oxide) are not suitable for this purpose.

Concrete

The properties of concrete depend on the proportions of cement, sand, crushed stone and water in the mixture. The proportions used depend on local conditions and the type of work you are doing, though low-strength concrete is usually adequate for the kind of construction described here. For foundation footings and solid slabs, combine the dry materials in a 1:4:4 cement:sand:stone ratio and add enough water to produce a workable mix (use a higher proportion of cement if you are building a large structure, or if the concrete is to be exposed to the elements). You will need about 230 kg of cement for every cubic metre of concrete (or more if you are making a stronger mix).

Dry mixed materials are available for minor concrete projects, but these are relatively expensive. For larger projects, ready-mixed concrete is often a viable proposition. You will, however, have to order a substantial quantity, and this must be placed as soon as it arrives.

Mortar mixes

Mortar is the conventional name given to various cement, sand and water mixes, and is used for bricklaying, rendering and floor toppings or screeds. Hydrated lime is often added to the mix to make it more pliable.

As with concrete, the proportions of dry materials vary when you mix mortar. You can rely on a cement:sand mix of 1:4 for any bricklaying or rendering required here. Concrete slabs may also be screeded with a 1:4 mix. If you are adding lime to the mortar, combine it in the ratio 2:1:8 (cement:lime:sand).

Plasters

Exterior render (see above) is some-times referred to as plaster, although the term refers more correctly to gypsum plasters for indoor use only. Mixed with water and applied with a trowel, plaster is used over bare brick, cement render or plasterboard. There

There are various types, including special finishing or skimming plaster which is also available ready mixed in buckets. Although they can be messy to apply, both gypsum and skimming plasters dry rapidly and create a really good, smooth finish.

INSULATION

Insulation can make the most basic structure habitable. It can also increase the potential uses a garden building can have. There are various insulation materials available, including fibreglass blankets, aluminium foil, treated vermiculite granules and loose fill sold in fibre form. Most may be placed in the ceiling space or fixed into dry-wall panelling. Fibreglass and foil are ideal for garden structures.

Fibreglass

Blankets of fibreglass are useful for both ceiling and wall insulation. Just trim the sheets to size with a utility knife or panel saw, then lay them in the ceiling space, or position them in the walls before the internal cladding is secured (see page 175). Fibreglass is easy to work with, but it can cause skin irritation so it is best to wear gloves and a mask.

Aluminium foil

Reinforced aluminium foil is manufactured in several grades, sometimes with a plastic vapour barrier on one side. It can be attached directly to both wall and ceiling panels prior to installation. If it is to be positioned once the roof trusses are in place, it should be affixed between the rafters and the purlins or battens with the waterproofing membrane uppermost.

FASTENERS

There is a wide range of fasteners and connectors suitable for use when building wooden structures. Nails are the most common, but screws, bolts and various special connectors are also useful. In addition, you may need reinforcing rods, hoop iron strapping and pieces of angle iron. Wherever possible, use rust-proof fasteners made from galvanised and anodised metal, brass, stainless steel or aluminium.

Aluminium foil is an effective material for insulating roofs.

Nails

Generally sold by weight and length, nails make a quick, strong and permanent joint provided the correct type is used. Various shapes and sizes are designed for different types and thicknesses of material; oval wire nails have an unobtrusive head, making them suitable for the attachment of floorboards, and round wire nails are intended for fairly rough carpentry. Masonry nails fix timber to concrete or brickwork, and ring-shank or twisted-shank nails will secure roof sheeting.

When joining two pieces of wood of roughly the same thickness, make sure the nail goes at least half-way through the second piece; if one section is much thinner, use a nail that is 2½ to 3 times the thickness of this piece.

Screws

Screws come in a variety of sizes and gauges. They are generally sold by number and diameter. Head shapes may be raised, rounded or countersunk, and the slot is either straight or crossed in one of three patterns – Phillips, Supadriv or Pozidriv. Common gauges range from no. 4 (which indicates a shank diameter of 2.7 mm) to no. 12 (5.6 mm). Each gauge is available in a range of lengths.

Apart from ordinary wood screws and chipboard screws (which have a deeper thread and do not taper as much), there are special-purpose screws. Coach screws are useful when erecting wooden structures. They have either a square or a hexagonal head. Sold by diameter rather than gauge number, they are tightened with a spanner instead of a screwdriver.

Bolts

Bolts, in a variety of sizes, are the usual choice for heavy-duty fixing. Coach (or cuphead) bolts have a rounded head and a short thread, while hexagonal bolts often have a thread which extends the full length of the shaft. Nuts and bolts are tightened with spanners. Rawl bolts are a good choice when bolting timber to bricks or concrete, as they expand in masonry to anchor your wood securely.

Staples

Heavy-duty staples are used with a staple gun for attaching awning material to pergolas or plywood to panels. They are 'shot' into place and then hammered lightly until the staple is flush with the surface.

Special connectors

There is a wide range of metal connectors and fastening plates such as joist hangers, post anchors, pole and truss hangers, angle brackets of various shapes, and spiky nail plates. They are usually made of galvanised or rust-proof metal and most of them are pre-drilled for easy use.

You do not have to be a highly skilled carpenter to erect most simple wooden structures. Nevertheless, your task will be simplified by using the correct tools. You should also master certain basic construction techniques which will help you to build something that looks professional, and that will last.

TOOLS

An extensive toolkit is unneccesary for most projects, but there are certain tools which are essential. If you need to buy tools, choose the best you can afford. If you are unlikely to use expensive equipment again, it is more sensible to hire rather than buy.

Setting out and levelling

All structures must be correctly set out before building work commences. Unless you are building an octagonal or hexagonal gazebo, you will need to ensure that all corners are square. The site or upper surface of foundations must be flat and level.

The most important tool you will need is a good quality retractable steel tape,

preferably with a locking mechanism. You will also need a metal builder's square and a spirit level with horizontal and vertical indicators. Choose a level that is at least 1.2 m long.

One of the cheapest and most useful tools is a water level, made with a length of transparent tubing. It works on the principle that water finds its own level and is an invaluable aid when setting out on a slope, establishing drainage levels or working out the correct height of poles and posts (see page 168). A dumpy level is ideal but is a particularly pricey tool.

You will need a pick if you are excavating hard or stony ground and a spade to dig foundations. Chalk (or even flour) may be used to mark the outline for footings, but it is better to use pegs and line to lay out the site accurately. Although you can buy pegs, any bits of wood may be used and ordinary string may be substituted for builder's line.

Where compaction of the ground is necessary, use a punner or tamper. This tool, made with a block of wood

or a lump of concrete set at the base of a pole is usually quite adequate. If the area to be flattened is fairly large, or if it is necessary to bring fill on to the site to level the ground, you may prefer to hire a compacting machine.

An auger is useful for boring holes if you are using the pole (or stick-frame) method of constructing a building (see page 166). It can also be used for sinking poles into the ground for a pergola, or for creating tube forms to contain concrete footings for decking post anchors. There are both manual and power-driven machines, but if concrete is to be poured around the posts once they are in place, make sure the holes are sufficiently wide to accommodate it.

Concrete and brickwork

Some of the tools used for setting out, including spirit levels and squares, are also indispensable for laying both concrete and bricks. Additional basic requirements include a builder's wheelbarrow and shovel for shifting dry materials and mixing concrete and mortar, and straightedges for levelling concrete and checking brick courses.

Of course, you will need trowels for bricklaying, plastering and possibly flattening concrete. A wooden float is essential for screeding a floor.

A brick hammer with a chisel end is useful for cutting bricks but an angle grinder is easier to use. Another tool used by bricklayers is the corner block, often home-made, which helps ensure that brick courses are level and even. Cut two L-shaped blocks from wood, saw a slot and groove through each and wrap builder's string around them. They can then be hooked on to either end of a brick wall at the same height, and held in place with builder's line to establish correct levels. As foundation walls are usually the only brickwork required for a wooden structure, these blocks are not essential.

A basic toolkit, including both hand and power tools.

A belt sander will save you hours of hard work.

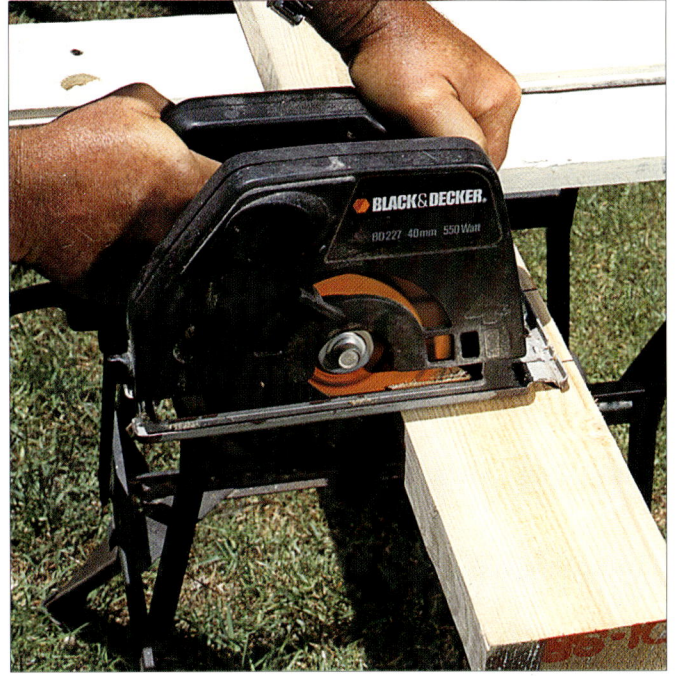
A circular saw will cut quickly, smoothly and in a straight line.

A concrete mixer is worth hiring if there is a lot of concrete to be placed, as hand mixing can be hard work. They are referred to by their capacity (which is measured in imperial units); a 10/7, for instance, can process 10 cu ft (or 0.3 m³) of dry materials in a reasonable period of time, to produce 7 cu ft (or 0.2 m³) of concrete.

Woodwork

Both hand and power tools are required in the carpenter's toolkit. You may be able to get by with the bare minimum, but there is no doubt that the better equipped you are, the easier it will be, and the result will be a more professional-looking structure.

First and foremost you will need suitable cutting tools, including saws, although you certainly do not need every type available. Although you can get by without the electric models, both power jigsaws and power circular saws make light work of many jobs, cutting more quickly and smoothly than handsaws. While a circular saw will cut in a straight line at any angle, a jigsaw may be used to make curved cuts, and is useful for creating interesting cut-out patterns, bargeboards and fascias (see page 171). On the other hand, it is easier to be more accurate with a

handsaw. For fine work, a stocky tenon (back) saw is invaluable, while a crosscut saw or smaller panel saw is the answer for slicing the ends of posts, battens, floorboards and so on. If you are going to be working with logs or poles, it is probably worth investing in a bowsaw. You may also want a ripsaw, designed for cutting along the grain of wood, and a general-purpose hacksaw, which will cut any metal you may need.

Planes, rasps and files are useful for shaping and finishing, while chisels are invaluable for trimming wood and for cutting notches and housings. While an electric planer is ideal for smoothing and sizing timber and bevelling or angling edges, you are unlikely to need one, especially for the projects in this book. If you have access to an electric router, you could use it for cutting grooves and rebates or for creating attractive chamfered edges on railings and so on, but this is not an essential tool for these projects.

While you will make use of an ordinary tape to measure wood, and a standard spirit level to ensure that it stands perfectly plumb or is flat and level, a small try square or carpenter's combination square (incorporating a spirit level vial) is a very useful tool to

have. A chalk line is ideal for marking the straight cutting lines on wood, especially when building with decking slats and floorboards.

You will need a claw hammer for driving nails and extracting bent or incorrectly angled nails, screwdrivers for ordinary wood screws, and spanners to tighten bolts and coach screws. Unless you plan to nail the entire structure together, you would be advised to invest in a good quality drill. A heavy-duty bit brace or hand drill will suffice, but an electric drill, even a small battery-powered model, is an invaluable tool to have. Do not forget to have a variety of appropriate wood drill bits on hand.

Another useful tool to consider buying is an electric sander. A belt sander may be used to level planks and boards which have been smoothly planed (or dressed). The smaller orbital sander is ideal for finishing a variety of small surfaces which might otherwise have to be sanded by hand.

Finally, you will need to have a flat and secure working surface. If you do not have a workbench in your tool shed, a portable workbench with built-in clamps is the answer. These usually fold flat, and may be packed out of the way when not in use.

SETTING OUT

Whatever you are going to build and whichever method of timber construction you use, it is essential to spend time laying out the site correctly.

Unless the structure is to be circular or have acute or obtuse angles, it is vital to ensure that all corners are square. This is a fundamental building principle which will help you achieve a professional finish.

With pegs and builder's line or string, mark the perimeter, using a steel square to create a 90° angle at each corner. Alternatively, you can use a larger home-made square, using what is known as the 3:4:5 method. For this, three pieces of wood are hammered together to form a right-angled triangle; the two outside lengths should measure units of three and four respectively (say 900 mm and 1.2 m), while the side which cuts the corners should measure a proportional unit of five (in this case, 1.5 m). If the structure is sufficiently large, it is ideal to measure 3 m, 4 m and 5 m respectively. You can also check the accuracy of your angle with this method, using the steel square and a tape, or by staking the required measurements along the string line and then measuring across the angle. Once you have done this, double-check for square, measuring the layout diagonally from opposite corners; the diagonal measurements should be exactly the same.

Once the basic layout has been established, mark the position of any foundation footings with chalk or flour (which is usually cheaper).

Levels

One advantage of pole buildings is their versatility on sloping ground. These may be structures built on a stick framework or decking, taking the form of a pole platform without sides or superstructure. What you need to establish is the ideal level for the floor and the best position for all the upright supports, avoiding rocky ground.

If you are working on a difficult site, you may require the services of an engineer, but for a gradual slope it is not difficult to determine these positions. Although many professionals use a dumpy level or a transit-theodolite, which is a surveyor's usual tool, the simplest and cheapest way to establish these points is by using a water level (see page 158).

Decide where the upright posts are to be positioned, and where the highest point of the floor structure will be (allowing for joists and bearers), then mark where bearers (or girders) should be secured by using a water level. This is done in the same way as illustrated on page 42, using the highest point as a datum level.

FOUNDATIONS AND CONCRETEWORK

Irrespective of the type of floor your structure has, poles or wall panels must be securely anchored on a solid foundation. This may be a solid slab (see page 164), or individual footings. Either way, the depth and dimensions of the foundation must be designed so that the building will withstand all possible loads – weighty materials, wind uplift, rain, hail and snow.

Setting·out a structure using the 3:4:5 method.

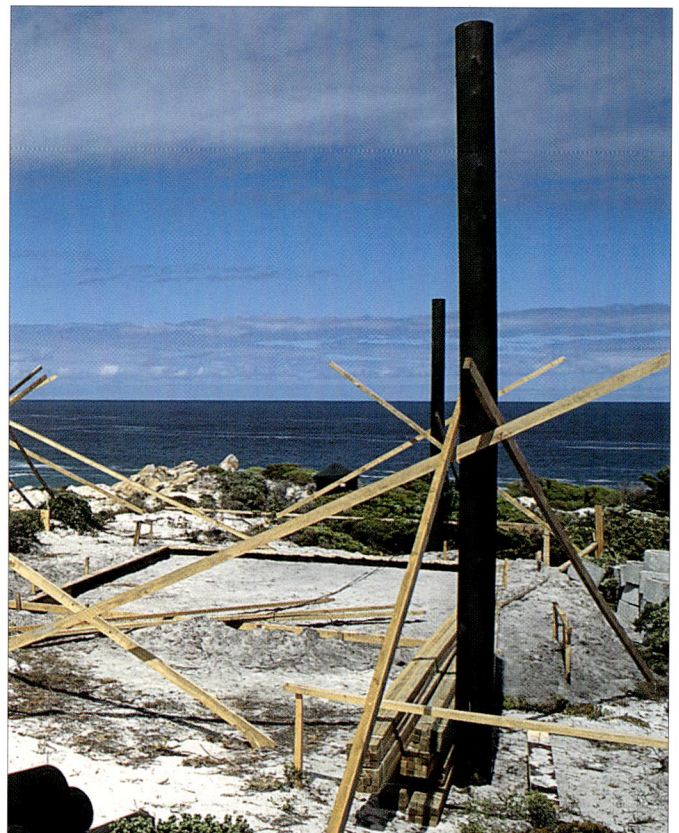

Upright poles are set in footings and braced in position.

The stilts of this A-frame play structure are securely anchored in concrete.

Concretework

The quantities of dry materials recommended for this type of concretework are given on page 156. Use a builder's bucket or clean 25 litre drum to measure accurately; it does not pay to rely on guesswork.

You can mix the materials with either a spade or a concrete mixer. It is hard work by spade, but unless you have a reasonably large volume to mix, it is not worth hiring a mixer.

To mix by spade, you will need a clean, level surface or a builder's wheelbarrow. Combine the cement and sand first, making a hollow in the centre for the water. Pour in a little at a time, shovelling the materials from the outside to the centre, until they are well mixed and have a soft, porridgy consistency. Add the stone last, with just a little more water if necessary.

When using a mixer, it is advisable to load the stone first, together with a little water. This prevents the cement from building up around the blades. Add the cement next, and then the sand and enough water to obtain a workable consistency. It should not take more than about two minutes.

The concrete mixture must not be allowed to dry out before it is poured. Since dry soil will absorb the moisture from wet concrete, it is essential to dampen the base of the hole before placing the mixture.

It is a simple matter to place concrete in footings; use the back of your spade or shovel to push it firmly into the holes to level the upper surface. The trickiest part is ensuring that the posts remain absolutely vertical.

If you are throwing a slab, you will need a straightedge to compact the concrete, using a chopping action to expel the air. At the same time, level the slab with a smooth, sawing action. Allow the concrete to set, ideally keeping it moist for five to seven days. This will aid curing and result in a really strong, solid base for the wooden structure.

It is usually necessary to screed the surface of a concrete floor to give it a smooth finish; this process is illustrated step-by-step on page 175.

Footings

If poles or posts are set directly into the earth, the hole (and consequently the length of timber underground) must be considerably deeper than if it is encased in concrete. Furthermore, it is essential to compact the soil at the bottom of the hole to minimise settling.

Although decks are often built on pier footings, with upright posts anchored on to the upper surface of the concrete, this is not recommended for larger structures. This type of footing should be at least 200 mm deep; a tube form, made from cardboard, will enable you to leave a portion of the footing protruding above ground.

Suggested foundation sizes are given in all the plans on pages 178-189, but these presume you are building on flat and stable ground where abnormal weather conditions are unusual.

If regular frost, snow and strong winds are a factor, all footings must be dug deeper. Numerous tables are available giving figures for greater loads; alternatively consult an expert or professional engineer for advice.

Where a structure is built on sloping land, it may be necessary to embed posts and poles deeper into the ground on the uphill slope for extra strength. The tops of all posts, apart from those at the apex of a roof, will be at the same level, but more timber will be visible at the lowest points under the floor level.

Foundation slabs

If you plan to cast a slab on solid, stable ground, it may be sufficient merely to compact the area thoroughly with a punner prior to pouring the concrete. If the ground is not firm and reasonably level, you may have to create a solid sub-base with sand and hardcore consisting of broken bricks, stones and rubble. This must be well compacted before covering with DPC and pouring the concrete.

The depth of a slab will also relate to the size and weight of the structure it will have to support. While a depth of 100 mm is adequate for a pergola or other light structure, you will need to throw a deeper strip foundation around the perimeter of a slab for a building.

A nail gun is used by the professionals.

A combination square is useful for marking cutting edges.

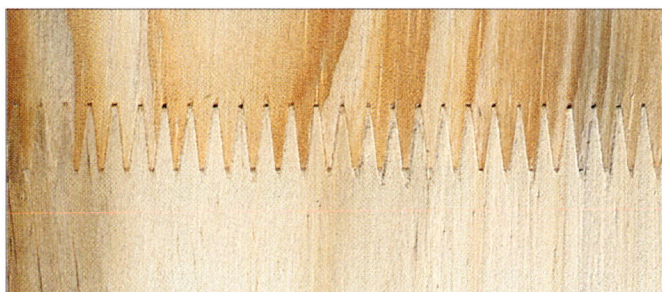
Finger joints are glued at the sawmill (see page 29).

CARPENTRY

Cutting timber and joining it to form various garden structures is reasonably elementary. Nevertheless, it is very important to ensure that the materials you are working with have the correct dimensions. Measure the wood two or three times; cut it once.

It also pays to be meticulous when working out your requirements. If you buy the wrong timber, you could end up having to redesign whatever you are planning to build, or even worse, find that it collapses during the first strong wind. It is usually advisable to buy timber that is a little longer than needed and cut it to size, rather than land up with pieces that are too short.

If you are uncertain about the optimum spacing of poles, posts and other timbers for your particular structure, local manufacturers or suppliers may be able to advise; otherwise seek professional assistance before you tackle your project (see pages 135, 137 and 138).

Cutting wood

Although you will find it easier to make a perfectly square, straight cut if you clamp the wood to a workbench, this is obviously not possible when you are sawing timber that has already been erected. You may have to ask somebody to support the other end of the wood. Start the cut in the correct place and then continue sawing in the same line. If you are working with a handsaw, make a small nick in the edge of the wood by drawing the saw towards you. The angle used to work different saws varies slightly (a flatter position is used with a tenon saw), but the movement is much the same. Whether you are using a handsaw or power tool, do not force the blade through the wood; let the blade or the machine do the work.

Working with electric saws takes practice and confidence. Remember that the narrow blade of a jigsaw cuts on the up stroke, so to minimise splintering, place boards and planks right-side down on the workbench.

Drilling

Wood is reasonably soft and easy to drill; the secret is to make the hole in the right place, and to prevent the bit from splintering the wood.

There are various drill bits available, but you will generally use either twist bits or wood bits. For screws with countersunk heads, you will need a countersink, and to make larger holes, a flat bit. Whichever drill bit you use, it must be the right size in relation to the nail, screw or bolt you are using. It is important that pre-drilled holes are the correct depth and that they align with one another. For screws, you will usually have to drill a pilot hole (which is shorter and narrower than the screw) in one piece of wood and a wider clearance hole in the other for the shank. If you are drilling pilot holes for nails, these should also be smaller than the nail itself.

Joining and fixing

Although some gazebo designs might require relatively complex joints and some intricate carpenter's work, most garden structures rely on quite simple joints. Many are nailed together with only simple butt joints.

Where the wood overlaps another piece, a T- or cross-butt joint may sometimes be used, but halving joints are generally more effective. A half-lap joint, where the ends of two lengths of timber are notched so that the pieces slot together, is used either to lengthen two shorter pieces or, if they are joined at right angles, to create a neat corner. A cross-halving joint is ideal for railings round the sides of a deck and for some pergola beams. Mitre joints are used where the ends of timber are cut at a 45° angle resulting in a 90° joint where the pieces abut neatly to form a corner. (See also page 177.)

Working with saws, nails, power tools, chemically-treated wood and with heavy timber can be potentially dangerous, so it pays to be sensible and to take precautions. If you stay alert and pay attention to what you are doing at all times, you can avert needless accidents.

Clothing

Although there is usually no need for DIY timber builders to don hard hats, boots and gloves, it is important to dress sensibly. Avoid loose clothing or jewellery that could become caught in the moving parts of power tools or machinery, tie back long hair, and wear gloves, boots and so on when necessary. Safety goggles may seem unnecessary, but they are invaluable in certain circumstances. A face mask is also a good idea where the job involves dust and grit, especially if you are sawing or planing wood that has been pressure-treated with toxic chemicals.

Treated timber

While structural timber should be treated with preservatives, there are certain precautions that should be taken when working with it.
• Wear a face mask (see above), especially if you are working in a confined space, as frequent or prolonged inhalation of the sawdust from treated wood can be harmful.

• If possible work outdoors so that airborne sawdust can disperse.
• Always wash yourself thoroughly after working with treated timber.
• Sawdust inevitably settles on clothing, so wash it separately.
• Never burn treated timber in an open fire, an indoor fireplace or on a barbecue. The toxic fumes may be dangerous if inhaled and the chemicals can affect food.

Preservatives

When applying preservatives to untreated timber, extreme caution is necessary. Toxicity varies but most preservatives are poisonous to humans, animals and plants, at least until they are thoroughly dry. Some are highly flammable, so do not smoke while working with these chemicals.

Tools and equipment

Always choose the correct tool for the job. If you do not have the right equipment, hire it. Always keep the work area properly illuminated, and clean up after every job. Cluttered spaces and untidy workbenches invite injury.

Power tools

Before using a power tool, check that its voltage requirements are compatible with your power supply. A power source with voltage greater than that specified for the tool can result in serious injury. Also keep

children away from these tools and store them so that little hands are not tempted to use them.

Power tools must be well maintained. Keep them clean and check the cords regularly for damage. It is especially important to keep handles dry and free from grease, and to avoid using these tools in a damp environment or near flammable gases and liquids. If you do not have a helper, use a clamp or vice to hold the timber while working. Always disconnect tools when they are not in use. Remove adjusting keys from tools before switching on.

Construction and maintenance

All structures must be safe. Make certain that all exposed wood is smooth and that, wherever possible, edges and corners are rounded. This is particularly important where a structure is intended for children. Check the structure regularly to ensure that it is sound, and make sure screws and nails do not protrude. Any rusty fasteners should be removed and replaced if they are in any way hazardous. If repairs are necessary, do them straight away, before the structure deteriorates further and becomes dangerous, and repairs become more expensive. Any rotten or badly split wood should be replaced, and surface areas should be regularly oiled, varnished or painted.

Bridges must be safe, stable and sturdy. Any timber submerged in a pond must not be treated with toxic chemicals.

STEP-BY-STEP BUILDING METHODS

While the basic techniques used when building wooden structures are discussed on pages 158 to 162 these detailed instructions take them a step further. Basic carpentry skills are illustrated, and two construction methods for garden buildings are shown. These guidelines incorporate two different floor types (a concrete slab which may be screeded and a suspended wooden floor) as well as decking, installation of doors and windows, and erection of a simple roof structure. They also show how to build basic internal walls (or partitioning) and how to insulate walls.

Even though the presentation follows construction of two simple buildings, these instructions are not intended as projects. Instead, they can be adapted and used when tackling the full range of garden structures, from the simplest arbour or pergola to a greenhouse, utilitarian shed or habitable cabin.

The pole structure illustrates a building method which is ideal not only for sheds and barns, but also for smaller-scale playhouses and even for animal shelters. The roof structure can be adapted for a pergola with a pitched roof, and the deck built as a freestanding feature.

The stud structure, built with pre-assembled panels, illustrates a method commonly used for garden buildings of all sizes. This is also an approach often suggested for DIY projects. Since the method is easily adapted, assembly of a typical panel is also explained.

CONCRETE SLAB

Whether you are casting concrete for foundation footings to support a simple timber structure, or for a solid slab which will form the floor of a garden building to be built from wood, the principles are exactly the same. Of course, if the slab is to act as a foundation, it must be designed and constructed to carry the load of the timber (and any other materials) used. Also, the method of construction will affect the size and type of all foundations and footings (see pages 160 to 161).

This slab supports a stud structure (see pages 173 to 176), and the 75 mm thick slab is laid on well-compacted fill. Low-strength concrete (cement, sand and stone mixed in the ratio 1:4:4), suitable for most garden buildings, is used.

1 Build the foundation walls on concrete and allow the mortar to set. Fill with hardcore and sand, moisten and compact well with a punner, leaving about 75 mm of blockwork above the fill.

2 Spread polythene over the hardcore, overlapping all joins by 100 mm. This damp-proof membrane forms a moisture barrier and is an essential measure to take against rising damp.

3 Working in batches, mix sufficient cement with sand and 19 mm stone in the ratio 1:4:4 and enough water to make it workable. Pour the mixture over plastic to top of blockwork to form the slab.

4 Use a straight-edged length of wood to compact and level the concrete with the top of the foundation walls. If the slab is not square and level, the wall panels will not fit.

5 While you are laying the slab, bend and insert galvanised hoop-iron strapping or steel strips in the concrete (or hollow blocks) at regular intervals around the perimeter, to coincide with the studs.

Pole-building is one of the oldest and most basic systems of construction. The method demands minimal preparation of the site, even on sloping ground, and structures are quick and easy to erect. Although basic carpentry skills (including experience with power tools and a knowledge of fixing and fastening techniques) will be a help, even an unskilled person can tackle a simple pole structure successfully.

The versatility of this building method creates many design possibilities, and it may be used for a structure of any size. The one illustrated here is only 7.5 m² in area, and has a covered deck 1 m wide. It is about 2 m high, which is quite adequate for a potting shed, tool shed or playhouse. A layout of the basic design (page 166) and a drawing of the stud framework (page 168) are included for convenience. The actual plan is featured on pages 178 to 179, and includes a materials list, or you may prefer to separate various elements and design a unique garden structure.

MATERIALS

Poles or sawn and planed posts may be used as vertical supports. These are embedded in the ground and attached to horizontal timbers which form a framework for the wall cladding (see pages 144 to 145).

In order to accommodate doors and windows, it is necessary to construct a stud framework to brace the walls. Ordinary, factory-assembled frames are easily installed; however the minimal dimensions of some structures, such as the one shown here, may demand that a smaller-than-usual door is used. The simplest solution is to construct a frame on site using wooden laths.

If relatively weak softwood decking slats are used, these should be quite thick (in this case 110 mm x 35 mm). If a tougher, more resistant wood is used, or if the bearers are closer together, thinner slats can be used.

Although standard bargeboard and fascias may be used to finish the little building, a less expensive and much prettier option is a plywood trim.

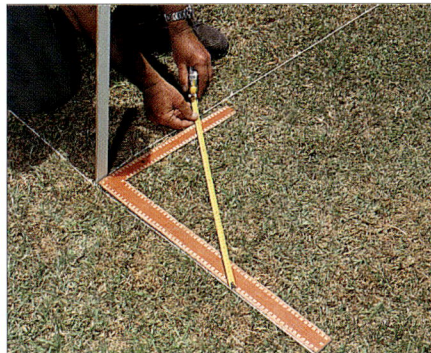

1 Mark the layout of the building on the ground using pegs and string (see plan on page 166). This shed measures 2.5 m x 3 m. Use the 3:4:5 method (see page 160) to ensure that all corners are at right angles and the building is absolutely square.

2 If there is a deck, you will need to indicate where this will be located. To do this, string a line 1 m from the front 2.5 m mark, using a builder's square for accuracy. To double-check that the layout is square, measure all the diagonals.

3 Cut as much wood to size as possible before you start work. These four bearers are 3 m long, and the five joists which support the floor-boards, 2.5 m long. If necessary, trim the wood now, using a combination or try square to mark the cutting line.

4 Although you can use a hand saw, it will be quicker, and the cut will be more accurate, if you use an electric circular saw. As neither the joists nor the bearers will be visible, it will not be necessary to plane the cut ends of the wood.

5 The upright posts will have to be firmly anchored in the ground, preferably in a concrete footing. A good way to prevent any vertical wind lift is to drill a hole and insert a metal rod through the timber a few centimetres from the base.

6 The holes for the 14 footings should be at least 500 mm x 500 mm x 500 mm in size (see page 161). Dig them all, but only insert the four outside posts, bracing them with battens and bricks to ensure that they are as vertical as possible.

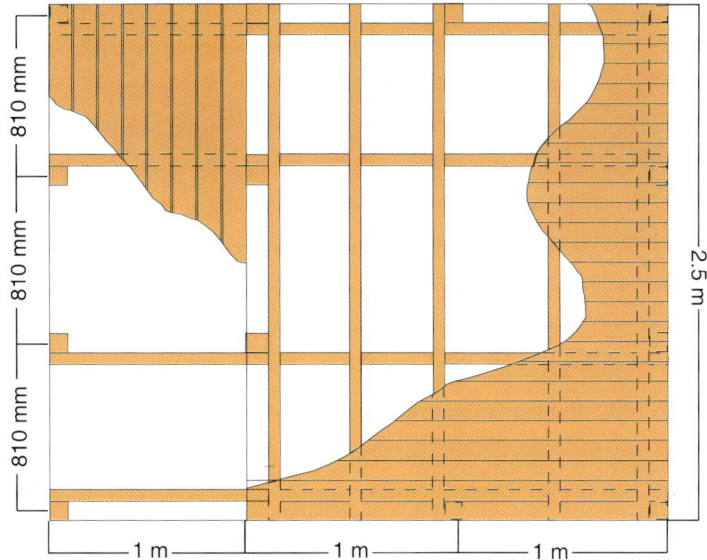

810 mm

810 mm

810 mm

810 mm

2.5 m

1 m   1 m   1 m

7 Although many people concrete the posts in at this stage, it is easier to keep the structure square and plumb if you start by securing all bearers, joists and uprights. Position the two outside bearers first, using blocks of wood to level them.

8 Use the correct drill bit to bore through the end of each bearer and the base of each of the four upright posts. You will need two suitable coach screws at each point to fasten the timber securely. Tighten the screws with a spanner.

9 It is vital that the outside bearers are affixed at exactly the same height, or your floor will be uneven. Use a straightedge with a spirit level placed over it to check. If the ground slopes, one end of the bearers will be off the ground.

10 Now you can position the first joist at the back of the building. Check that it is level and pre-drill holes as before. Use the same length coach screws to secure the joist to the two posts. Then attach the central and front joists of the structure.

11 The next step is to position the remaining upright posts (see step 12) and two inner bearers. This way you will not have to brace the posts. Once these are securely fixed, position the last two joists as shown on the plan and skew-nail to the bearers.

12 The two longest upright posts should be positioned opposite one another, to coincide with the apex of the roof. The four shorter posts should be placed at 810 mm centres at the front of the building, to support the railing and verandah roof.

13 Remove the bracing, but before you go any further, double-check the upper plane of the joists and bearers. Do this at numerous points to make absolutely certain your workmanship is straight and level. It is easier to rectify errors now than later.

14 If you have used sawn (rather than planed) timber, you may have to use a rasp or file to trim, flatten or even out sections of some of the pieces. You are unlikely to need a plane unless the wood is badly bowed; there is no need to sand the wood.

15 Now you can concrete the posts in place. Use a 1:4:4 mixture of cement, sand and stone and place it in the holes with a spade. If all the posts were vertical when they were bolted, the building will be square. Allow the concrete to set overnight.

16 The first decking slat will have to be cut and notched to accommodate the posts. Position it on the bearers, and then draw a line where you are going to cut out. Accuracy is extremely important, so is best to use a combination square.

17 The best way to notch timber is with a handsaw and chisel. This gives you better control than with a power saw. Work on a stable surface, like a portable workbench, and use a crosscut saw which is designed to cut across the grain.

18 Although you can use a saw or a chisel to finish cutting the end joint, you will have to use a chisel to cut the back of the notches which will accommodate the two inner posts. Use a hammer to drive the chisel blade gradually into the wood.

19 String a line along one end of the deck as a guide, then secure the slats with anodised nails. Use a block of wood, planed to the width of the gap you wish to leave between the slats, as a spacer. Trim the other end of the decking as shown in steps 22 and 23.

20 Moving on to the inside of the structure, cut the tongue off the first floorboard and nail the board in place with two oval nails at each of the joists. Continue laying the flooring, slotting the tongue of each board into the groove of each previous one.

21 Line up the ends of all the boards at the front of the building. You will need to notch some of these ends to accommodate the posts, and to trim those which lie at the point where the door is to be hung (see plan on page 168).

22 Now you can trim the boards at the back of the building. These must line up with the edge of both the bearer and the upright posts. The best way to ensure that the cutting line is straight is to make use of a chalk line, snapping it between two posts.

23 You can use either a handsaw or a power tool to cut the boards. Although you could use a circular saw, it is easier to obtain a really flush cut with a jigsaw. Otherwise use a crosscut saw, following the line marked previously.

24 Before you affix the cladding, assemble the roof structure. Use a water level to determine the correct height of all the upright posts. The height of the middle posts will be determined by the required pitch; these are 200 mm higher.

25 Once you have measured and marked all the upright posts, you can cut the excess ends off with a crosscut saw; it is too awkward to use a power saw. Note that the two higher posts should be cut at a slight angle to support the rafters.

26 Before securing the beams, cut a notch at the top of each post, in a dimension which will support the rafters. Then, using coach screws, fasten the beams to the uprights, so that the upper surface of each is flush with the newly cut wood.

27 To prevent the two central beams below the apex of the roof from bowing and bending, sandwich a block of wood between them at the centre, and secure with a hexagonal bolt and washer, using a spanner and ratchet to fasten it.

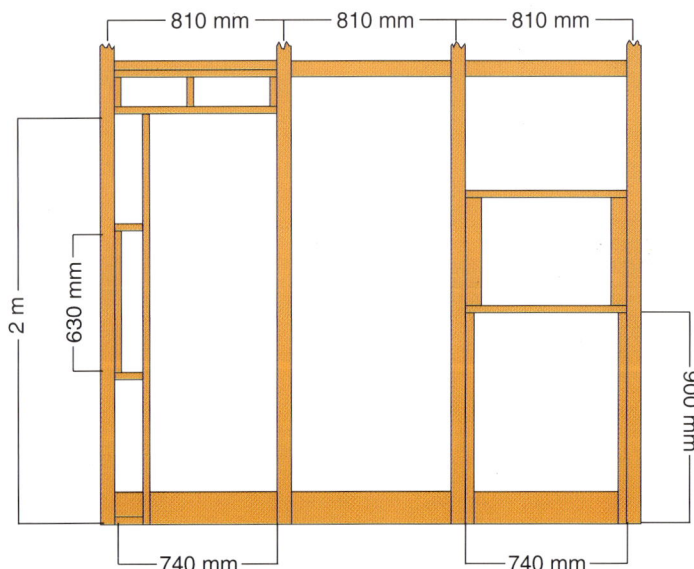

810 mm — 810 mm — 810 mm

2 m

630 mm

900 mm

740 mm — 740 mm

28 You will need eight lengths of timber for the rafters which will have to be cut at a slight angle to ensure that they join properly at the apex. Position a shorter length on the cut-out posts and use a combination square to determine the angle.

29 Mark the same angle for all the rafters, checking before cutting the ends. Drill through the rafter and post, then fasten the wood to form a half-lap joint, using a smaller sized coach screw. Repeat at both ends of each rafter.

30 The rafters are best joined at the apex with nail plates (timber connectors), available in various sizes. Working on the ground, simply hammer a plate on each side of the wood over the join. Alternatively you can make a plywood gusset.

31 Once all the rafters have been positioned and secured, string a line along the apex of the roof. Use this as a guide when measuring and marking where the purlins should be affixed. Remember to leave a space at the apex for the capping.

32 Now attach the purlins to the rafters with 75 mm long anodised nails. Use the marks made in step 31 as well as the string line to ensure they are nailed on absolutely straight. If the purlins are crooked, the roofing nails will not be neat.

33 Before you lay the roof sheeting, nail the cladding to the posts. This splayed lapboard is designed to create a weatherproof wall. Use two nails at each post and check your spirit level periodically to see that the boards are horizontal.

34 While the cladding is nailed across the posts on three walls, the front wall incorporates a door and a window. To brace these openings, it is necessary to build a stud framework (see plan on page 168). Secure timber with anodised nails.

35 Studs around the window are nailed to the upright posts, to create an opening exactly the same size as the frame. Although any type of window may be fitted, a PVC frame is one of the easiest to work with as it simply slots into position.

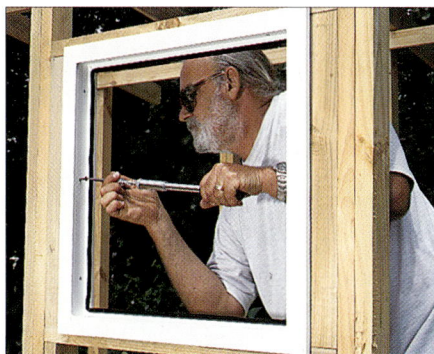

36 Before the window can be glazed, the frame is screwed to the studs. The inner PVC frame is removed and holes drilled through the frame and into the wood. Countersunk brass screws are used to ensure the frame is flush when it is reassembled.

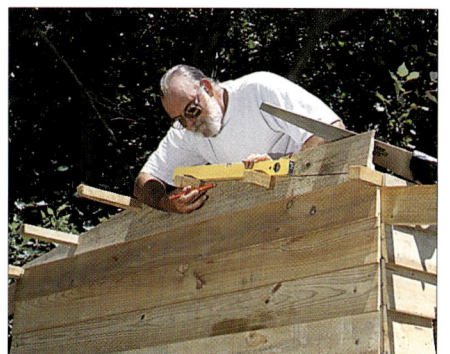

37 When you reach roof height, it will be necessary to notch the cladding around the purlins and cut it to the angle of the rafters. Use a spirit level as a straightedge to mark the cutting line and then saw the timber with a crosscut saw.

38 Buy longer lengths of sheeting than required and cut to size. The flexible corrugated sheeting used here is made from organic fibre, which can be cut with an angle grinder or well-oiled handsaw. Mark a line with a chalk line and carefully cut a straight edge.

39 String lines along all edges of the roof to help you keep the roof sheeting straight. Note that the sheeting must overlap at the joins to ensure that it is waterproof. Align the sheets carefully so that the corrugations overlap exactly.

40 Although it is usually necessary to pre-drill holes for roofing nails, this is not necessary for organic-fibre sheeting as long as you hammer gently. Knock in the nails, using a spirit level and lines to gauge the position of the underlying purlins.

41 The ends of the rafters should line up neatly with the ends of the roof sheeting. Use a carpenter's square to mark this point accurately. Then use a crosscut saw to cut all the excess pieces of timber at the front and back of the shed.

42 The purlins must also be cut so that they are flush with the roof sheeting on both sides. Bargeboard, or in this case a decorative trim, can then be nailed to the ends of the timber. Once again it is best to use a handsaw to cut the wood.

43 Now affix the capping to close the gap between the sheets which cover the two halves of the shed. Capping is supplied in standard lengths and must be overlapped in the same way as the sheeting. Secure with roofing nails along the purlins.

44 Most of the work has been done, and now you can make the railing around the deck. First affix a supporting strut to the shed at the corners of the deck, opposite the two outer posts. Then mark cutting lines on all your crosspieces.

45 As the crosspieces below the rails are angled, the ends of each piece must be cut to form a V at both top and bottom. Use a carpenter's square to draw a straight line down one side of each piece to help you cut in a straight line.

46 Preferably clamp the wood to a portable workbench and use a tenon saw to angle the corners. It is best to cut all the wood before you start assembling the railing. It is also a good idea to check that you have cut the correct angle.

47 Now cut a housing in the centre of each crosspiece so they slot together neatly. It will be slightly angled, depending on the length of the diagonals and where they meet. Mark this position and make a series of cuts halfway through the wood.

48 Chisel out the excess wood from the notch. If the cuts made previously are accurate, you will find that you can simply trim the wood at the base line. Otherwise you will need to pare away the remainder with the chisel blade.

49 The two diagonals should now slot together neatly. There is no need to affix them at this point, although you can glue them if you wish. Once the crosspieces have been secured to the posts and support struts, the railing will be quite sturdy.

50 You can nail or screw the crosspieces into place, but to avoid splitting the wood, it is best to pre-drill the holes. Use the appropriate drill bit and angle each hole. The upper sections are affixed to the posts and lower pieces to the decking.

51 If you are using nails, use ones that are anodised and will not rust. Make sure you hammer them in so that the tops are flush with the wood. It is also a good idea to countersink them with a punch and fill the holes with wood filler.

52 Now fit the top railings over the criss-cross by skew-nailing them to the upright posts on each side. A drilled pilot hole will help to prevent the timber from splitting. Make use of an orbital sander to smooth the edges and round them off neatly.

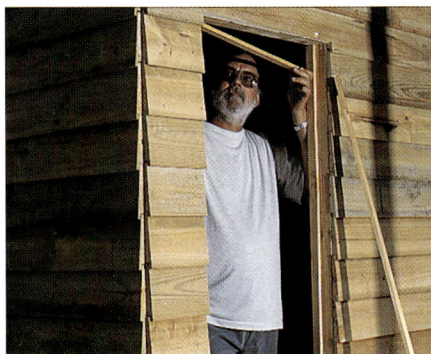

53 Nail the laths to the inside of the doorway to form a narrow frame along the top and sides, using 50 mm long nails. Then hang the door so that it opens outwards, above the upper surface of the deck. Fit the lock and the handles.

54 The quadrant can now be nailed to the four outside corners of the building using suitable nails. This finishes off the corners neatly. You could also use square lengths of wood or PVC capping similar to that illustrated on page176.

55 Mark the design for your trim on the plywood and cut it out with a jigsaw. Any holes can be made by drilling, using a flat drill bit. Attach it at the front and sides of the structure with 50 mm nails. Also cut out closures for the capping ends from the plywood.

STUD-FRAME PANEL

Simple stud frame structures are often built with prefabricated panels which are bolted together on site. These are simple to make and no special skills are required.

The method illustrated may be adapted for panels of practically any size, and a range of cladding materials may be used. Note that this panel incorporates an optional bracing layer of plywood, which strengthens the structure and improves its insulation qualities.

These guidelines illustrate construction of a typical external panel measuring 3 m x 2.17 m and incorporating a 1.14 m x 1.2 m window. You can make it bigger or smaller, depending on your particular design, although the larger the panel, the more studs you will need to ensure a sturdy framework.

1 The framework of the panel is made with 70 mm x 35 mm PAR (DAR) timber. You will need two 3 m, six 2.1 m, three 1.14 m and one 790 mm lengths, plus two 790 mm x 50 mm x 38 mm supports for the window.

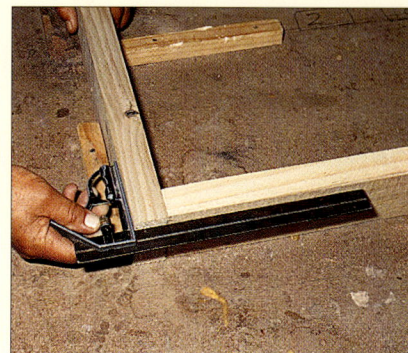

2 Ensure that all panels are absolutely square. Work on a flat surface and use a carpenter's square to check all corners. If you have a large table, affix short horizontal and vertical battens to guide you.

3 Using 100 mm wire nails, join a 2.1 m length of wood to one of the two 3 m lengths. Note how the smaller battens, secured to the table, help keep the woodwork straight and square. Nail all the pieces together.

4 Make sure the gap you have left for the window is exactly the same size as the frame – in this case, 1.14 m x 1.2 m. If it is, you can slot the window frame into place. Wooden, PVC and aluminium frames may be used.

5 Nail or screw the window frame securely into place, depending on the type of frame you have used. Note the two 1.14 m lengths of wood which must be inserted above the top of the window frame to ensure a snug fit.

6 You will need four pieces of 4 mm plywood for the bracing layer; 2 x 930 mm x 2.17 m, 1 x 1.14 m x 860 mm and 1 x 1.14 m x 110 mm for the small section above the window. This should give the structure added strength.

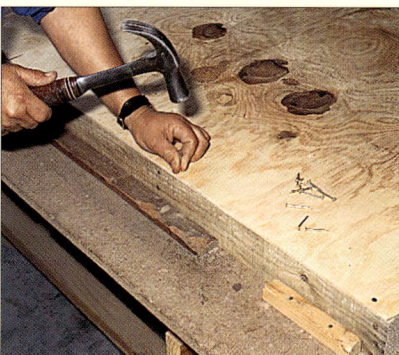

7 Make sure that the plywood is cut accurately and fits neatly over the framework, then use clout nails or round-head nails to secure it firmly to the wood. You can also use heavy-duty staples, inserting them with the aid of a staple gun.

8 Use wire nails to affix the cladding to the plywood, with the first board about 100 mm from the bottom; this allows you to overlap the foundation with cladding on site. Also overhang boards by 70 mm on one side of each corner panel.

Stud-frame buildings may be erected on a concrete slab with a prefabricated board floor, or built with wooden strip flooring. Many prefabricated sheds, as well as smaller structures available in kit form, have timber flooring. However, concrete is an inexpensive option and is the base illustrated here.

There are several ways to assemble a stud-frame structure, and you must decide whether to use pre-made panels (see page 172). or to build the frame on site and then clad it. The framework must be anchored to the foundation or floor, using strapping or steel strips (as shown here), or by bolting it on with ragbolts. Whichever of these fasteners you use, they should be concreted in when the floor or foundation is laid.

While a pole building has vertical supports extending to roof height, a stud-frame structure has a conventional roof with trusses. Interior dry walls are also made from preconstructed panels which, like the outer walls, are insulated before being clad with plasterboard. Joints are taped then skimmed with gypsum plaster for a smooth finish.

MATERIALS

All studs and rails are made with planed timber, the dimensions depending on the size and design of the structure. The panels here were made in the same way as those on page 46. Blankets of fibreglass insulation material are set in all panels after erection and plasterboard is used to finish internal walls.

If you are building a habitable building, it is wise to insulate the roof and walls. Other cladding materials, roof sheeting and insulation are discussed on pages 144, 145, 148 and 157 respectively.

In addition to the timber required, you will need cement, sand and stone for the foundations and the concrete slab; a relatively small number of bricks or blocks for the foundation walls; cement and sand for the mortar and screed; and skimming plaster to skim the walls (see page 156 for quantities). A damp-proof membrane of 250 micron polythene must be laid under the slab and you will also need rolls of thicker 375 micron DPC for the base of all wall panels.

Various nails, bolts and screws are also vital to the project.

1 Before you start erecting the wall panels, prepare the concrete foundation or slab (see page 164). Nail DPC to base of each panel with clout nails. This should be slightly wider than the timber used. Position panels on the ground around the slab.

2 Make sure all strapping or steel strips are bent towards the centre of the slab. Starting at one of the corners, raise the first panel into a vertical position and brace it with a spare batten. This is a cumbersome job and you will need some assistance.

3 The next panel you erect must be at right angles to the first one. Tack the two sections together with nails, preferably electroplated ones. It also helps to brace the two panels with a horizontal stay across the top corner.

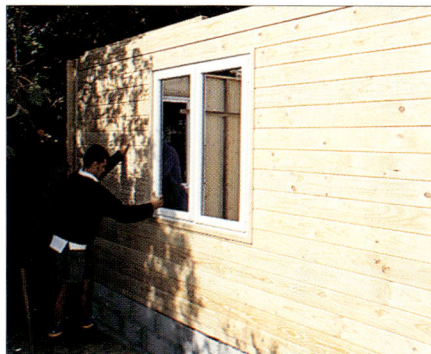

4 It is essential to check periodically that the erected panels are in fact vertical. You can use a spirit level or plumb line to do this (see page 158). If any of the panels are out of line, you will have to remove the nails and reposition them.

5 To simplify construction, a panel with overhanging boards (see page 172, step 8) is used at each corner. To ensure a neat, secure and watertight join where the panels meet on a straight wall, sandwich foam between the sections at these points.

6 ·Continue to erect all the external panels in a systematic manner. As the building takes shape, you will be able to remove the temporary bracing. Note that the bottom skirt of cladding is not affixed to the structure at this stage.

7 No matter how many panels are used for the structure, continue slotting these into place and nailing adjacent sections together. Do this carefully to ensure that the strips of cladding line up perfectly at the corners of the building.

8 If internal panels are to be erected, this will be the next step. These are pre-made in the same way as the external panels, but without the shiplap cladding. Instead, plasterboard is later nailed to both sides to create a solid wall surface.

9 The internal panels slot together at right angles, partitioning different sections and adding stability to the structure. You will need about five nails to secure adjacent panels to one another and bolts to anchor them into the concrete.

10 When all the panels are in place, but before you bolt them together permanently, check again that each one is vertical and all are correctly aligned with one another. If necessary, use a large, heavy hammer to knock the studs and rails straight.

11 Now you can nail the hoop-iron strapping or steel strips to the framework (each should be directly in front of a vertical stud). Pull each piece of metal up straight and, using a sharp punch and a hammer, make a hole to facilitate nailing.

12 Use 75 mm long anodised nails to secure the strapping or steel strips to the studs. It is important to realise that the strapping or strips anchor the building to the foundation. Aligning them accurately with the studs will ensure maximum strength.

13 Before you put the roof on, bolt all the wall panels securely together at the top, middle and bottom of each join. Various fasteners are suitable (see page 157), in particular, coach screws or wood-fix screws, which are used here.

14 Erecting roof trusses and gable ends takes practice and you will need assistance. Although experienced and agile carpenters may be able to raise the roof sections into position without scaffolding, you will probably find this equipment indispensable.

15 The two gable ends are placed on top of the gable walls and securely braced in position with temporary battens. Then the trusses are positioned and fastened with hoop-iron strapping at the points where they meet the wall panels.

16 Bolt the roof panels at the truss and gable ends, as in step 13. If there is a verandah, secure the posts, lean-to rafters and ceiling panels before installing fascia boards, roof sheeting, flashing, capping and finally bargeboards at the gable ends.

17 Now you can screed the floor with mortar mixed in a 1:5 cement:sand ratio. You can use the concrete slab as a mixing platform, provided it is clean and you smooth the area out carefully later. First mix the dry materials and then add water.

18 Use a shovel to mix thoroughly until you have a thick paste that will spread easily. If the foundation walls were built with hollow concrete blocks, these must be filled before you start covering the slab. Allow to set before screeding.

19 Make sure the surface of the slab is clean before you start laying the screed. It should also be reasonably rough to achieve good bonding. To improve adhesion further, dampen the floor and roughly brush on a cement-sand slush.

20 It is important to lay the screed before the slush dries. The screed should be about 25 mm thick and well compacted on the slab. Use a wooden float to smooth and level the mortar, checking the accuracy of your work regularly with a spirit level.

21 You can achieve a reasonably flat, uniform surface with a wooden float, or the screed may be lightly smoothed with a steel trowel to get a really even finish. Do not overwork it, or water will rise to the surface and the screed may crack later.

22 If plumbing and electrics are required, get a professional to channel the wiring and pipework in and through the dry walls before you finish the internal cladding. Then cut the fibreglass insulation to size and pack it into the wall cavities.

23 Working from the floor upwards, use galvanised nails to affix the plasterboard cladding to the studs and horizontal rails at 150 mm centres. Make sure the top of each piece of board is perfectly horizontal and that they join at a stud.

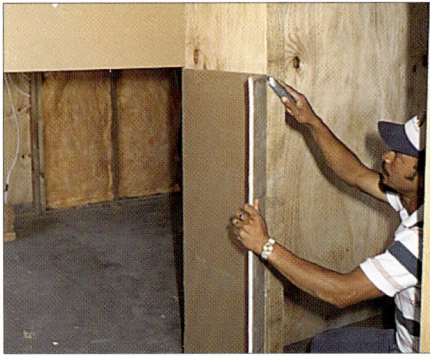

24 Attach plasterboard to both sides of the internal panels, covering the plywood (on one side) and the framework itself. This improves the visual finish as well as sound insulation. Cut excess board with a sharp utility knife.

25 A simple way to install plasterboard around doors and windows is to cover the opening, mark its position, and then cut a hole with a panel saw. If more than one sheet of cladding covers an opening, cut away the first piece before affixing the next.

26 Once the board is in place, attach skirtings at floor level. If you wish to plaster around window openings to finish them off neatly, rather than affixing a wooden trim or frame, you can nail or staple on steel or aluminium corner beading.

27 If internal doors do not have their own frames, you will have to use wooden laths to cover the rough edges of the plasterboard. You can then hang the door, using two hinges and screws. Prop it up while you work so that it clears the floor.

28 Even though the pieces of plasterboard are abutted against one another, there are invariably slight gaps between them. To disguise these, first fill with a small amount of skimming plaster, then press jointing tape across the filler.

29 The same skimming plaster, which is mixed with water according to the manufacturer's instructions, can then be used to skim over all the joints and nail heads. Alternatively, you can skim the entire wall with gypsum plaster.

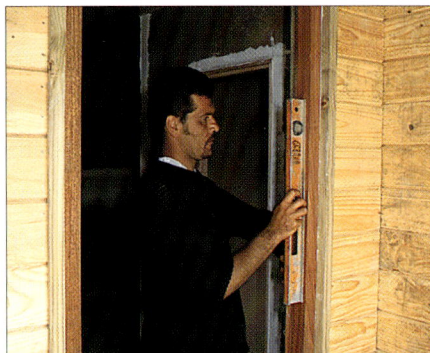

30 The front door can now be positioned. It is best to use a door that is supplied with its own frame. This should be nailed or screwed into the opening left in the front wall panel. Use a spirit level to make sure that the door frame is vertical.

31 You will need four hinges to hang a stable door, as well as handles, a lock and bolts. Since the bottom of the door is difficult to reach once it has been hung, seal this surface before hanging to protect it from excessive weathering.

32 The final steps include installing guttering and downpipes (if required) and affixing the external skirting to overlap the foundation walls. The outside corners of the building can be neatly finished with a PVC cover or with timber.

JOINTS

Whatever you are going to build, it will be necessary to join separate pieces of timber together. In most instances, relatively simple joints may be used, but it is always essential to ensure that the connection is strong enough to withstand the strains it will be exposed to.

BUTT JOINTS
The simplest of all timber connections, butt joints involve abutting wood without making any special cuts in the wood, such as rebates or tongues. Glue, nails, screws and other fastening devices are used to fix the timbers in place.

Butt joints may be used at a corner or where two lengths of timber meet to form a T. Although a cross-butt joint may be created where two lengths of timber interconnect, halving joints are usually preferable in this situation.

HALVING (OR HALF-LAP) JOINTS
Simple to perfect, neat halving joints are used for many garden structures including the connection of pergola beams to posts. Cross-halving joints are particularly useful where diagonal timbers cross beneath the railing of a deck.

As their name suggests, halving joints necessitate cutting a rebate equal to half the thickness of the wood, usually from both the timbers to be connected. This results in a strong, interlocking join with a flush surface.

With experience, you will find that measuring tools are not necessary to cut halving joints. Simply mark out the cutting lines with the second piece of timber, and remember to cut inside the marked line.

HOUSING JOINTS
Similar to halving joints, housing joints involve only one rebate or groove to support the adjoining piece of timber. These are useful when constructing a stud framework.

MITRED JOINTS
Essentially decorative butt joints, these are found wherever two pieces of wood meet at 45°. Although a standard mitre is not particularly strong, it is a neat joint for many simple garden structures. Alternatively, a mitred halving (or half-lap) joint may be used.

MORTISE-AND-TENON JOINTS
Not common in the average garden structure, mortise-and-tenon joints are sometimes used for pergolas. These involve cutting a rectangular 'mortise' or hole in one

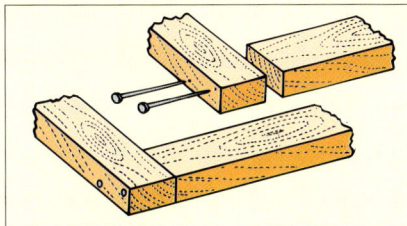

Simple butt joint

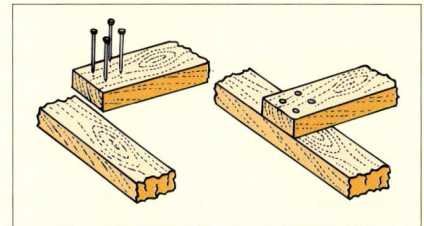

T-butt joint

Corner halving joint

Cross-halving joint

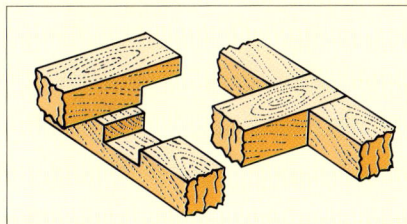

T-halving joint

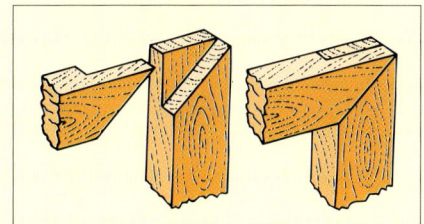

Mitred halving joint

Three-cut scarf joint

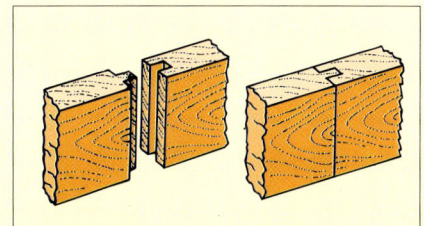

Tongue-and-groove joint

piece of timber, and a 'tenon' or tongue to fit into the second. The two lengths of wood then slot together. Although the standard mortise-and-tenon joint is neat, it is not always strong enough.

POLE JOINTS
Even though most structures built with poles do not require elaborate joints, it is useful to know how to adapt methods to fit their cylindrical form. In some instances, poles may be abutted to one another, but simple halving joints are usually a more adequate option, and housing joints are particularly useful where horizontal and vertical timbers need to be connected.

SCARF JOINTS
Used to lengthen timbers, rails, beams and so on, scarf joints are usually glued, clamped and pinned. The simplest kind is made by cutting the ends of both pieces of wood at an angle and attaching them in a straight line This type of joint will be considerably stronger if made with three saw cuts, but they must be accurately marked.

TONGUE-AND-GROOVE JOINTS
Particularly common for floorboards and cladding, tongue-and-groove joints are often found where manufactured timber boards have been used. The tongue fits into the groove, creating a nice, snug finish.

This charming garden shed may be used as a storeroom for tools and garden equipment, or even as a workroom or children's playhouse. Designed with a narrow deck in front, the building is constructed by assembling a pole (or stick) frame on site. The roof is covered with organic-fibre sheeting, a flexible, corrugated roof covering which is lightweight and easy to install. It could be insulated and clad with plasterboard inside. Simple wooden cut-outs and a criss-cross railing add charm and character, while paint gives it a traditional look.

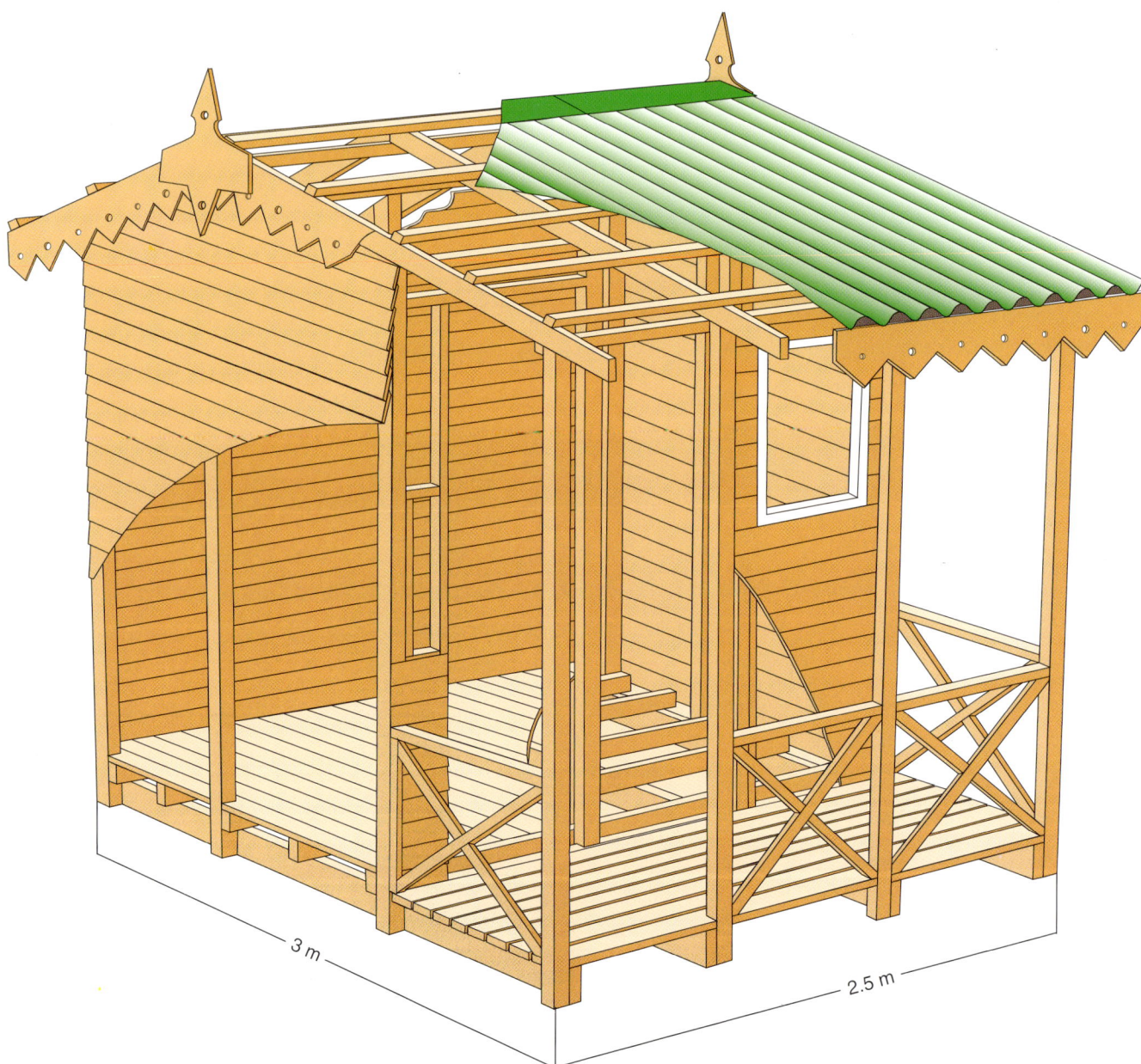

MATERIALS

Footings
400 kg cement
1.2 m³ sand
1.2 m³ stone

Timber
4 x 3 m x 228 mm x 50 mm
  bearers
5 x 2.5 m x 150 mm x 50 mm
  joists
14 x 3.2 m x 70 mm x 70 mm
  upright posts
8 x 2.5 m x 110 mm x 35 mm
  decking slats
25 x 2 m x 100 mm x 22 mm
  tongue-and-groove
  floorboards
1 x 2 m x 70 mm x 22 mm
  stud
2 x 740 mm x 70 mm x 22 mm
  studs
1 x 630 mm x 70 mm x 22 mm
  stud
3 x 130 mm x 70 mm x 22 mm
  studs
3 x 114 mm x 70 mm x 22 mm
  studs
2 x 900 mm x 70 mm x 36 mm
  studs
1 x 740 mm x 70 mm x 36 mm
  studs
2 x 600 mm x 70 mm x 36 mm
  stud
1 x 600 mm x 35 mm x 13 mm
  laths
2 x 1.9 m x 35 mm x 13 mm
  laths
5 x 2.5 m x 75 mm x 36 mm
  beams
1 x 100 mm x 70 mm x 36 mm
  spacer block
4 x 2.07 m x 106 mm x 36 mm
  rafters
4 x 1.07 m x 106 mm x 36 mm
  rafters
8 x 2.6 m x 50 mm x 38 mm
  purlins
40 x 3 m x 130 mm x 22 mm
  lapboards
42 x 2.5 m x 130 mm x 22 mm
  lapboards
2 x 710 mm x 70 mm x 22 mm
  rail supports
8 x 1.2 m x 36 mm x 36 mm
  crosspieces
2 x 900 mm x 70 mm x 36 mm
  rails
2 x 750 mm x 70 mm x 36 mm
  rails
4 x 2.7 m x 19 mm quadrants
3.5 m x 200 mm x 4 mm piece
plywood

Roof covering
3 x 900 mm wide roof cappings

3 x 1 m x 970 mm corrugated
  organic-fibre roof sheeting
3 x 2 m x 970 mm corrugated
  organic-fibre roof sheeting

Doors and windows
600 mm x 1.9 m door
600 mm x 600 mm PVC window
  frame
547 mm x 547 mm safety glass
lock set with handles

Fasteners
14 x 300 mm long reinforcing
  rods
62 x 8 mm x 100 mm coach
  screws
16 x 6 mm x 65 mm coach
  screws
1 x 8 mm x 150 mm hexagonal
  bolt with washer
100 mm anodised wire nails
75 mm anodised wire nails
50 mm anodised wire nails
oval flooring nails
10 x 65 mm no. 8 countersunk
  brass screws
2 x nail plates
  (timber connectors)
80 x 70 mm ring-shank roofing
  nails with cover
2 x hinges with screws

1 Insert reinforcing rods into each post, 25 mm from the base.
2 Dig 14 foundation footings, 500 mm x 500 mm x 500 mm.
3 Set four corner uprights in holes and brace.
4 Secure two outer bearers with 100 mm coach screws.
5 Secure the central two outer joists with 100 mm coach screws.
6 Position remaining 10 uprights and fasten inner bearers with 100 mm coach screws.
7 Skew-nail last two joists to bearers.
8 Pour concrete into footings and allow to set overnight.
9 Trim tops of uprights to size, as indicated.
10 Affix decking slats to bearers at front of building, using 75 mm nails.
11 Affix floorboards to joists using oval nails.
12 Assemble stud framework to accommodate door and window as shown on page 41. Secure with 75 mm and 50 mm nails.
13 Screw window frame into place.
14 Assemble the roof structure by securing the beams with 100 mm coach screws and the rafters with 65 mm coach screws, creating a half-lap joint. Join central rafters with nail plate.
15 Affix purlins to rafters with 75 mm nails, leaving space for capping at the apex.
16 Nail the cladding on horizontally. Notch around purlins and cut to angle of rafters.
17 Nail roof sheeting to purlins and affix capping at apex.
18 Trim all excess timbers from roof structure.
19 Cut decorative trim from plywood and nail across ends of rafters at the front, and purlins at the sides with 50 mm nails.
20 Cut plywood closures for the capping ends and nail in place.
21 Nail rail supports to front wall opposite corner posts and then assemble railings. Notch crosspieces so they fit snugly.
22 Nail quadrant to outside corners with 50 mm nails.
23 Glaze window.
24. Hang door, fit lock set and handles, and finally paint the structure.

This charming shelter can be nailed together in a weekend and erected anywhere in the garden. Upright poles, machined to a reasonably uniform size, combine with sawn and planed timber to create a rustic venue for seating and alfresco summer meals. Although the surface under the timber umbrella is grass, it could be paved at a later stage.

MATERIALS

Foundations
115 kg cement
465 kg or 0.35 m³ sand
465 kg or 0.35 m³ stone

Framework
4 x 2.5 m upright poles, 90 mm in diameter
1 x 500 mm pole for roof, 90 mm in diameter
2 x 3.5 m x 70 mm x 42 mm beams
12 x 1.7 m x 30 mm x 25 mm roof timbers
8 x 1.36 m x 30 mm x 25 mm roof timbers

4 x 1.26 m x 30 mm x 25 mm roof timbers
70 mm x 10 mm slats to cover 6.6 m²
4 x 2.5 m x 70 mm x 25 mm fascia boards
4 x 1.7 m x 70 mm x 10 mm cover strips
1 x 200 mm x 200 mm x 30 mm capping to fit on central apex of roof

Fasteners
100 mm anodised wire nails
50 mm anodised wire nails

1 Dig four foundation footings, 500 mm x 500 mm x 500 mm.
2 Set upright poles in holes, brace and pour in concrete. Allow to set thoroughly, at least overnight.
3 Assemble basic roof framework by joining two beams at centre with a lap joint and nailing the short pole above the joint. Create the umbrella shape by nailing four 1.7 m roof timbers to connect the top of the pole with the four ends of the beams.
4 Working on a flat surface, nail five roof timbers to each side of the roof, as illustrated, to form a support grid for slats.
5 Nail fascia to secure the loose ends of roof timbers.
6 Cut slats to fit and nail over grid, overlapping each one slightly.
7 Nail the cover strip along the upper surface to strengthen and neaten the four corners and affix the capping to the central apex.
8 Cut a 70 mm deep notch in the top of each pole (see detail photograph) and slot the assembled roofing into place. Use 100 mm long nails to fasten.
9 Coat with a suitable wood sealer.

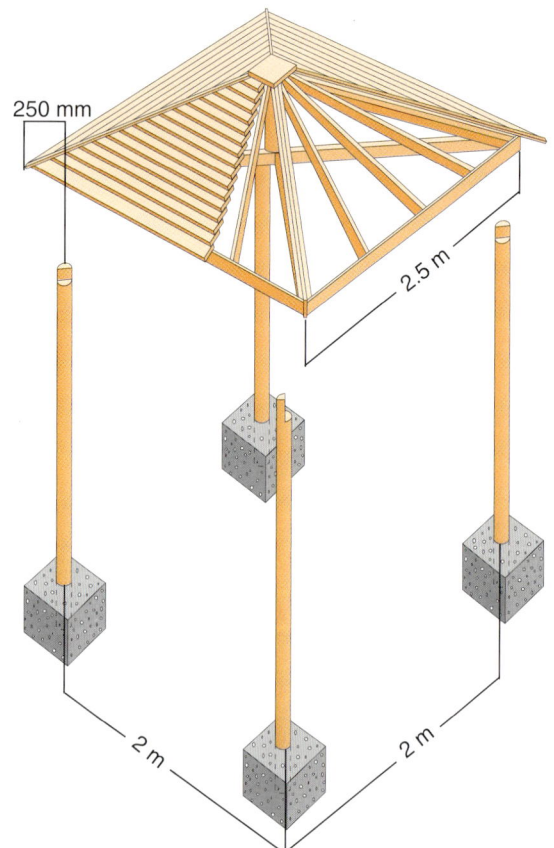

This perfectly proportioned pergola will be a decorative addition to any garden. Designed to provide a sturdy and stable support for climbing plants, it incorporates a series of criss-crossed rails which add a feeling of intimacy by partly enclosing the structure. The floor surface features reconstituted flagstones with groundcover planted between them. All the timber has been planed to a smooth finish and the dimensions given relate to the finished size. Upright posts, measuring 140 mm x 130 mm, are made from two lengths of 130 mm x 70 mm timber, glued together and chamfered for effect.

1 Dig 12 foundation footings, 500 mm x 500 mm x 500 mm, to support 2.4 m upright posts, and four smaller ones measuring 300 mm x 300 mm x 300 mm for the short uprights.
2 Bolt the post-anchor bracket or metal shoe to the 2.4 m posts and drill a hole in the 770 mm uprights to accommodate the galvanised pipe.
3 Place anchors (with uprights attached) and pipe in holes and brace.
4 Pour concrete into all footings and allow to set overnight.

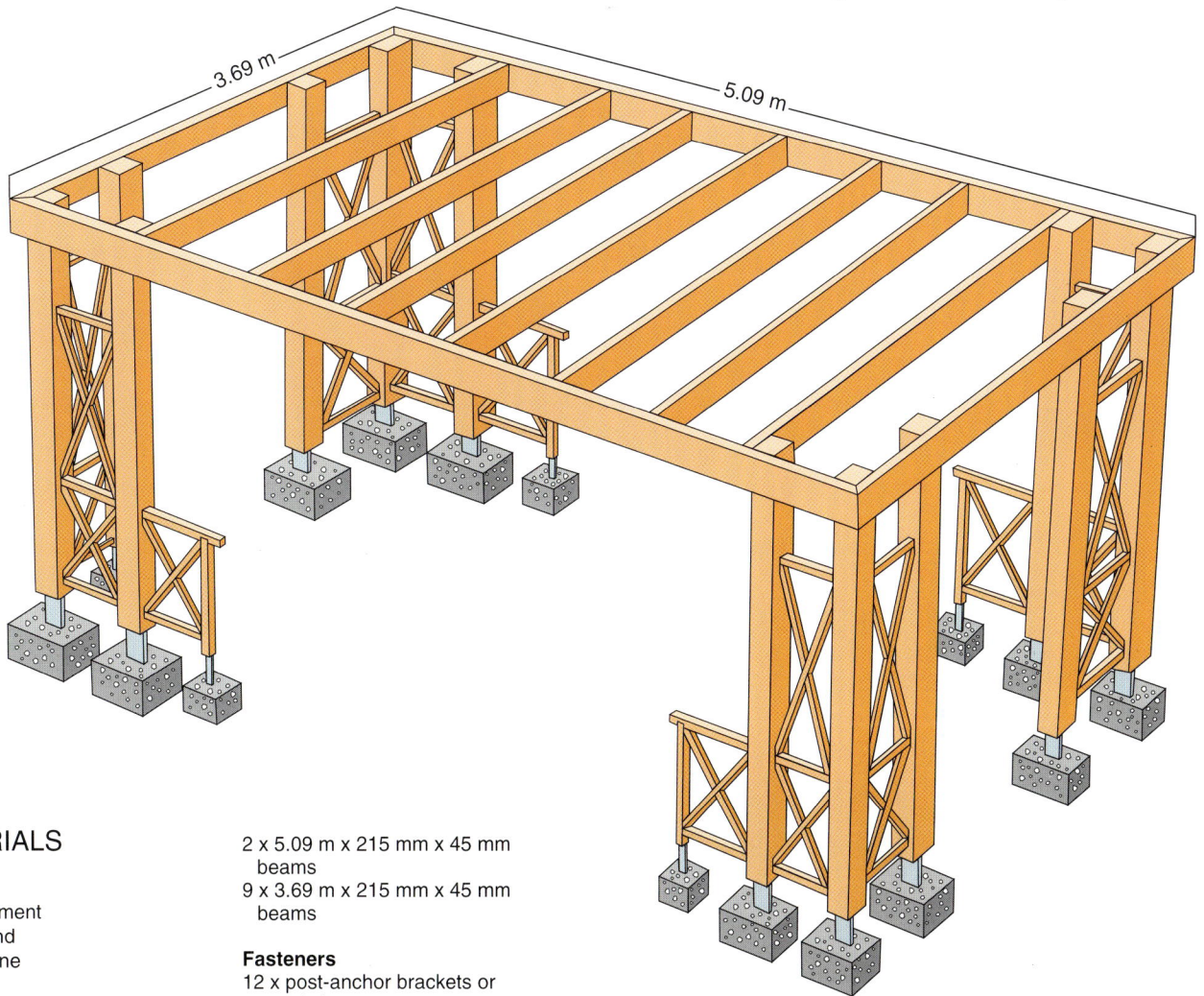

MATERIALS

Footings
370 kg cement
1.1 m³ sand
1.1 m³ stone

Framework
12 x 2.4 m x 140 mm x 130 mm upright posts
4 x 770 mm x 70 mm x 45 mm upright posts
28 x 500 mm x 70 mm x 45 mm rails
4 x 550 mm x 70 mm x 45 mm rails
16 x 1.2 m x 45 mm x 30 mm crosspieces
24 x 760 mm x 45 mm x 30 mm crosspieces

2 x 5.09 m x 215 mm x 45 mm beams
9 x 3.69 m x 215 mm x 45 mm beams

Fasteners
12 x post-anchor brackets or metal shoes
4 x 300 mm galvanised pipes, 25 mm in diameter
24 x 10 mm x 150 mm hexagonal bolts with washers
60 x 8 mm x 100 mm coach screws
60 mm oval, anodised wire nails
4 x 210 mm x 210 mm sheets galvanised metal
50 mm anodised wire nails
8 x 210 mm x 165 mm sheets galvanised metal
25 m galvanised wire (optional)

5 Slot remaining uprights securely onto protruding pipe.
6 Affix all rails and crosspieces with oval nails as indicated, trimming timber where necessary.
7 Cut the ends of all four beams to allow for mitred joints at the corners.
8 Position the two longer beams and then, starting at one end, secure shorter beams at equal intervals (approximately 620 mm centres) using coach screws.
9 Bend 10 mm over on each side of the metal to be used for capping. Nail the larger pieces to the tops of the corner uprights, and the smaller ones to the remaining posts.
10 Stretch and secure wire over beams for extra plant support, if desired.
11 Paint, varnish or seal.

MATERIALS

Perfect for adventurous children, this delightful play structure incorporates a hide-out, ladders and ramps, a deck for outdoor play, and two swings. Essentially a pole structure, the covered hide-out is enclosed with rounded loglap cladding, while both inside and outside decking slats are planed (or dressed) timber. The ladder into the hide-out is constructed with poles, while the net ladder, leading from it, is made by knotting synthetic rope to form sturdy webbing between two sturdy poles. A climbing frame for budding gymnasts has galvanised pipe rungs. Although the structure photographed is on a slope, to simplify the project, these instructions assume you are building on flat ground. When building on a slope, start from the lowest point and vary the footing depths where necessary.

Footings
325 kg cement
1 m³ sand
1 m³ stone

Pole framework
4 x 3.6 m poles, 120 mm in diameter
1 x 3 m x pole, 120 mm in diameter
3 x 2.1 m poles, 120 mm in diameter
2 x 3 m poles for swing A-frame, 90 mm in diameter
2 x 1.8 m pole beams, 90 mm in diameter
2 x 1.14 m pole beams, 90 mm in diameter

Decking and cladding
4 x 1.1 m x 110 mm x 38 mm decking slats
3 x 1 m x 110 mm x 38 mm decking slats
2 x 890 mm x 110 mm x 38 mm decking slats
14 x 900 mm x 110 mm x 38 mm decking slats
1 x 1.8 m x 75 mm rail
1 x 900 mm split-pole rail, 90 mm in diameter
4 x 710 mm x 50 mm x 36 mm battens
16 x 1.4 m x 100 mm x 20 mm lengths loglap cladding

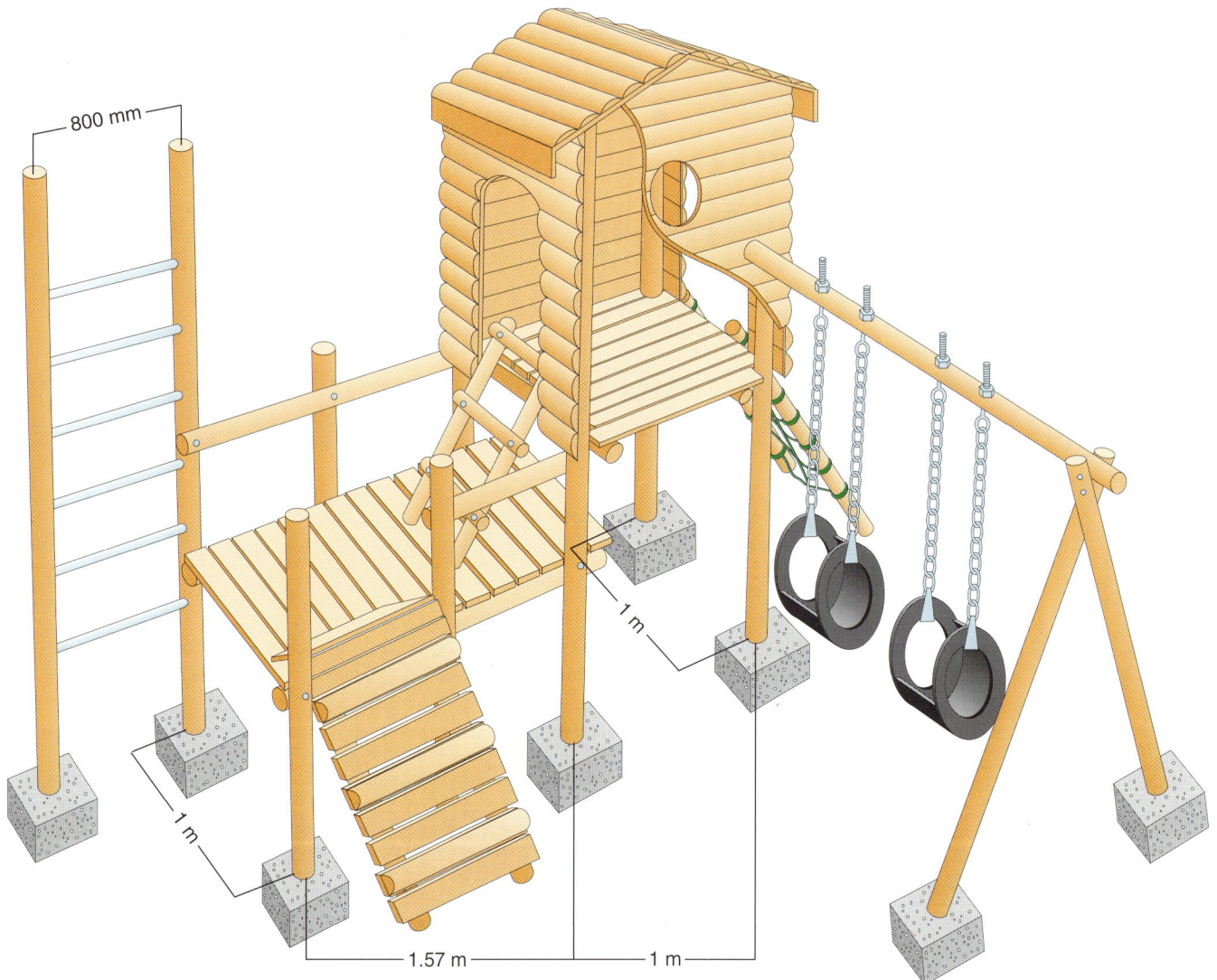

38 x 1.14 m x 100 mm x 20 mm lengths loglap cladding

38 x 310 mm x 100 mm x 20 mm lengths loglap cladding

2 x 1 m x 100 mm x 20 mm lengths loglap cladding

4 x 1.41 m x 25 mm x 20 mm timber corner pieces

4 x 900 m x 25 mm x 15 mm cover strips

Ladders

2 x 3 m poles, 120 mm in diameter

6 x 800 mm galvanised pipes, 30 mm in outside diameter

2 x 1.5 m poles, 90 mm in diameter

2 x 1.4 m poles, 90 mm in diameter

2 x 800 mm poles, 70 mm in diameter

3 x 550 mm poles, 70 mm in diameter

9 x 900 mm x 100 mm x 20 mm slats (treads)

2 x 680 mm x 100 mm x 20 mm slats (treads)

3 x 900 mm split poles, 90 mm in diameter

Synthetic rope for webbing

Swings

4 x 1.3 m lengths galvanised chain with 5.6 mm link

4 x swing fittings (including bolts etc.)

2 x bucket tyre seats

Fasteners

1 x 12 mm x 230 mm coach bolt

12 x 12 mm x 200 mm coach bolts

125 mm anodised wire nails

100 mm anodised wire nails

75 mm anodised wire nails

50 mm clout nails

50 mm anodised wire nails

50 mm oval nails

2 x small nail plates (timber connectors)

1 Mark the layout of the structure and then dig all 11 footings to at least 500 mm x 500 mm x 500 mm.

2 Assemble pipe ladder using two 3 m long poles, inserting metal rungs into holes drilled out at 300 mm centres.

3 Place ladder and rest of upright poles into footings and brace. Ensure that the end supports for swings meet to form the A-frame.

4 Secure the A-frame with 200 mm coach bolts.

5 Pour concrete into the footings and allow to set overnight.

6 Bolt pole beams to uprights to form firm, level support for decking.

7 Affix 900 mm long decking with clout nails to form lower deck.

8 Nail balance of decking to upper-level beams, with 1 m slats in centre to accommodate pole ladder, and short slats between corner poles.

9 Now assemble simple roof structure of hide-out using 710 mm battens, mitred and joined with connectors at centre. Height at the apex should be about 1.44 m from the floor of the enclosed area.

10 Using oval nails, affix cladding to all four sides of hide-out, placing shorter pieces to create two entrances. Using a jigsaw, cut archways at the top of each entrance to the hide-out.

11 Continue to nail cladding over battens to form roof; use two 1.14 m lengths on two sides as fascias.

12 Cut two 1 m cladding timbers to shape to fill triangular spaces between the roof and the walls; if necessary trim timbers below to fit roof shape.

13 Nail the cover strip on the sides of entrances to finish.

14 Use a jigsaw to cut a circle and a triangle on the other two walls to create windows.

15 Cut another hole, 120 mm across, in one wall to allow the 3 m long horizontal pole of swing frame to enter enclosure. Secure to upright pole with 230 mm long coach bolt and to A-frame with smaller bolt.

16 Nail safety rails to lower deck structure, leaving space alongside split-pole rail for ramp entry.

17 Make the pole ladder by nailing 70 mm thick poles together with 125 mm wire nails. Cut one end of longer poles at a slight angle and skew-nail firmly to deck and upper platform.

18 Construct ramp using 1.5 m long poles as stringers (on sides). Nail two 680 mm treads at top to accommodate poles supporting deck.

19 Nail split poles on 2nd, 5th and 8th tread for extra foothold.

20 Cut out the last slat to accommodate the stringer poles and attach at 45° to the platform.

21 Position poles for net ladder 800 mm apart and skew-nail to structure. Knot rope to form webbing.

22 Affix swing chains and tyre seats securely to horizontal pole.

23 Sand and oil or seal.

MATERIALS

A charming wooden entrance creates instant appeal and ambience, with the craftsman's attention to detail giving the structure a period feel. The basic structure is made from decorative timber posts and neat latticework, while corrugated organic fibre, a flexible sheeting, is used as the roof covering, providing shelter at the front door during bad weather. The design is essentially quite simple, the only complicated carpentry being the turned finial.

Footings
60 kg cement
235 kg or 0.18 m³ sand
235 kg or 0.18 m³ stone

Timber
2 x 2.37 m x 92 mm x 92 mm upright posts
2 x 2.2 m x 92 mm x 32 mm upright posts
4 x 1.8 m x 96 mm x 32 mm rafters
1 x 2.2 m x 104 mm x 32 mm beam
1 x 2.2 m x 96 mm x 32 mm beam
2 x 955 mm x 96 mm x 32 mm beams
6 x 693 mm x 92 mm x 32 mm rails
1 x 350 mm x 96 mm x 32 mm brace
6 x 955 mm x 42 mm x 32 mm purlins
1 x 975 mm x 96 mm x 32 mm strut
1 x 785 mm x 96 mm x 32 mm ridge beam
2 x 540 mm x 78 mm x 32 mm corner pieces, cut to shape from 104 mm x 32 mm timber
100 mm x 22 mm lapboard, to cover 2.2 m²
2 x 963 mm x 142 mm x 22 mm fascias
2 x 1.8 m x 142 mm x 22 mm bargeboards
2 x 1.8 m x 96 mm x 22 mm cover strips
26 x 1 m x 30 mm x 12 mm laths
26 x 935 mm x 30 mm x 12 mm laths
70 x 693 mm x 30 mm x 12 mm laths
8 x 192 mm x 50 mm x 22 mm timbers, mitred at each end
16 x 156 mm x 32 mm x 32 mm curved mouldings, mitred at each end
1 x 300 mm turned finial

Roof covering
2 x 1.7 m x 955 mm sheets corrugated organic-fibre roof sheeting
955 mm roof capping

Fasteners
10 x 8 mm x 75 mm Rawlbolts
2 x 3 mm galvanised anchor plates
4 x 8 mm x 75 mm coach screws

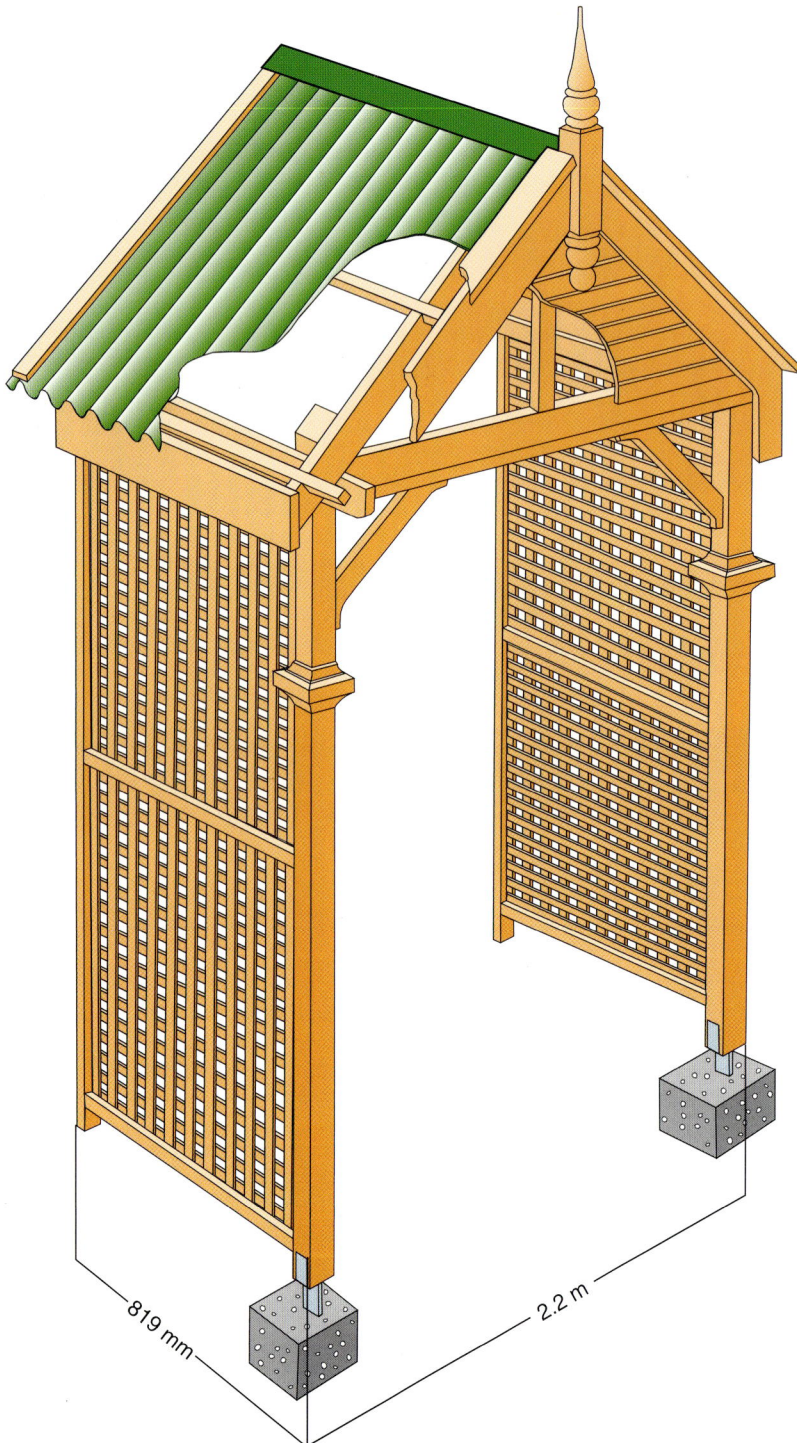

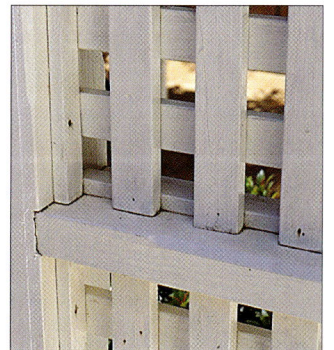

819 mm

2.2 m

various brass screws (preferably
  countersunk)
panel pins

24 x 70 mm ring-shank roofing
  nails with covers
2 x 1.6 m flashing

1 Cut and bolt 2.2 m upright posts to wall about 2 m apart, ensuring doorway is centred.

2 Cut 33 mm x 42 mm notches in 4 rafters to accommodate purlins on edge. Bolt two rafters against wall to form apex of roof.

3 Measure 825 mm from wall and dig two holes. Concrete anchor plates into these and allow to set.

4 Assemble upright front section of framework on the ground using brass screws. Notch the broader 2.2 m beam to accommodate upright posts and set 96 mm beam on edge above it.

5 Lift front section into position, brace temporarily, and fasten to anchor plate using coach screws. Ensure height aligns with framework on wall.

6 Cut notches in upright posts to accommodate 955 mm long beams, and notches 130 mm from one end of each beam for the rafters. Lay these beams on edge under the eaves (there will be a 130 mm overhang in front).

7 Affix the 693 mm long rails between the posts, with the top one flat against the underside of the top beam. Allow a gap of 935 mm and 1 m to the middle and bottom beams respectively.

8 Now assemble remaining rafters, bracing at the apex.

9 Cut ends of timber at the required angles to fit.

10 Screw rafter to upright posts, slot purlins into position and secure.

11 Screw perpendicular strut at front of the structure, behind the rafters and beam.

12 Secure ridge beam in position.

13 Screw corner pieces in place.

14 Now affix the lapboard, working from the bottom up.

15 Nail roof sheeting to purlins and affix capping at apex.

16 Screw fascias to bottom ends of rafters and bargeboard to front of structure. Glue and screw a decorative shaped end (cut from offcuts) to bargeboard if desired.

17 Neaten top of bargeboard with cover strip.

18 Attach laths vertically on sides of structure.

19 Reserve eight 693 mm laths. Make up four lattice panels (two 1 m x 693 mm, two 935 mm x 693 mm) with a grid of 30 mm x 30 mm, using panel pins to join horizontal and vertical laths.

20 Slot the panels into place and then secure by affixing the remaining laths to the rails.

21 Screw mitred timber around front posts as shown, finishing off with decorative moulding above and below each piece.

22 Screw decorative finial to apex of roof.

23 Fill any screw holes and paint as desired.

24 Attach flashing between the entrance roof and the wall of house.

Even if you do not have any suitable trees, with a little imagination you can erect this tree-house in any garden. The little building, which incorporates a 750 mm wide verandah, is set on two dead, but sturdy, tree trunks which have been concreted into the ground so that they emerge from the tree-house in a natural way. Much of the house is made from exterior-grade plywood, while shutterboard provides a solid floor. Plywood for cladding was ripped to 150 mm widths from standard sheets. Although there is no glazing, open spaces in the wall could be adapted to incorporate window frames. A timber ladder leads onto a covered deck, while a prefabricated slide suggests an easy escape for little people. If softwood is used for bearers, V-bracing and joists, use similar dimensions to those in the Garden Shed on page 178.

MATERIALS

Footings
100 kg cement
0.75 m² sand
0.75 m² stone

Timber
2 x 2.52 m x 105 mm x 85 mm
  hardwood bearers
4 x 1.1 m x 110 mm x 30 mm
  lengths hardwood for
  V-bracing
5 x 2.8 m x 100 mm x 38 mm
  hardwood joists
4 x 2 m x 70 mm x 70 mm
  upright posts
2 x 2 m x 55 mm x 50 mm
  upright posts
3 x 850 mm x 55 mm x 32 mm
  upright posts
1 x 750 mm x 55 mm x 50 mm
  upright post
2 x 2.44 m x 1.22 m x 22 mm
  pieces shutterboard
1 x 1.2 m x 70 mm x 32 mm
  sole plate
2 x 1.1 m x 70 mm x 32 mm
  sole plates
2 x 900 mm x 70 mm x 32 mm
  sole plates
4 x 750 mm x 70 mm x 32 mm
  sole plates
1 x 650 mm x 70 mm x 32 mm
  sole plate
5 x 1.968 m x 70 mm x 32 mm
  vertical studs
2 x 1 m x 70 mm x 32 mm
  vertical studs
1 x 936 mm x 70 mm x 32 mm
  vertical stud
2 x 2.3 m x 70 mm x 32 mm
  horizontal studs
3 x 1.55 m x 70 mm x 32 mm
  horizontal studs
2 x 900 mm x 70 mm x 32 mm
  horizontal studs

1 x 2.44 m x 70 mm x 32 mm
  beam
8 x 1.65 m x 70 mm x 32 mm
  rafters
9 mm exterior plywood to cover
  14 m², ripped to 150 mm
  widths
2 x 2.44 m x 1.65 m x 9 mm
  pieces exterior plywood
2 x 2.5 m x 55 mm x 50 mm rails
1 x 820 mm x 55 mm x 50 mm
  rail
2 x 2.4 m x 70 mm x 45 mm
  stringers
6 x 600 mm x 70 mm x 36 mm
  rungs
1 x 980 mm x 650 mm x 22 mm
  piece shutterboard
1 x 800 x 650 mm x 22 mm
  piece shutterboard

1 x 1.8 m x 30 mm x 15 mm lath
1 x 630 mm x 50 mm x 22 mm lath

Fasteners and hardware
16 x 250 mm threaded bolts
  with washers
5 x 8 mm x 120 mm
  coach bolts
20 x 5 mm x 100 mm
  coach bolts
40 mm brass screws
40 mm anodised clout nails
  (optional)
30 mm anodised clout nails
4 x brass hinges with screws
handle set
1 x brass barrel bolt with screws
bituminous felt (or geofabric) to
  cover 8 m²
fibreglass slide (optional)

2.44 m

2.4 m

1 Dig two 600 mm x 600 mm x 600 mm footings in which to 'plant' suitable dead trees. First place 200 mm of concrete at bottom of holes, allow to set, then stand trunks on foundations and fill holes with more concrete. Allow to set again, overnight. Tops of bearers should be 1.7 m from ground level.

2 Erect supportive framework of two bearers and V-bracing (see detail photograph). Use 12 threaded bolts to secure timber to trees and bearers to bracing.

3 Set joists across bearers, skew-nailing into position.

4 Affix shutterboard in position with screws to form the floor.

5 Erect four main (70 mm x 70 mm) upright posts at corners of building, securing to bearers with threaded bolts.

6 Attach 2 m high verandah posts to two outside corners with four 120 mm cuphead bolts.

7 Assemble studs for walls, with sole plates on the floor (see illustration), securing with brass screws.

8 Now position and secure the roof timbers. First anchor a beam to the two trees at the apex using threaded bolts. Affix rafters so that they can be screwed just above the beam. You can overlap interior rafters, but mitre those at the end of the verandah.

9 Use clout nails or screws to affix plywood cladding horizontally to outside of stud framework. Start at the bottom and allow each to overlap the next. See illustration for windows and door openings.

10 Use 30 mm clout nails to secure plywood roof to rafters, allowing it to overhang walls by about 150 mm.

11 Fill triangular space between cladding and roof with cladding nailed or screwed vertically to top stud and rafter.

12 Secure three 850 mm posts to joists along front of verandah using six of the smaller cuphead bolts.

13 Screw long rail to top of posts; nail shorter rail along one side, overlapping side of house slightly.

14 Now assemble the ladder, using 100 mm coach bolts to attach the rungs to the stringers.

15 Use a large coach bolt to affix the 750 mm high post at 600 mm centre to second verandah post.

16 Using smaller bolts, secure ladder to these two posts.

17 Screw hinges to remaining pieces of shutterboard and then screw to house, with the 980 mm length on top.

18 Screw 1.8 m lath to opposite side of the opening in place of a door jamb, and shorter lath along the inside top of lower section of the door.

19 Cut a diamond in the top section of the door (optional) and fit handles and a barrel bolt.

20 A covering of bituminous felt on the roof will repel water. Overlap all edges and affix with clout nails.

21 Position and fix slide if desired.

22 Finally, paint the door and coat the timber as desired.

An imaginative addition to any garden, this beautifully ornamental aviary incorporates a pitched roof which is constructed in exactly the same way as the Timber Umbrella on page 180. The rest of the structure is made up of four simple panels which incorporate attractive latticework. These, like the roof structure, are pre-assembled and bolted together on site. All four sides are covered with wire mesh, while a neat door at the back of the aviary enables one to enter to clean the area and feed the birds.

MATERIALS

Framework

12 x 2.47 m x 45 mm x 45 mm horizontal timbers, notched to accommodate uprights
16 x 2 m x 45 mm x 45 mm upright timbers, notched to fit into horizontal notching
3 x 770 mm x 45 mm x 45 mm arches, cut from 190 mm wide timber
6 x 760 mm x 45 mm x 45 mm arches, cut from 190 mm wide timber
11 x 2.47 m x 22 mm x 22 mm horizontal laths
8 x 2.38 m x 22 mm x 22 mm horizontal laths
4 x 1.65 m x 22 mm x 22 mm horizontal laths
8 x 2 m x 22 mm x 22 mm vertical laths
4 x 1.26 m x 22 mm x 22 mm vertical laths (above door)
36 x 785 mm x 22 mm x 22 mm vertical laths
4 x 760 mm x 22 mm x 22 mm laths
8 x 695 mm x 22 mm x 22 mm laths
2 x 760 mm x 45 mm x 45 mm timbers
2 x 695 mm x 45 mm x 45 mm timbers
1 x 520 mm pole for roof, 90 mm in diameter
2 x 3.5 m x 70 mm x 42 mm beams

12 x 1.7 m x 30 mm x 25 mm roof timbers
8 x 1.36 m x 30 mm x 25 mm roof timbers
4 x 1.26 m x 30 mm x 25 mm roof timbers
70 mm x 10 mm slats to cover 6.8 m²
4 x 2.5 m x 70 mm x 25 mm fascia boards
4 x 1.7 m x 70 mm x 10 mm cover strips
1 x 200 mm x 200 mm x 30 mm capping
1 x decorative finial (optional)

Fasteners and hardware

35 mm countersunk brass screws
75 mm countersunk brass screws
30 mm brass screws
8 x 8 mm x 90 mm hexagonal bolts with nuts and washers
100 mm anodised wire nails
50 mm anodised wire nails
netting staples
2 x brass hinges with screws
latch
wire mesh to cover 20 m²

1 Assemble the panels first, by joining timber together with lap joints, using 35 mm screws. Affix arches in position on three of the panels using 75 mm screws, positioning shorter lengths at the corners.
2 Lift the first panel into position and brace. Bolt adjacent panels at right angles.
3 Screw four 695 mm long laths to the inside of the upright posts (under rail) on two side panels.
4 Now attach wire mesh to inside of structure using netting staples to secure. Leave a 695 mm x 760 mm high gap for the door.

5 Affix laths to three panels to create latticework between rail and sole plate, with four equally spaced horizontal timbers on each.
6 Affix laths to remaining panel, leaving gap for door.
7 Use 760 mm and 695 mm x 45 mm x 45 mm timbers to make framework of door; cover with wire mesh and latticework constructed with remaining laths. Hinge to corner post so it opens outwards. Affix latch.
8 Assemble roof structure by following steps 3 to 5 on page 180 (Timber Umbrella). Affix finial if required.
9 Slot roofing in position and skew-screw at each corner.
10 Follow steps 6 and 7 on page 180 and paint.

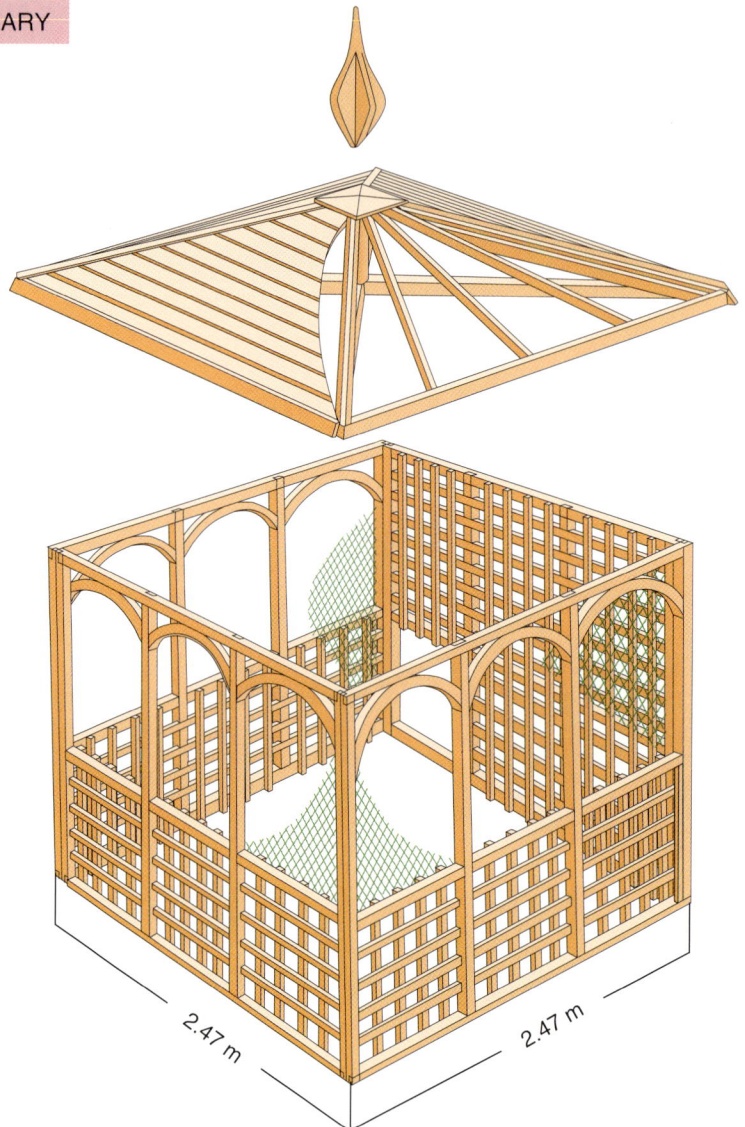

Perfect for the traditional English garden, this period-style gazebo incorporates seating on five sides. Not only is it a feature, but it is a pleasant and practical place for alfresco meals. The basic structure of the gazebo is made from planed (or dressed) timber and the roof is covered with corrugated iron sheeting. A weathervane adds a charming finishing touch. It is a good idea to provide a solid floor underfoot; this one has been paved with clay bricks.

5 x 1.4 m x 160 mm x 9 mm pieces hardboard, cut to form decorative trim
5 x 1.45 m x 68 mm x 22 mm beams
5 x 985 mm x 94 mm x 22 mm timbers
6 x 428 mm x 68 mm x 22 mm timbers
6 x 378 mm x 68 mm x 22 mm seat posts
68 mm x 22 mm slats, total length 30 m, cut to fit seating
5 x 1.35 m x 144 mm x 22 mm rails
5 x 1.35 m x 92 mm x 22 mm rails
10 x 786 mm x 22 mm x 22 mm laths
75 x 1.1 m x 22 mm x 5 mm laths
12 x 340 mm x 94 mm x 22 mm decorative corners, cut to shape

Roof covering
corrugated iron (or other sheeting) to cover 10 m²
14 m corrugated iron capping

Fasteners and hardware
6 x galvanised post-anchor brackets
12 x 50 mm coach screws

50 mm brass screws
75 mm wire nails
50 mm wire nails
panel pins
66 x galvanised roofing nails (drive screws)
weathervane on cone

1 Dig six holes for footings, 500 mm x 500 mm x 500 mm. Concrete post anchors in position and leave to set overnight.
2 Affix posts to anchors with coach screws and brace temporarily.
3 Nail beams to uprights, allowing an overlap of 47 mm on outside of posts. There should be a 22 mm gap at the top of each post to accommodate rafters.
4 Slot rafters into place and nail to posts and at the apex, using offcuts of timber to secure.
5 Cut ends of rafters vertically to overlap the upright posts by 140 mm.
6 Now affix purlins at 880 mm centres.
7 Nail roof sheeting onto purlins. Nail capping over joins and affix cone of weathervane at the apex.
8 Use 50 mm nails to attach bargeboard to outside ends of rafters.
9 Screw beams between upright posts with the underside at a height of 310 mm above the ground. Trim pieces where necessary.
10 Assemble rest of seat framework, with 428 mm lengths resting on beam and seat posts. Screw each join to secure.
11 Screw remaining timber to outside of seat post, flush with upper surface of framework. Trim timber where necessary.
12 Measure seating area to check for correct slat lengths. Cut and affix five parallel slats on each.
13 Attach back rail by skew-nailing 92 mm timber on edge, between two uprights, with bottom surface 786 mm above ground level. Check lengths of wider rails, trimming if necessary, and round two corners with a sander. Affix on top of 92 mm rail so rounded edge protrudes outwards.
14 Screw 22 mm x 22 mm laths to inside of upright posts between back rail and ground.
15 Use panel pins to attach thin laths vertically between rail and posts. Use offcuts for shorter lengths.
16 Place decorative trim over top of latticework under rail, trimming hardwood where necessary.
17 Attach decorative corners at top of upright posts on either side under the eaves, and paint.

1.35 m

1.35 m

MATERIALS

Footings
175 kg cement
700 kg or 0.55 m³ sand
700 kg or 0.55 m³ stone

Framework
6 x 2.1 m x 94 mm x 68 mm upright posts
6 x 2.3 m x 94 mm x 22 mm rafters

6 x 1.5 m x 94 mm x 22 mm beams, cut and mitred to fit
44 mm x 44 mm purlins, total length 18 m, cut to fit roof

Seating and decorative timber
6 x 1.65 m x 220 mm x 9 mm pieces hardboard, cut to form decorative bargeboard and trimmed where necessary

USEFUL ADDRESSES

AUSTRALIA

Banner Timber Centres, Head Office: 191 Main Road, Blackwood, South Australia, 5051
Tel: (08) 278 8211 (5 branches in South Australia)

BBC Hardware, Head Office: Building A, Cnr Cambridge & Chester Streets, Epping NSW 2121
Tel: (02) 876 0888 (Branches throughout Australia)

Bunnings Building Supplies, Head Office: 152 Pilbara Street, Welshpool, Western Australia, 6106
Tel: (09) 365 1555 (24 branches in Western Australia)

Harcros Timber & Building Supplies, Head Office: 586 Doncaster Road, Doncaster, Victoria, 3108
Tel: (03) 848 7577 (5 branches in Victoria)

Harley's Landscapes, 52 Strickland Street, Mt Claremont, Western Australia, 6010
Tel: (09) 384 0756

Hudson Timber and Hardware, Head Office: Cnr Showground Road & Victoria Avenue, Castle Hill, NSW 2154
Tel: (02) 634 5344 (10 branches in NSW)

Marion Sand & Metal Paving Centre, 917 Marion Road, Mitchell Park, South Australia, 5043
Tel: (08) 296 5122

Mitre 10, Head Office: 1367 Main North Road, Para Hills West, South Australia
Tel: (08) 281 2244

Pine Rivers Landscaping Supplies, 93 South Pine Road, Strathpine, Queensland, 4500
Tel: (07) 3205 6708

Sundown Landscape Supplies, 199 Fairfield Road, Fairfield, NSW 2165
Tel: (02) 632 8677

Terraforce, Head Office: Boral Besser, P O Box 6, Seven Hills, NSW 2147
Tel: (02) 896 4222 (Branches throughout Australia)

Wilson Timbers, Head Office: 13 Davey Street, Moorooka, Queensland, 4105
Tel: (07) 277 1988 (3 branches in Queensland)

NEW ZEALAND

Birkdale Timbermart Ltd, 2-4 Bay Park Place, Birkdale
Tel: (09) 483 8428

Carters, 640 Great South Road, Manukau City
Tel: (09) 262 0951

Herman Pacific, 110 Foundry Road, Silverdale
Tel: (09) 377 1425

Mitre 10, Home & Trade, 3037 Great North Road, New Lynn
Tel: (09) 827 5809

Terraforce, P O Box 3910, Auckland

Westside Landscaping Supplies, 2 Akatea Road, Glendene, Auckland

UNITED KINGDOM

B&Q plc, Portswood House, Hampshire Corporate Park, Chandlers Ford, Eastleigh, Hants S03 3YX
Tel: (01703) 256256 (Branches throughout the UK)

Brick Development Association, Woodside House, Winkfield, Windsor, Berks SL4 2DX
Tel: (01344) 885651

Building Centre Group, 26 Store Street, London WC1E 7BT
Tel: (0171) 637 1022 (Technical advice)
Tel: (01344) 884999 (Useful literature)
Also in Bristol, Glasgow and Manchester

Do-It-All, Falcon House, The Minories, Dudley, West Midlands DY2 8PG
Tel: (01384) 456456, (Branches throughout the UK)

Homebase Ltd, Beddington House, Wallington, Surrey SM6 0HB
Tel: (0181) 7847200, (Branches throughout the UK)

Jewson Ltd, Intwood Road, Cringleford, Norwich NR4 UXB
Tel: (01603) 456133, (Branches throughout the UK)

Onduline Building Products, (organic-fibre roof sheeting), Eadley Place, 182-184 Campden Hill Road, Kensington, London W8 7AS
Tel: (0171) 7277 0533

Texas Homecare, Homecharm House, Parkfarm, Wellingborough, Northampton NN5 7UG
Tel: (01933) 67 9679, (Branches throughout the UK)

Travis Perkins, Lodge Way House, Lodge Way, Harlestone Road, Northampton NN5 7UG
Tel: (01604) 752424, (Branches throughout the UK)

Wickes, 120-138 Station Road, Harrow, Middlesex HA1 2QB
Tel: (0181) 8635696, (Branches throughout the UK)

UNITED STATES OF AMERICA & CANADA

Decor Concrete, 682 Arvin Avenue, Stoney Creek, Ontario, L8E 5RH

Terraforce, 1728 Sprucewood Place, Victoria BC, V8N 1H3

Terraforce, 2246 North Durfee Avenue, El Monte, CA 91732-3902

SOUTH AFRICA

Airton Timbers, Paarden Eiland Road, Paarden Eiland, Cape Town
Tel: (021) 511 2318; fax: (021) 511 6771
Timber Lane, Retreat, Cape Town
Tel: (021) 72 9835; fax: (021) 75 6164

Buildex, 433 Commissioner Street, Johannesburg
Tel: (011) 618 1252; fax: (011) 614 3818

The Building Centre, 209 Cartwrights Corner, Adderley Street, Cape Town, 8001
Tel: (021) 461 6095/461 1121; fax: (021) 461 9265

Concrete Society of Southern Africa/Portland Cement Institute (PCI), Head Office: Portland Park, Halfway House, P O Box 168, Halfway House, 1685
Tel: (011) 315 0300; fax: (011) 315 0584
P O Box 13019, Humewood, 6013
Tel: (041) 53 2141; fax: (041) 53 3496
P O Box 12, Vrijzee, 7495
Tel: (021) 591 5234; fax: (021) 591 3502
P O Box 1393, Wandsbeck, 3631
Tel: (031) 86 1306/7; fax: (031) 86 7241

Corobrick, P O Box 1517, Durban, 4000
Tel: (031) 560 3111; fax: (031) 84 6752
P O Box 49, Germiston, 1400
Tel: (031) 871 8600; fax: (011) 45 3221
P O Box 38, Stellenbosch, 7599
Tel: (021) 887 3311; fax: (021) 887 2766
P O Box 20, Swartkops, 6210
Tel: (041) 66 2701; fax: (041) 66 2704

Federated Timber Industries, Head Office: Johannesburg
Tel: (011) 609 7873; fax: (011) 452 1870
Cape Town
Tel: (021) 54 5111; fax: (021) 54 7714
Durban
Tel: (031) 42 2011; fax: (031) 42 6958
Bloemfontein
Tel: (051) 47 3171; fax: (051) 47 7407
Port Elizabeth
Tel: (041) 54 2535; fax: (041) 57 1855
East London
Tel: (0431) 43 3733; fax: (0431) 43 5240

Institute for Timber Construction, Branches throughout South Africa, P O Box X686, Isando, 1600
Tel: (011) 974 1061; fax: (011) 974 9779

Natal Master Builder's & Allied Industries' Association Exhibition Centre, 40 Essex Terrace, Westville, 3630
Tel: (031) 86 7070; fax: (031) 86 6348

SA Lumber Millers' Association, 6 Hulley Road, Isando
P O Box X686, Isando, 1600
Tel: (011) 974 1061; fax: (011) 974 9779

Smartstone, 101 Retreat Road, Retreat, 7945
Tel: (021) 75 7083-6; fax: (021) 75 7087
24 Villiers Road, Walmer, 6075
Tel/fax: (041) 51 5400

Terraforce, P O Box 1453, Cape Town, 8000
Tel: (021) 465 1907; fax: (021) 465 4047